Winning the White House, 2008

Winning the White House 2008

*Kevin J. McMahon, David M. Rankin,
Donald W. Beachler, and
John Kenneth White*

palgrave
macmillan

WINNING THE WHITE HOUSE, 2008

Copyright © Kevin J. McMahon, David M. Rankin, Donald W. Beachler, and John Kenneth White, 2009.

First published in 2009 by
PALGRAVE MACMILLAN®
in the United States—a division of St. Martin's Press LLC,
175 Fifth Avenue, New York, NY 10010.

Where this book is distributed in the UK, Europe and the rest of the world, this is by Palgrave Macmillan, a division of Macmillan Publishers Limited, registered in England, company number 785998, of Houndmills, Basingstoke, Hampshire RG21 6XS.

Palgrave Macmillan is the global academic imprint of the above companies and has companies and representatives throughout the world.

Palgrave® and Macmillan® are registered trademarks in the United States, the United Kingdom, Europe and other countries.

ISBN: 978–0–230–60768–2 (hardcover)
ISBN: 978–0–230–61933–3 (paperback)

Library of Congress Cataloging-in-Publication Data is available from the Library of Congress.

A catalogue record of the book is available from the British Library.

Design by Newgen Imaging Systems (P) Ltd., Chennai, India.

First edition: September 2009

10 9 8 7 6 5 4 3 2 1

Printed in the United States of America.

For my son Brooks and my parents
—K. J. M

For Noah and Liam, future voters
—D. M. R

For Brigid
—D. W. B

For Professor Norman L. Zucker
—J. K. W

The 2008 Presidential Election Results by State.

The 2008 presidential election results

Northeast	Obama #	%	EV	McCain #	%	EV
Connecticut	997,772	60.6	7	629,428	38.2	—
Delaware	255,459	61.9	3	152,374	36.9	—
DC	245,800	92.5	3	17,367	6.5	—
Maine	421,923	57.7	4	295,273	40.4	—
Maryland	1,629,467	61.9	10	959,862	36.5	—
Massachusetts	1,904,097	61.8	12	1,108,854	36.0	—
N. Hampshire	384,826	54.1	4	316,534	44.5	—
New Jersey	2,215,422	57.2	15	1,613,207	41.6	—
New York	4,769,700	62.8	31	2,742,298	36.1	—
Pennsylvania	3,276,363	54.5	21	2,655,885	44.1	—
Rhode Island	296,571	63.1	4	165,391	35.2	—
Vermont	219,262	67.6	3	98,974	30.5	—
West Virginia	304,127	42.6	—	398,061	55.7	5
Total	**16,920,789**	**59.1**	**117**	**11,153,508**	**39.0**	**5**

Midwest	Obama #	%	EV	McCain #	%	EV
Illinois	3,419,673	61.9	21	2,031,527	36.8	—
Indiana	1,374,039	49.9	11	1,345,648	48.9	—
Iowa	828,940	53.9	7	682,379	44.4	—
Kansas	514,765	41.8	—	699,655	56.6	6
Michigan	2,872,579	57.4	17	2,048,639	40.9	—
Minnesota	1,573,354	54.1	10	1,275,409	43.8	—
Missouri	1,441,911	49.3	—	1,445,814	49.4	11
Nebraska	333,319	41.6	1	452,979	56.5	4
N. Dakota	141,278	44.5	—	168,601	53.1	3
Ohio	2,933,388	51.4	20	2,674,491	46.8	—
S. Dakota	170,924	44.8	—	203,054	53.1	3
Wisconsin	1,677,211	56.2	10	1,262,393	42.3	—
Total	**17,281,381**	**53.9**	**97**	**14,290,589**	**44.6**	**27**

South	Obama #	%	EV	McCain #	%	EV
Alabama	813,479	38.7	—	1,266,546	60.3	9
Arkansas	422,310	38.9	—	638,017	58.7	6
Florida	4,282,074	50.9	27	4,045,624	48.1	—
Georgia	1,844,137	46.9	—	2,048,744	52.1	15
Kentucky	751,985	41.1	—	1,048,462	57.4	8
Louisiana	782,989	39.9	—	1,148,275	58.6	9
Mississippi	554,662	43.0	—	724,597	56.9	6
N. Carolina	2,142,651	49.7	15	2,128,474	49.4	—
Oklahoma	502,496	34.4	—	960,165	65.6	7
S. Carolina	862,449	44.9	—	1,034,896	53.9	8
Tennessee	1,087,437	41.8	—	1,479,178	56.9	11
Texas	3,528,663	43.6	—	4,479,328	55.4	34
Virginia	1,959,532	52.6	13	1,725,005	46.3	—
Total	**19,534,834**	**45.8**	**55**	**22,727,311**	**53.0**	**113**

West	Obama #	%	EV	McCain #	%	EV
Alaska	123,594	37.9	—	193,841	59.4	3
Arizona	1,034,707	44.9	—	1,230,111	53.4	10
California	8,274,473	61.0	55	5,011,781	36.9	—
Colorado	1,288,568	53.6	9	1,073,584	44.7	—
Hawaii	325,871	71.9	4	120,566	26.5	—
Idaho	236,440	35.9	—	403,012	61.3	4
Montana	231,667	47.1	—	242,763	49.4	3
Nevada	533,736	55.2	5	412,827	42.0	—
N. Mexico	472,422	56.9	5	346,832	41.8	—
Oregon	1,037,291	56.8	7	738,475	40.4	—
Utah	327,670	34.3	—	596,030	62.3	5
Washington	1,750,848	57.4	11	1,229,216	40.3	—
Wyoming	82,868	32.6	—	164,958	64.8	3
Total	**15,720,155**	**56.1**	**96**	**11,763,996**	**41.9**	**28**

	Obama #	%	Electoral Votes	McCain #	%	Electoral Votes
Obama National	**69,456,897**	**52.9**	**365**			
McCain National				**59,934,814**	**45.7**	**173**

Contents

Tables

Preface

As a first-time candidate for the U.S. Senate seat from Illinois, 42-year-old Barack Obama rocketed onto the landscape of American politics as the keynote speaker at the 2004 Democratic national convention in Boston. In a nation divided, at times bitterly, into Democratic "blue" and Republican "red" states in recent presidential elections, the son of an African father from Kenya and a white mother from Kansas noted, "[T]here's not a liberal America and a conservative America—there's the United States of America. There's not a black America and white America and Latino America and Asian America; there's the United States of America." Four years later, Obama would be back at the Democratic national convention in the mile-high city of Denver, shattering historic racial barriers as the first black major party nominee for president of the United States. And on Election Night 2008, Obama would be the first Democratic presidential candidate to win a majority of the national popular vote since 1976 while winning in states that Democrats had not carried since Lyndon B. Johnson's landslide victory in 1964.

Building on Democratic dominance in the Northeast, the Obama campaign surged in what had been a competitive upper Midwest, winning the bellwether state of Ohio, the swing state of Iowa, and even the traditionally Republican Indiana. In what has become the regional foundation for Republicans in the Electoral College, Obama picked up the southern states of Florida, Virginia, and North Carolina, which have undergone rapid development and demographic shifts that have altered their politics. In addition, Obama won three previously red western states also undergoing change, namely, Colorado, New Mexico, and Nevada.

In an historic election, including the candidacies of New York Senator Hillary Clinton for the Democratic nomination and Alaska Governor Sarah Palin as the GOP vice presidential nominee, there were many "firsts" but also some predictable trends. Making a claim to a national mandate Obama added three states each in three different regions to Kerry's 2004 total. The rest of the electoral map remained unchanged as John McCain was unable to turn a single blue state to red. Much like George W. Bush, his strength laid in the central plains and Deep South. For McCain, President Bush's reach extended to voter concerns with the war in Iraq, the economy, and social issues, including increasingly unfavorable policy ties associated with the administration and the Republican Party.

In the chapters that follow, we consider the election through an analysis of critical issues and electoral groupings across America's four main geographic regions. Each of us has contributed two chapters, and they stand as individual contributions. As a result, we do not always offer a unified interpretation of the election. Rather, it might be said that we each participate—from the vantage point of the process, issue, or region in focus—in a discussion of the meaning of the election. In many ways, we are at the beginning of what will be a long national conversation about the historical and enduring significance of this election.

John Kenneth White begins the book by exploring an historic path to the 2008 nomination, describing how Obama overtook early frontrunner Hillary Clinton in a lengthy primary campaign, and how a relatively easy nomination process for McCain still stirred up damaging intra-party conflict. Considering a particularly important issue for voters in the 2008 general election, Donald Beachler focuses on the electoral fallout of the economic downturn while also considering the influence of political and demographic trends to the final results. John White then turns our attention to foreign policy, including the war in Iraq and war on terrorism, in what many thought would be as pressing an issue area for voters as it had been in 2004, until the financial collapse pushed America in another direction. In 2004 "moral values" was the most important issue of the election and although less prominent in 2008, Kevin McMahon searches for and discovers the role of social issues in this election.

In the third section of the book, we closely consider each of the nation's four main regions. Examining each region's electoral history and trends in the context of the 2008 presidential and congressional elections, we also focus special attention on one battleground state. Kevin McMahon begins in the Northeast, a region that cemented its status in 2008 as a Democratic stronghold both in presidential and congressional elections. Donald Beachler takes us through the South, where Republicans maintained their own longstanding advantage, but where population change and growth are opening up Democratic opportunities in several states. In the Midwest, David Rankin explores a region in which upper Midwest states vital to both parties Electoral College count all voted Democratic in 2008 yet the central plains states remain reliably Republican. With the eastern half of the electoral map flipping the party strengths upside down since the 1960s, Rankin also examines how the rapidly expanding states in the west region represent the electoral frontier in the competition for the Congress and the presidency.

KEVIN J. MCMAHON
Hartford, CT

DAVID M. RANKIN
Fredonia, NY

DONALD W. BEACHLER
Ithaca, NY

JOHN KENNETH WHITE
Gaithersburg, MD

Part I

The Nomination

A Campaign to Remember

John Kenneth White

It was the primary campaign of a century—or, at least, the last half century. Not since 1952 had there been a contest in which either an incumbent president or vice president had *not* sought their party's presidential nomination.

In 1952, Democrat Harry S. Truman was one of the most unpopular presidents in history, garnering just 29 percent support thanks to the Korean War stalemate.[1] Truman was so out-of-favor that a popular saying took hold: "To err is Truman"—a play off the old adage, "to err is human." Given these political circumstances, Truman's vice president was an unlikely presidential contender. In 1948, when Truman appeared to be an improbable winner, Democrats chose elder statesman Alben W. Barkley to be their vice presidential candidate. Truman later observed that it took Barkley "five minutes to sign his name," and in 1952 he concluded that the presidency would kill him within three months.[2] The eventual Democratic nominee was a man from Illinois, the state's governor Adlai E. Stevenson.

Republicans, too, had their political problems that year. Having lost five straight presidential elections, the party was desperate for a winner. Conservatives preferred a more isolationist foreign policy abroad and balanced budgets at home. They backed "Mr. Republican," Ohio Senator Robert A. Taft. Eastern Establishment Republicans wanted to win, and their man was ex-World War II General Dwight D. Eisenhower. The Eisenhower-Taft battle rage continued into the Republican Convention, when Eisenhower squeaked out a narrow victory. That November, the change candidate (Eisenhower) easily defeated the status-quo candidate (Stevenson).

In many respects, the political history of 1952 bears an eerie resemblance to the memorable contests of 2008. On the Republican side, the race was shaped by a crucial decision made by George W. Bush when he selected Dick Cheney in 2000 to be his vice presidential running mate. Cheney, a respected ex-congressman, ex-secretary of defense, and ex-White House Chief of Staff, harbored no presidential ambitions. But Cheney's dim political star made it possible for him to be a kind of supernova within the Bush administration when it came to making public policy. Cheney became the most powerful vice president in history, exerting exorbitant influence in domestic and foreign affairs (not just in a few policy areas, as previous vice presidents had done). But Cheney's growing unpopularity (only 18 percent approved of his job performance) meant that the Republican Party faced a succession crisis—a crisis that came to pass in 2008.[3]

For Democrats, the political history of 1952 also reverberated in their 2008 primary contests. Democrats have never subscribed to a hierarchal culture favored by Republicans—namely, that it is a senior party leader's "turn" to be their presidential nominee. When New York Senator Hillary Rodham Clinton argued that her experience and the successes of her husband's administration made her the only realistic choice, many Democrats were unpersuaded. A gargantuan dissatisfaction with the status-quo in general and George W. Bush in particular meant that Democrats (and the rest of the country) were ready for something new. That new thing turned out to be the junior senator from Illinois, Barack Obama. Obama's rhetorical skills, his appeal to young voters, and his ability to woo African-Americans away from their long-standing love affair with the Clintons (recall Toni Morrison's famous line that Bill Clinton was "the first black president"[4]) caught Hillary Clinton unprepared for a powerful challenge to her status as the presumptive Democratic nominee.

The Democrats: A New Politics of Identity

The Democratic nomination fight between Hillary Clinton and Barack Obama was more than a contest between two powerful personalities. By 2008, Democrats had crossed an important threshold: no longer would ideology be the dominant feature of their nomination struggles. Ever since the disastrous Democratic Convention in 1968, when Hubert H. Humphrey was chosen to be the nominee amidst street riots that presidential chronicler Theodore H. White likened to a "sea of blood,"[5] Democrats had been split into two warring camps. For nearly forty years, Old Guard Democrats—led by Lyndon B. Johnson, Hubert H. Humphrey, and their heirs—and New Democrats—led by Eugene J. McCarthy, Robert F. Kennedy, George S. McGovern, and their offspring—battled for supremacy.[6] Old Guard Democrats were hawkish Cold Warriors who were deeply suspicious of the Soviet Union's intentions. They were strong supporters of the Vietnam War (at least at the outset) and were among the last to back away from it. On social issues (including abortion, gay rights, and women's rights), Old Guard Democrats adhered to more conservative, traditional stances (although they were in the vanguard of the civil rights revolution). New Democrats, on the other hand, strongly opposed the Vietnam War, were less suspicious of Soviet intentions, and pleaded with Old Guard Democrats to leave foreign ventures aside and "come home, America" (the refrain McGovern employed in his 1972 acceptance speech) and concentrate on domestic problems.[7] On social issues, New Democrats were staunch liberals: supporting abortion, gay rights, and women's rights (as well as civil rights—the one area where Old Guard Democrats and New Democrats were in agreement).

With these battle lines set, the Democratic Party split apart. Only in 1976 did the warring factions temporarily declare a truce. That year the Watergate and Nixon scandals gave Democrats the greatest opportunity in a dozen years to recapture the presidency, and they did not disappoint. Jimmy Carter consolidated his intra-party support by emphasizing human rights—a stance that appealed to Old Guard Democrats and New Democrats alike. Old Guard Democrats saw human rights as a bludgeon from which to bash the Soviets and their allies, while New Democrats saw Carter's human rights emphasis as a break from ossified Cold War–like thinking. Carter also opposed Gerald Ford's vetoes of domestic spending bills passed by a Democratic Congress, even as he presented himself as a budget-deficit hawk. By making his character and persona his chief qualifications for the presidency (something that attracted support following the Nixon experience), Carter obscured his positions on the issues and, thus, gave the Democrats a respite from their internecine party warfare.

But the Democratic cease-fire did not last. By 1980, Carter was a very unpopular president, as only 31 percent approved of his job performance.[8] Massachusetts Senator Edward M. Kennedy challenged Carter's renomination, and the battle between Old Guard Democrats and New Democrats resumed. Carter's election as an outsider in 1976 left him estranged from his party's base, thereby making him especially vulnerable to an intra-party challenge. Kennedy carried the banner of the Old Guard Democrats and argued that Carter was hardly a Democrat (too conservative on domestic matters, especially health care), while he wanted a more vigorous, proactive, New Deal-like government. In 1984, former Vice President Walter F. Mondale and Colorado U.S. Senator Gary Hart took up their assigned roles: Mondale, Old Guard Democrat; Hart, New Democrat, and the two fought to a near draw. Four years later, the party remained divided. But for the first time, New Democrats claimed victory with the nomination of Massachusetts Governor Michael S. Dukakis. Like many New Democrats, Dukakis eschewed Old Guard, New Deal-like thinking—especially on domestic matters. He saw himself belonging to a professional class, given to technological approaches to solving the nation's problems. Political scientist Edgar Litt was one of the first to spot the emerging New Democrats, whom he termed the "managerial class." A decade before Dukakis was first elected governor of Massachusetts, Litt saw the appeal of the managerial class to a changing Massachusetts electorate and he neatly summarized their worldview:

> The managers are in favor of constitutional reform and increased aid to private and public education. Because they are cosmopolitan they are the least class-conscious and the least party-bound group. Because they have high educational and occupational attainments their political emphasis is on merit rather than personalized reward. They have a penchant for rational criteria in government. They are the least likely to respond to ethnoreligious appeals, for example, and they form an electorate that is more concerned with policy than patronage, charisma, and the politics of revenge.[9]

But Dukakis's perceived weakness on foreign policy (remember his tank ride in 1988?)—coupled with a contented, happy country during the Reagan regime—meant that Vice President George H. W. Bush was able to win Ronald Reagan's third term. Still, New Democrats savored their first taste of power and hungered for more victories.

In 1992, the United States was a much less happy place than it had been at the start of George H. W. Bush's term as president. The end of the Cold War had caused many economic dislocations. As one unemployed defense worker memorably stated, "We won the Cold War, and now they're saying here's a pink slip."[10] Making George H. W. Bush's reelection prospects especially bleak were unemployed defense workers (like the aforementioned laid-off Groton, Connecticut shipyard worker) who had enjoyed what they believed to be lifetime jobs during the 40-year-long Cold War. Thus, the recession of 1992 had a larger political impact than it might have had otherwise. Bill Clinton told voters that he "felt their pain," even as he sought to mitigate the divisions between Old Guard Democrats and New Democrats. On the eve of his nomination, Clinton told *The New York Times* that since 1968 "the Democrats have had a lot of trouble," adding:

> The American people have voted for Republican presidents and Democratic congresses, a situation which has given us gridlock and quadrupled our investments and our economic potential. But I think largely on something like this, you know [voters say]: "Republicans would be better presidents because they manage the economy better, keep taxes low, stick up for the country abroad, but the Congress should be Democratic because they care more about the people that really need help."[11]

Clinton promised that he would focus "like a laser beam" on the economy, even as he cast himself as a New Democrat who would be different from Old Guard Democrats of the past.[12] The 1992 party platform promised to eschew big government solutions (favored by Old Guard Democrats) in favor of a "third way" favored by New Democrats that would make government a partner (but not a principal one) with community volunteers and local businesses:

> We offer a new social contract based neither on callous, do-nothing Republican neglect, nor an outdated faith in programs as the solution to every problem. We favor a third way beyond the old approaches—to put government back on the side of citizens who play by the rules. We believe that by what it says and how it conducts its business, government must once again make responsibility an instrument of national purpose. Our future as a nation depends upon the daily assumption of personal responsibility by millions of Americans from all walks of life—for the religious faiths they follow, the ethics they practice, the values they instill, and the pride they take in their work.[13]

It also helped that Clinton chose as vice president, Tennessee senator, Al Gore, who, like Clinton, was the first of the post–World War II generation to rise to the apex of political power. For eight years, Clinton and Gore perfected their New Democratic, small-bore solutions, with their mantra of "opportunity, community, and responsibility."[14] In his 1996 State of the Union Address, Clinton sounded much like Ronald Reagan when he famously declared, "The era of big government is over."[15]

The Clinton-Gore years solidified the dominance of New Democratic thinking within the party. The Democratic Leadership Council, which was founded after the party's 1984 shellacking in the Reagan-Mondale contest, became a center of

New Democratic ideas. Bill Clinton, Al Gore, and Joe Lieberman became important leaders of this party-within-a-party, and their influence was reflected in subsequent platforms and in the selection of its nominees. By 2000 Al Gore became
the party's standard-bearer without much of a fight, and he continued to espouse
Bill Clinton's New Democratic approach to solving the country's problems.[16]

Following the disputed election of George W. Bush in 2000, Democrats had
a spirited contest in 2004. John F. Kerry, John Edwards, Howard Dean, and others sparred for the right to carry their party's banner. But this time there was an
important difference: the issue differences among the candidates were muted, and
the party's rank-in-file were united in their antipathy toward George W. Bush.
Among likely Democratic voters in the 2004 Iowa caucuses and New Hampshire
primary, more than eight-in-ten Democrats disapproved of the way Bush was
handling his job as president.[17] Moreover, half of those polled said they disliked
Bush *personally*.[18] In effect, the forty-third president became the great peace-
maker between Old Guard Democrats and New Democrats. Antipathy toward
Bush and the passage of time meant that the cup of bitterness the Democrats had
drunk from in 1968 had finally been cleansed from the party's soul.

One effect of George W. Bush's outsized influence within the Democratic Party
was an energized Democratic vote. As table 1.1 demonstrates, Democrats who
decided to cast a primary ballot in 2008 more than doubled from four years earlier. Of course, some portion of that increase came because the race boiled down
to a contest between two historic candidates: Hillary Rodham Clinton was the
first woman to have a serious shot at winning the Democratic nomination; Barack
Obama, the first black. Still, the hostility of so many voters toward George W.
Bush was yet one more motivating factor in spiking Democratic primary turnout
to record heights. At the beginning of the primary contests in 2008, only 31 percent
of Americans approved of the way Bush was handling his job as president.[19]

Given that the Democrats were united in their opposition to George W. Bush,
just what, then, distinguished Hillary Rodham Clinton from Barack Obama? In
fact, very little. Clinton claimed, rightly, to have more government experience than
Obama (35 years, to be precise), while Obama had been elected to the Illinois state

Table 1.1   Democratic primary turnout, 1972–2008

Election	Votes cast (in millions)	Major candidates
1972	16.0	McGovern-Humphrey-Wallace
1976	16.1	Carter-Brown-Udall
1980	18.7	Carter-Kennedy
1984	18.0	Mondale-Hart-Jackson
1988	23.0	Dukakis-Jackson-Gore
1992	20.2	Clinton-Brown-Tsongas
1996	10.9	Clinton
2000	14.0	Gore-Bradley
2004	16.2	Kerry-Edwards
2008	37.2	Obama-Clinton

Source: Rhodes Cook, *The Rhodes Cook Letter*, June 2008, p. 5.

senate only at the beginning of her husband's second term in 1996. Even Obama tacitly conceded his lack of experience by titling his 2008 campaign book *The Audacity of Hope*.[20] But when it came to the crucial issues the next president would face, there were few differences between Clinton and Obama. Clinton voted to give George W. Bush authorization to wage war in Iraq; Obama decried Iraq as a "dumb war," saying his judgment on this issue (and others) had proven correct over time. On health care, Clinton offered universal coverage; Obama covered most people but made exceptions for healthy, younger Americans to opt out of the system. (Both Clinton and Obama favored universal coverage for children.) Clinton and Obama disagreed as to whether the next president should meet unfriendly foreign leaders: Clinton argued such meetings should be carefully prepared with set preconditions; Obama wanted no preconditions and announced he would engage our enemies using vigorous diplomacy. Finally, Clinton wanted to suspend the federal gas tax during the summer months; Obama maintained this was a gimmick and that the oil companies would not lower their prices but pocket the additional profits.

Instead of debating issues, the Clinton and Obama campaigns forged a new politics of identity. Consider the most "memorable" moments of the 2008 Democratic contest:

> A protestor in New Hampshire yelled at Hillary Clinton: "Iron my shirt!"
> In a debate, Barack Obama turned to his opponent and said, "You're likable enough, Hillary."
> *Saturday Night Live* presented a mock Clinton-Obama debate in which the moderator asked if Obama was comfy and needed another pillow.
> Bill Clinton belittled Barack Obama's impending victory in South Carolina, where blacks composed 55 percent of the vote, as nothing more than blacks voting for one of their own.[21] (Jesse Jackson had won there in 1988.)
> will.i.am, a black rap singer, issued an internet hit combining his music with Obama's mantra, "Yes, We Can!"
> Barack Obama shattered all fund-raising records, beating Hillary Clinton and the Democratic Party establishment in the quest for dollars. (Obama continued to set records all year, raising more than $500 million and leading to federally regulated filings so huge that the computers at the Federal Election Commission could not handle them.)
> A video of Reverend Jeremiah Wright, Barack Obama's longtime pastor surfaced on YouTube. In a sermon following the terrorist attacks of September 11, 2001, Wright said, "Not God bless America; God damn America." Wright maintained that the U.S. was responsible for the terrorist attacks, not Osama bin Laden.
> Barack Obama told a fund-raiser in San Francisco that those he encountered in rural areas were "bitter" about the poor economy and lacked faith in government. Therefore, he argued, they "cling" to their guns and religious beliefs.

Taken together, these "memorable moments" have more to do with image, style, and values than with any real issue disagreements. Left without any serious ideological disputes, Democrats cast their ballots for either Hillary Clinton or Barack Obama based on their race, gender, and identification with a particular educational and income class. In fact, the outcomes did not differ much from place to place when it came to these important subgroups. Women were firm Clinton supporters; blacks were solidly behind Obama. Downscale whites backed Clinton; those who were college-educated (especially those with postgraduate degrees) liked Obama. Younger voters were overwhelmingly in Obama's camp; seniors strongly preferred Clinton. Gun owners liked Clinton; those without guns preferred Obama. Urban dwellers (which included significant minority populations) backed Obama; rural residents (mostly white) stuck with Clinton. Suburbanites split their votes, with Obama frequently obtaining a majority in most places. The April 22 Pennsylvania Democratic primary provided a microcosm of how the new identity politics split the 2008 Democratic electorate (see table 1.2).

As the primary season progressed, the voting patterns depicted in table 1.2 hardened and the results became predictable. States that were upscale—that is, with high incomes and greater exposure to college, had a significant African-American population, and were immersed in the new economy (think high-technology, twenty-first-century jobs)—were Obama territory. Thus, the Illinois

Table 1.2   Pennsylvania 2008 democratic primary results by key subgroups

Demographic group	Clinton %	Obama %
Male	46	**53**
Female	**56**	44
Less than $15,000	47	**53**
$15,000–$30,000	**55**	45
$30,000–$50,000	**56**	44
$50,000–$75,000	**57**	43
$75,000–$100,000	**51**	49
$100,000–$150,000	**60**	40
$150,000–$200,000	47	**53**
$200,000+	40	**60**
High school graduate	**64**	36
Some college	**51**	49
College graduate	46	**53**
Postgraduate	48	**52**
18–24 years old	34	**66**
25–29 years old	45	**55**
30–39 years old	43	**57**
40–49 years old	**53**	47
50–64 years old	**56**	44
65+ years old	**63**	37
Gun owner	**63**	37
Not gun owner	**50**	**50**
White	**63**	37
African-American	10	**90**
Weekly church attendance	**59**	41
Occasionally attend	**56**	44
Never attend church	45	**55**
Urban	40	**60**
Suburban	**59**	41
Rural	**63**	37

Source: Edison Media Research and Mitofsky International, Pennsylvania exit poll, April 22, 2008.

Note: Winner's percentage is denoted in **boldface type**.

senator easily won Maryland (61 percent), Virginia (64 percent), Wisconsin (58 percent), South Carolina (55 percent), North Carolina (56 percent), District of Columbia (75 percent), and Vermont (59 percent). But in those states with mostly blue-collar populations (think manufacturing, twentieth-century-related jobs), lower incomes, and less exposure to college, Hillary Clinton often prevailed. Thus, the New York senator easily won Pennsylvania (55 percent), Ohio (53 percent), West Virginia (67 percent), Kentucky (65 percent), Rhode Island (58 percent), and Arkansas (70 percent). Of course, there were exceptions, most of them favoring Clinton: Massachusetts voted 56 percent for Clinton, a place where the managerial class had its origins. Likewise, California gave Clinton 51 percent of its ballots, despite last-minute support for Obama from the state's First Lady, Maria Shriver, and talk show host Oprah Winfrey. But these were early states in the primary calendar, and the twentieth-and twenty-first-century rule hardened as the Clinton-Obama race was transformed into an endurance contest.[22]

As the twenty-first century progresses, the Obama coalition is only becoming stronger. The United States is becoming an increasingly less white, less rural, and less-churched country. According to recent Census Bureau estimates, whites are expected to be a minority throughout the United States by 2042.[23] Church attendance has hovered for decades around 40 percent.[24] And suburban counties continue to expand (although so-called exurban counties, many of which lie in rural areas, are also growing exponentially). Thus, the demographic and values differences are very likely to favor Obama over Clinton in the future (as they did in 2008). The only positive for Clinton is that women continue to be a majority of the electorate, particularly in Democratic primaries.

But ideology no longer holds the powerful sway it once did. For example, in Ohio the deviation among liberals moderates and conservatives from Hillary Clinton's statewide percentage was as follows: liberals, 0; moderates, +3; conservatives, –5.[25] Wisconsin, a state that gave Barack Obama 58 percent of its votes, also showed little deviation by ideology: liberals +2, moderates, 0; conservatives, +1.[26] In her speech at the Democratic Convention, Clinton conceded that there were few issue differences, and urged her followers to abandon their politics of identity and back Obama based solely on the issues:

> I ran for President to renew the promise of America. To rebuild the middle class and sustain the American Dream; to provide the opportunity to work hard and have that work rewarded; to save for college, a home, and retirement; to afford the gas and groceries and still have a little left over each month.
> To promote a clean energy economy that will create millions of green collar jobs.
> To create a health care system that is universal, high quality, and affordable so that parents no longer have to choose between care for themselves or their children or be stuck in dead-end jobs simply to keep their insurance.
> To create a world class education system and make college affordable again.
> To fight for an America defined by deep and meaningful equality—from civil rights to labor rights, from women's rights to gay rights, from ending discrimination to promoting unionization to providing help for the most important job there is: caring for our families. To help every child live up to his or her God-given potential.
> To make America once again a nation of immigrants and a nation of laws.

>To bring fiscal sanity back to Washington and make our government an instrument of the public good, not of private plunder.
>
>To restore America's standing in the world; to end the war in Iraq; bring our troops home, and honor their service by caring for our veterans.
>
>And to join with our allies to confront our shared challenges, from poverty and genocide to terrorism and global warming.
>
>Most of all, I ran to stand up for all those who have been invisible to their government for eight long years.
>
>Those are the reasons I ran for President. Those are the reasons I support Barack Obama. And those are the reasons you should, too.
>
>I want you to ask yourselves: Were you in this campaign just for me?...Were you in it for that mom struggling with cancer while raising her kids? Were you in it for that boy and his mom surviving on the minimum wage? Were you in it for all the people in this country who feel invisible?[27]

In 1959, sociologist Daniel Bell argued that those on the political Left had entered a new, ideologically free political era. Bell argued that liberals were exhausted by the struggles of the 1930s and 1940s—including a worldwide economic depression, the rise of fascism, and a great World War that resulted in the murders of millions in concentration camps. The result, Bell claimed, was "an end to chiliastic hopes, to millenarianism, to apocalyptic thinking—and to ideology. For ideology, which once was a road to action, has come to a dead end."[28]

In effect, something very similar to what Bell described in 1959 has happened within today's Democratic Party. The ideological battles between Old Guard Democrats and New Democrats have ended—thanks to the exhaustion felt by both sides and the passage of time. The only question for Democrats is whether, like Bell's premature prediction to ideology's end, the truce is temporary, or will be revived around a new set of issues. Much of that, it seems, will be up to President Obama to determine.

The Search for a Republican Regency

The Republicans entered 2008 a dispirited group. George W. Bush remained an unpopular figure, even though he continued to retain a high level of core backing from self-identified Republicans. Yet even majority Republican support could not save Bush. From 2006 onward, numerous opinion surveys revealed a presidency in its final death throes: 42 percent were "ashamed" to have Bush as president; 64 percent thought he had abused his powers; 54 percent believed those actions warranted impeachment; and 23 percent named Bush as the "worst president ever"—an extraordinary finding given the historic failures of James Buchanan, Ulysses S. Grant, Warren G. Harding, Herbert Hoover, and Richard M. Nixon.[29] Things were so dire that even Bush's own pollster, Matthew Dowd, broke with him, claiming the president had lost "his gut-level bond with the American people."[30]

Things were hardly better at the state level. In California, Republican Governor Arnold Schwarzenegger noted that the GOP had shed more than 370,000 registered voters following the 2006 midterm elections. Schwarzenegger told his fellow Republicans that the party faced a dire situation: "In movie terms, we are dying at the box office. We are not filling the seats."[31] Virginia Republican Congressman Tom Davis told his colleagues that the GOP brand was "in the trash can," adding: "[I]f we were a dog food, they would take us off the shelf."[32] Adding to the many alarums were surveys showing that Bush's historic unpopularity had begun to translate onto the Republican Party itself. Back when Bush assumed the presidency in 2001, the GOP had a 56 percent favorable rating; six years later, it was just 40 percent.[33]

Given these numbers, the 2008 Republican candidates faced a serious dilemma. No serious contender could risk offending George W. Bush or his substantial bloc of remaining Republican supporters. On the other hand, a successful Republican candidate needed additional support from independents (who thought Bush was an anathema) in order to win a general election. In an attempt to solve this problem, the candidates collectively decided not to mention Bush publicly but, instead, channel the ghost of Ronald Reagan who had assumed an iconic standing among all Americans. In their first debate, the nine GOP candidates mentioned Bush only once, even as they tripped over creating their own modern-day analogies to Reagan, citing him an extraordinary *nineteen times*.[34] *New York Times* columnist Frank Rich exposed the Republican quandary: "You don't see Democratic candidates changing the subject to J.F.K. and F.D.R. They are free to start wrestling with the future while the men inheriting the Bush-Rove brand of Republicanism are reduced to harking back to a morning in America on which the sun set in 1989."[35]

But summoning Reagan's ghost did not solve the Republican Party's fundamental problems. Reagan's mid-twentieth-century-based conservatism was hell-bent on battling communism, reducing the size of government, and cutting taxes. In many ways, conservatism was an exhausted philosophy—not because of the many failures associated with George W. Bush—but because of Reagan's (and conservatism's) many *successes*. For example, the Cold War ended with a whimper in 1991, as the Soviet Union fell onto the ash heap of history (as Reagan had predicted). While government did not shrink under Reagan and the Bush presidencies, the rate of its growth was slowed. Both Reagan and George W. Bush had successes when it came to reducing federal taxes—to a point where further reductions were fiscally unsound. Writing in the *Wall Street Journal*, Brendan Miniter concluded that tax cutting had run its course:

> It was bound to happen eventually, but Republicans may now be concluding that there is no longer any political benefit to pushing for deep tax cuts....The reason is that the Laffer Curve applies to politics, too. There's a point after which they won't win any more elections....On both the national and state level, some Republicans are starting to bet that they know where the point of diminishing political returns is, and that for tax cuts, we've already reached it.[36]

Having enjoyed successes (most of them in the decade before George W. Bush became president), conservatism entered a period of crisis as the Bush years drew to a close. Exactly what did it mean to be a conservative? Some argued that Bush had betrayed the cause, maintaining that "compassionate conservatism" was nothing more than a euphemism for big government. Former American Enterprise Institute scholar Bruce Bartlett wrote that Bush was a "pretend conservative," who masqueraded as a "partisan Republican, anxious to improve the fortunes of his party, to be sure. But he is perfectly willing to jettison conservative principles at a moment's notice to achieve that goal."[37] To these conservatives, Bush's No Child Left Behind education program symbolized his willingness to expand government's reach into areas best left to the states. After voting for the bill, then-House Majority Leader Tom DeLay expressed regret, saying, "I came here to eliminate the Department of Education." DeLay explained that his "yea" vote was cast only because he wanted to support Bush: "I'm ashamed to say it was just blatant politics."[38] During Bush's first term, federal spending grew by an astounding 30.2 percent.[39] (Only Lyndon B. Johnson's Great Society had outspent Bush.) New York City Mayor Michael Bloomberg, who left the GOP to become an independent, maintained that Bush was guilty of fiscal "lunacy" for the federal indebtedness future taxpayers will have to absorb.[40]

Libertarian-minded conservatives were also unhappy, especially over Bush's unauthorized eavesdropping on millions of private telephone conversations and his demand that telecommunications companies provide the government with records of calls made—all without court approval. House Minority Leader John Boehner was skeptical: "I am not sure why it would be necessary to keep and have that kind of information."[41] Former Republican congressman and MSNBC commentator, Joe Scarborough, was even more passionate:

> Memo to the President and congressional leaders who signed up on this lousy program: We don't trust you anymore. We don't trust you with our phone bills. We don't trust you with our bank records. We don't trust you with our medical histories. From now on, if you want to look at Americans' private records, get a damn search warrant![42]

These intra-party disputes were compounded by the fact that in 2008 the Republicans lacked an heir apparent. Ever since 1960, Republicans have quickly settled on a prospective presidential nominee because it was his "turn." It was Vice President Richard M. Nixon's turn in 1960. That year, Nixon was able to turn away a half-hearted challenge from New York Governor Nelson A. Rockefeller.

It was Nixon's "turn" again in 1968, as he thwarted challenges from Rockefeller on the Left and Ronald Reagan on the Right. In 1972, Nixon was an incumbent president seeking reelection. Though challenged on the Left by California Congressman Pete McCloskey and on the Right by Ohio conservative Congressman John Ashbrook, Nixon coasted to an easy renomination.

Four years later it was supposed to be Ronald Reagan's "turn." But his succession was upended by Watergate and Nixon's resignation, making Gerald Ford an incumbent president who wanted a full term for himself. It was clearly Reagan's turn in 1980, although he had to initially rebuke a serious challenge from George H. W. Bush. In 1984, there was no one standing to challenge Reagan.

In 1988, Vice President George H. W. Bush was Reagan's heir apparent, and he easily bested his most serious challenger, Kansas Senator Bob Dole. In 1992, Bush sought reelection and easily beat conservative commentator Patrick J. Buchanan and his Buchanan Brigades. Bush's loss to Bill Clinton meant that it was Bob Dole's "turn" in 1996. Dole faced some stiff competition but none of his opponents could overcome the fact that the Kansas senator had spent decades toiling in the GOP trenches and, therefore, "deserved" the prize.

In 2000, it was George W. Bush's "turn," as the Bush family pressured Republican donors to accept the choice and made sure that they did not contribute to any other GOP candidate. As an incumbent president, Bush was unchallenged for renomination in 2004.

Only in 1964 did the Republicans not quickly settle on a candidate whose "turn" it was to be nominated. Richard Nixon's defeat in 1960 and his gubernatorial loss in California two years later had left the Republican Party without a regent. In the ensuing chaos, Arizona Senator Barry M. Goldwater emerged victorious. Goldwater's victory marked the conservative takeover of the Republican Party machinery, making them future kingmakers who would decide which conservative's "turn" it was for the party's presidential nomination.

In 2008, Republicans faced a situation akin to that of 1964. George W. Bush had no natural heirs. Jeb Bush, the popular ex-governor of Florida (a crucial state for the GOP in a general election), might have been the anointed one. But Jeb's problem was that his last name was Bush, an appellation that was toxic in 2008. As would-be nominees put their names forward, the question as to who would be the Republican regent became something more than merely answering who would be the party's nominee. It would determine, in some measure, the direction the party would take after Bush. Would Republicans like their conservatism undiluted? If so, Ron Paul was their man. But Paul's pure libertarianism and his strident opposition to George W. Bush made him a persona-non-grata to most Republicans. (Paul was booed at several Republican debates.) Did they prefer a Ronald Reagan-like figure who could command the stage and carry the conservative torch? If so, then Fred Thompson was attractive. But Thompson lacked Reagan's sense of timing and delayed his presidential announcement until the fall of 2007. Would Republicans prefer a social liberal on cultural issues and someone who would still make the war on terror a key issue? If so, former Mayor Rudolph W. Giuliani was their man. But as Democratic vice presidential nominee Joseph Biden so memorably stated, Giuliani could not construct a sentence without "a noun, a verb, and 9/11."[43] Would a successful businessman and ex-governor from the Northeast be able to fill the Reagan mold? If so, then Mitt Romney fit the bill. But two problems beset Romney's candidacy. First, to win the governorship of Massachusetts in 2002, Romney had to run as an economic conservative committed to cutting taxes and balancing budgets (no problem here for the GOP) *and* as a social liberal (Romney pronounced himself to be "pro-choice" on abortion and said he would enforce laws guaranteeing a woman's right to choose.) Second, Romney was a Mormon, an insurmountable obstacle for Republican-minded evangelicals who viewed Mormonism not as a form of Christianity but as a cult. Would Republicans prefer a folksy social conservative who had Reagan's affability? Then, former Arkansas Governor Mike Huckabee was their man. But the personable Huckabee could not expand his base beyond the Religious Right.

In effect, John S. McCain became the last man standing. McCain, who had lost a bitter nomination contest to George W. Bush in 2000, was the only Republican in 2008 who, because of his perceived longtime opposition to Bush, stood a chance of winning a general election. McCain's orthodox, balance-the-budget conservatism stood him in good stead with the party faithful. But McCain's espousal of campaign finance reform alienated social conservatives, especially pro-life groups who saw the 2001 McCain-Feingold bill as an impediment to their advocacy of traditional family values. In 2000, McCain alienated social conservatives by labeling Reverends Jerry Falwell and Pat Robertson as "agents of intolerance." Four years later McCain parted company with Bush and voted against his proposal to amend the U.S. Constitution and prohibit gay marriage. On domestic matters, McCain's apostasy continued with his strident opposition to the 2001 tax cuts. That year McCain was just one of two Republicans to oppose the reductions, saying they were fiscally irresponsible and skewed to the wealthy.[44] He also voted against three of George W. Bush's most conservative judicial nominees by preventing a rules change that would have made it possible to cut off debate. McCain also joined forces with Massachusetts Senator Edward M. Kennedy to support a patient's bill of rights. And he famously aligned himself with Kennedy to push for immigration reform in 2006 that included tighter border security (which was fine with conservatives) and gave illegal immigrants a path toward citizenship (which was not).[45]

While McCain won most Republican primaries, starting with an impressive win in New Hampshire (which became a second home after his 19-point upset win against Bush in 2000), he became the first to win the Republican presidential nomination without a majority of registered Republican voters—winning the support of just 47 percent of Republican voters.[46] To accomplish this extraordinary feat McCain garnered some Republican support, and added independents and wayward Democrats to score his primary victories.

In this respect, McCain's path to the nomination resembled that of Wendell Willkie's in 1940. Willkie was a utilities executive and corporate lawyer who supported Franklin D. Roosevelt's New Deal and had twice voted for him. In fact, Willkie was a lifelong Democrat who had attended the 1924 and 1932 Democratic Conventions. Willkie left the Democratic Party only in 1939, following a disagreement over TVA and the sale of his company's assets to that newly created government entity. Maintaining that the New Deal had failed ("What about the $60 billion you've spent and the 10 million persons that are still unemployed?" he asked FDR[47]), a groundswell began for his candidacy. Like McCain, Willkie was able to secure the Republican nomination thanks to overwhelming support from independents and so-called party amateurs who joined the "Win with Willkie Clubs" that mushroomed across the country. These outsiders pressured the party bosses to nominate Willkie over better-known partisans—including New York Governor Thomas E. Dewey and Ohio Senator Robert A. Taft. Like McCain, Willkie claimed to put country above partisanship. A 1940 issue of *Newsweek* magazine described Willkie's nomination as an anomaly: "Nothing exactly like it ever happened before in American politics. Willkie had never held public office or even sought it. Virtually a neophyte in politics, he had entered no primaries, made no deals, organized no campaign.... His backers were uninitiated volunteers, as strange to the ways of ward bosses and state chairmen as their hero."[48]

Willkie and McCain bore many political resemblances, particularly in their appeals to independents. But what also gave them common ground was the weakened stature of the Republican Party. In the presidential campaigns of 1932 and 1936, Republicans won only 8 out of a possible 96 states. The new Democratic majority was based not only on FDR's winning persona, but because Republicans were recast as a Great Depression Party whose sole clientele was satisfying the needs of its wealthy, fat cat constituents. This caricature was so powerfully implanted in the public's brain that it was accepted as a truism for nearly five decades (even though the facts suggested otherwise)—until 1980, when inflation and high unemployment eroded the Democrats' advantage as the party best for the economy. In a similar vein the Republican Party's weakened state in 2008 made McCain's nomination not only possible, but necessary. Republicans concluded that the only way to win was to nominate the least Bush Republican-associated candidate they could find. And that man was John McCain. McCain, for his part, seemed to delight in excoriating his party, declaring in his acceptance speech:

> I fight to restore the pride and principles of our party. We were elected to change Washington, and we let Washington change us. We lost the trust of the American people when some Republicans gave in to the temptations of corruption. We lost their trust when rather than reform government, both parties made it bigger. We lost their trust when instead of freeing ourselves from a dangerous dependence on foreign oil, both parties and Senator Obama passed another corporate welfare bill for oil companies. We lost their trust, when we valued our power over our principles.
>
> We're going to change that. We're going to recover the people's trust by standing up again for the values Americans admire. The party of Lincoln, Roosevelt and Reagan is going to get back to basics.[49]

McCain's scolding of the Republican Party did not diminish interest in the contest, however. Just as the Democratic primary turnout broke all records, so, too, did Republican turnout. As table 1.3 demonstrates, Republicans and independents took a keen interest in determining George W. Bush's successor.

Table 1.3   Republican primary turnout, 1972–2008

Election	Votes cast (in millions)	Major candidates
1972	6.2	Nixon
1976	10.4	Ford-Reagan
1980	12.7	Reagan-Bush-Anderson
1984	6.6	Reagan
1988	12.2	Bush-Dole
1992	12.7	Bush-Buchanan
1996	14.0	Dole-Buchanan-Forbes
2000	17.2	G. W. Bush-McCain
2004	7.9	G. W. Bush
2008	20.8	McCain-Romney-Huckabee

Source: Rhodes Cook, *The Rhodes Cook Letter*, June 2008, p. 5.

New Hampshire prides itself on being the first presidential primary in the nation. While its record for picking eventual party nominees is not perfect (Hillary Clinton won there in 2008), the state often does choose candidates who eventually win their party's presidential nomination. That was true for John McCain in 2008. McCain edged former Massachusetts Governor Mitt Romney in the Granite State, 37–32 percent. More telling perhaps was the coalition that McCain managed to assemble in New Hampshire and elsewhere. McCain *lost* Republican voters in New Hampshire—winning just 34 percent of their votes as compared to 35 percent for Romney. Among independents, McCain scored a resounding 40–27 percent victory. And among those who were dissatisfied or angry with the Bush administration, McCain won most of their votes. In fact on *every* issue that could be considered to be anti-Bush, McCain won plurality backing from New Hampshire voters (see table 1.4).

Table 1.4 John McCain's anti-Bush New Hampshire coalition

Issue	McCain % Favor	Romney % Favor
Highest priority for the next president is cutting taxes (pro-Bush position)	27	**37**
Highest priority for the next president is reducing the deficit (anti-Bush position)	**46**	26
Abortion should be illegal (pro-Bush position)	**36**	30
Abortion should be legal (anti-Bush position)	**37**	33
Positive opinion of Bush administration (pro-Bush)	32	**37**
Negative opinion of Bush administration (anti-Bush)	**40**	26
Compared to Bush, the next president should continue Bush policy (pro-Bush)	**35**	27
Compared to Bush, the next president should be more conservative (pro-Bush)	31	**35**
Compared to Bush, the next president should be less conservative (anti-Bush)	**56**	17
Enthusiastic about Bush administration (pro-Bush)	30	**37**
Satisfied with Bush administration (pro-Bush)	33	**37**
Dissatisfied with Bush administration (anti-Bush)	**41**	31
Angry with Bush administration (anti-Bush)	**37**	16
Oppose civil unions in New Hampshire (pro-Bush position)	32	**36**
Support civil unions in New Hampshire (anti-Bush position)	**43**	26
Give illegal immigrants a path to citizenship (pro-Bush position)	**54**	40

Continued

Table 1.4   Continued

Issue	McCain % Favor	Romney % Favor
Give illegal immigrants temporary worker status (pro-Bush position)	**42**	32
Deport illegal immigrants (anti-Bush position)	24	**40**
Strongly approve of U.S. war in Iraq (pro-Bush position)	23	**44**
Somewhat approve of U.S. war in Iraq (pro-Bush position)	**39**	33
Somewhat disapprove of U.S. War in Iraq (anti-Bush position)	**49**	22
Strongly disapprove of U.S. War in Iraq (anti-Bush position)	**38**	16

Source: Edison Media Research and Mitofsky International, New Hampshire exit poll, January 8, 2008.

Note: Winning issue percentage is denoted in **boldface type**.

The Future of Intra-Party Politics

Both parties crossed their own political rubicon in 2008. For Republicans, the election loss signals a period of introspection and internal party squabbling. Despite John McCain's many liabilities, he performed about as well (or better) than Republicans had a right to expect. The postelection challenge for the GOP is twofold: (1) on what grounds do they oppose President Obama, and (2) how do they retool their conservative philosophy for a twenty-first-century America whose demography is increasingly less friendly? Not only is Ronald Reagan dead, but so, too, is the powerful coalition he built that became the cornerstone for a Republican-dominated era. Undoubtedly, the 2012 Republican primaries will provide some answers to these challenges. But the selection of a new nominee will pale in contrast to the choice Republicans will make in finding some firmer ideological footing than it had when George W. Bush left office in disgrace in January 2009. Whether the party can do this quickly remains to be seen. After all, it took the GOP six elections after Franklin D. Roosevelt's 1932 victory before it found a winning formula in the person of Dwight D. Eisenhower. Wendell Willkie's nomination in 1940 was a tell-tale sign that Republicans were aware that they were a party in distress (and that their troubles were deeper than Herbert Hoover's many failures). Already, there are some indications that the GOP realizes it cannot revel in the traditional postelection mortems of blaming the losing candidate for its troubles. Yes, John McCain was temperamental; yes, McCain had no consistent political message; yes, McCain's choice of Sarah Palin was an admitted "Hail Mary pass" that failed; and yes, the McCain campaign lacked the discipline and powerful financial apparatus that Barack Obama managed to direct. But Republicans seem to understand that blaming the candidate, while cathartic, does nothing to solve their substantial party problems. Having come to this consensus sooner rather than later means that a GOP recovery, though not easy, will take less time.

Barack Obama's victory has significant consequences for Democrats. For the first time since Jimmy Carter in 1976, a Democrat won more than 50 percent of the popular vote. But unlike Carter, Obama won without an intra-party ideological struggle (as this chapter has described). As a result, Obama inherits a Democratic-controlled Congress with padded majorities. Unlike Jimmy Carter and Bill Clinton, who also had Democratic majorities in the House and Senate, Obama has something else from these lawmakers that these other Democratic presidents did not have: loyalty. Carter's and Clinton's Democratic Congresses did not believe that a presidential failure would have any lasting impact on them. After all, Democratic candidates ran substantially ahead of the top of their tickets in 1976 and 1992. But the 1994 midterm elections proved that Democrats could lose control of Congress. No longer could they take their 40-year reign in the House for granted. Memories of the 1994 loss are still fresh, and Obama's Democrats (besides having no real disagreements with him) want to follow his direction. Instead of a presidential system with Congress acting independently of the White House, the Congress is increasingly acting like a parliamentary body—especially when one party controls both the executive and legislative branches. As it was for George W. Bush from 2001–2006, when he set the agenda and got the votes from Republican-controlled Congresses for his domestic and foreign programs, so the once fractious Democrats appear capable of doing the same thing. How long the Democrats walk in lockstep and whether the party fractures around a set of issues that are unknown at this point are, of course, open questions. But the lack of intra-party conflict gives Barack Obama a chance to be the most successful Democratic president since Franklin D. Roosevelt. If he succeeds, intra-party unity will follow. If he does not, then the intra-party battles will start anew.

Notes

1. See Gallup poll, July 13–18, 1952. Text of question: "Do you approve or disapprove of the way Truman is handling his job as President?" Approve, 29%; disapprove, 59%; both (volunteered), 1%; no opinion, 12%.
2. See David McCullough, *Truman* (New York: Simon and Schuster, 1992), p. 889.
3. Harris Interactive, poll, June 4–8, 2008. Text of question: "And how would you rate the job Vice President Dick Cheney is doing—excellent, pretty good, only fair, or poor?" Excellent/pretty good, 18%; only fair/poor, 74%; not sure, 8%.
4. Toni Morrison, "Comment," *New Yorker*, October 5, 1998.
5. Theodore H. White, *The Making of the President, 1968* (New York: Atheneum, 1969), p. 376.
6. For more on this see Ted Van Dyk, "How the Election of 1968 Reshaped the Democratic Party," *Wall Street Journal*, August 25, 2008, p. A-11.
7. George McGovern, Acceptance Speech, Democratic National Convention, Miami, Florida, July 14, 1972.
8. Gallup poll, November 21–24, 1980. Text of question: "Do you approve or disapprove of the way Carter is handling his job as President?" Approve, 31%; disapprove, 56%; no opinion, 13%.
9. Edgar Litt, *The Political Cultures of Massachusetts* (Cambridge, MA: MIT Press, 1965), p. 22.

10. Quoted in John Kenneth White, *Still Seeing Red: How the Cold War Shapes the New American Politics* (Westview, CO: Westview Press, 1997), p. 199.
11. Excerpts from Interview with Clinton on "Goals for Presidency," *New York Times*, June 28, 1992, p. 17.
12. Bill Clinton, Interview with Ted Koppel, ABC News, "Seventy-Two Hours to Victory," broadcast, November 4, 1992.
13. *The Democratic Party Platform, 1992* (Washington, DC: Democratic National Committee, 1992), p. 7.
14. See especially John Kenneth White, *The New Politics of Old Values* (Lanham, MD: University Press of America, 1998), especially Chapter 9, pp. 243–278.
15. Bill Clinton, State of the Union Address, Washington, DC, January 23, 1996.
16. New Jersey U.S. Senator Bill Bradley challenged Gore for the party's nomination. But it was difficult for most political analysts and voters to see the differences between the two contenders.
17. See John Kenneth White, *The Making of the Candidates, 2003* (Utica, NY: Zogby International, 2003).
18. Zogby International, Iowa survey, September 8–9, 2003. Fifty percent said they disliked George W. Bush as a person; only 35% liked him. Zogby International, New Hampshire survey, September 24–25, 2003. Fifty percent disliked George W. Bush as a person; only 38% liked him.
19. Gallup Poll, January 30–February 2, 2008. Text of question: "Do you approve or disapprove of the way George W. Bush is handling his job as president?" Approve, 34%; disapprove, 61%; no opinion, 5%.
20. Barack Obama, *The Audacity of Hope: Thoughts on Reclaiming the American Dream* (New York: Crown Publishers, 2006).
21. Edison Media Research and Mitofsky International, South Carolina Democratic primary exit poll, January 26, 2008.
22. Obama's organizational skills helped him to win 13 of 15 caucuses—an organization strength that proved decisive in the delegate count.
23. See Sam Roberts, "A Generation Away, Minorities May Become the Majority in U.S.," *New York Times*, August 14, 2008, p. A-1.
24. For example, see NBC News/*Wall Street Journal*, poll, August 15–18, 2008. Text of question: "How often do you attend services at a church, synagogue, mosque, or other place of worship?" Never, 14%; once a year, 6%; a few times a year, 20%; once a month, 7%; about twice a month, 10%; once a week or more often, 39%; not sure, 4%.
25. Edison Media Research and Mitofsky International, Pennsylvania Democratic primary exit poll, April 22, 2008.
26. Edison Media Research and Mitofsky International, Wisconsin Democratic primary exit poll, February 19, 2008.
27. Hillary Clinton, Speech to the Democratic National Convention, Denver, Colorado, August 26, 2008.
28. Daniel Bell, *The End of Ideology: On the Exhaustion of Political Ideas in the Fifties* (New York: The Free Press, 1962), p. 393.
29. See Zogby International, poll, May 17–20, 2007. Text of question: "Are you proud or ashamed that George W. Bush is the President of the United States?" Proud, 45%; ashamed, 42%; not sure, 14%. See American Research Group, poll, November 9–12, 2007. Text of question: "Which one of these four statements do you agree with about President Bush? #1. President Bush has not abused his powers as president. #2. President Bush has abused his powers as president, but the abuses are not serious enough to warrant impeachment under the Constitution. #3. President Bush has

abused his powers as president which rise to the level of impeachable offenses under the Constitution and he should be impeached and removed from office." #1, 36%; #2, 9%; #3, 21%; #4, 34%. See "Poll: Public Not Pleased with President Bush," CNN press release, November 9, 2007. According to a CNN/Opinion Research poll, 23% said Bush was the worst president ever, 35% said Bush was doing a poor job compared to his predecessors, and 40% said Bush was doing a good job compared to other presidents.

30. Quoted in Jim Rutenberg, "Ex-Aide Details a Loss of Faith in the President," *New York Times*, April 1, 2007.

31. Arnold Schwarzenegger, Address to Republican Party Fall Convention, September 7, 2007.

32. Tom Davis, "Where We Stand Today," memo to Republican Leadership, May 14, 2008.

33. See Pew Research Center, "Political Landscape More Favorable to Democrats: Trends in Political Values and Core Attributes," p. 8.

34. Frank Rich, "Earth to GOP: The Gipper Is Dead," *New York Times*, May 13, 2007. Fred Thompson was still an undeclared candidate.

35. Ibid.

36. Quoted in Bruce Bartlett, *Imposter: How George W. Bush Bankrupted America and Betrayed the Reagan Legacy* (New York: Doubleday, 2006), p. 203.

37. Ibid., pp. 1, 16.

38. Quoted in "Washington Wire," *Wall Street Journal*, July 27, 2001, p. A-1.

39. See Veronique de Rugy, "President Reagan, Champion Budget-Cutter," American Enterprise Institute, June 9, 2004. The discretionary spending figures were LBJ, +33.4%; Nixon, −15.2%; Carter, +10.1%; Reagan (first term), +8.3%; Reagan (second term), +7.0%; George H. W. Bush, −3.4%; Clinton (first term), −3.4%; Clinton (second term), −8.0% George W. Bush (first term), +30.2%.

40. Quoted in Jackie Calmes, "GOP Is Losing Grip on Core Business Vote," *Wall Street Journal*, October 2, 2007, p. A-1.

41. Quoted in Eric Lichtblau and Scott Shane, "Bush Is Pressed over New Report on Surveillance," *New York Times*, May 12, 2006, p. A-1.

42. Joe Scarborough, "Joe Scarborough on NSA Phone Database: 'Be Very Afraid,'" MSNBC post, May 12, 2006; MSNBC.com.

43. Joe Biden, Democratic presidential debate, October 30, 2007.

44. See Jonathan Weisman, "McCain Offers Tax Policies He Once Opposed," *Washington Post*, April 25, 2008, p. A-1. The other Republican senator opposed to the bill was Rhode Island's Lincoln Chafee. See Lincoln Chafee, *Against the Tide: How a Compliant Congress Empowered a Reckless President* (New York: Thomas Dunne Books, 2008), p. 61.

45. See Joseph Lelyveld, "John and Sarah in St. Paul," *New York Review of Books*, October 9, 2008, p. 10 and Elizabeth Drew, *Citizen McCain* (New York: Simon and Schuster, 2002), passim.

46. See Rhodes Cook, *The Rhodes Cook Letter*, June 2008, p. 12.

47. Quoted in Louis L. Gould, *Grand Old Party: A History of the Republicans* (New York: Random House, 2003), p. 280.

48. Quoted in Stefan Lorant, *The Presidency* (New York: The Macmillan Company, 1951), p. 626.

49. John McCain, Acceptance Speech, Republican National Convention, St. Paul, Minnesota, September 4, 2008.

Part II

The Issues

2

It Was the Economy, Mostly

Donald W. Beachler

O ver the course of 2008, the issue that would seem most determinative of the presidential election outcome changed several times. In January, as the nominating contests got under way, it appeared that the war in Iraq, which was in its fifth year with no foreseeable conclusion, might be the focus of the election. In the first caucus of the year in Iowa, the war in Iraq and the economy were tied at 35 percent as the issue Democratic caucus attendees listed as most important. In the Iowa Republican caucus, illegal immigration was listed most frequently (33 percent) as the most important issue by caucus participants.[1] In New Hampshire, the first primary was held just a few days after the Iowa caucuses. The economy was selected over Iraq as the most important issue by a 38–31 percent margin among voters in the Democratic primary. In the Republican primary in New Hampshire the economy was listed as the most important issue by 31 percent of the voters, but when the Iraq and terrorism responses are combined the national security voters total 42 percent of the Republican electorate.

By late spring and through the summer, world oil prices soared and the cost of gasoline and home heating oil rose dramatically. It appeared as though energy might be the dominant issue in the campaign, and Republicans thought they might have an advantage as they argued for more domestic energy production through methods such as offshore drilling. Most Democrats had opposed such drilling as a threat to the nation's ocean and coastal environments.

In the fall, an economy that had been slowing all year cratered in the wake of a financial crisis of a scale not seen since the 1930s. While few commentators thought the nation was headed for a depression, many said that such a catastrophic outcome was not impossible or wholly unthinkable. In the final weeks of the campaign many topics were discussed, but the economic crisis seemed to overshadow all other matters.

On the various issues related to the economy, the voters were treated to fairly traditional campaign by the candidates. Both candidates promised to increase the number of Americans covered by health care, but Barack Obama's program consisted largely of an expansion of government programs whereas

John McCain proposed a system of changes in tax law that he believed would reduce costs and allow more Americans access to health insurance.[2] Health policy analyst Jonathan Oberlander argued that the programs were similar to what each party had been offering 16 years before.[3] As Republicans had done with much success in many prior presidential elections, John McCain said that his Democratic opponent would raise taxes on hardworking Americans. Barack Obama frequently accused McCain of favoring more tax breaks for the rich. In 2008, some of the policy proposals and political rhetoric of each candidate may have been standard fare, but the circumstances preceding the election were extraordinary.

The American Political Economy

As did the rest of the developed world in 2008, the United States combined a capitalist or market economy with a democratic electoral system. Political parties that wish to be rewarded by the voters, and governments that inevitably desire to be reelected, must preside over a period of relative economic prosperity. Voters use the ballot box to punish poor economic performance. In a market economy, growth depends to a significant degree upon the investment decisions of the private sector. All governments must induce investment from capitalists if they wish to succeed in a democratic capitalist society.[4]

Despite the need to create conditions for private sector growth there is still a great deal of variation in the politics and economic policies of various capitalist democracies. The balance of power between capital, labor, and government varies widely across different political systems. Levels of taxation and government-provided or -mandated social services vary greatly from country to country across the developed world. For example, in many European countries the government mandates that workers receive five or six weeks of annual paid vacation. In the United States, there are no legally mandated minimum vacations and the average worker receives just 13 days paid vacation each year.[5] In most European nations, workers receive extended paid leave when they give birth or adopt a child. In the United States, certain workers are legally entitled to unpaid leave for 12 weeks while many workers in small businesses are excluded from this mandated benefit. In a measure of access to healthcare and nutrition, the United States ranked thirty-second in the world in its infant mortality rate in 2008.[6]

The limited welfare state in the United States renders American workers especially vulnerable in times of economic upheaval. The British news magazine, *The Economist*, summed up just one aspect of the rather weak safety net that is available to Americans when they face economic difficulties,

> Compared with the systems in other industrialized countries, the American unemployment-insurance (UI) scheme pays lower benefits for less time and to a smaller share of the unemployed. In expansions this encourages the jobless to return quickly to work and unemployed Americans do indeed work harder at finding jobs than their European counterparts.... But in recessions, when there is less work to return to, it causes hardship.[7]

Unemployment benefits are comparatively stingy with an average benefit of just $300 per week, or less than half the average private sector wage. Because of restrictions on eligibility, only about 40 percent of unemployed workers qualify for unemployment insurance.[8]

The United States occupies a unique position among economically developed countries with respect to taxation and the level of government benefits provided to citizens. While they often complain of high taxes, Americans pay relatively low taxes compared to their Canadian and European counterparts. For example, in 2001 it was estimated that Americans paid taxes equivalent to about 31 percent of the entire economy as measured by Gross Domestic Product. By contrast, Canadians paid over 40 percent, the French nearly 50 percent, and the Swedes nearly 56 percent of GDP.[9] While they retain far greater portions of their income, Americans live in a nation where one-fifth of children are raised in poverty, more than double the rate in most other wealthy nations. The United States is the only industrialized nation without some form of universal health insurance. Moreover, the gap between the rich and poor is much greater than in most European nations.[10]

The dual results of America's exceptional path are well summed up by Andrew Hacker at the conclusion of his 1997 book, *Money*. Hacker states that,

> America's chosen emphasis has been on the offering of opportunities to the ambitious...America has more self-made millionaires and more men and women who have attained a $100,000 than any other country...less is left for those who lack the opportunities or the temperament to succeed in competition. The United States has a greater percentage of its citizens in prison, on the streets, and more neglected children, than any of the nations with which it is appropriately compared.[11]

The United States is different from most democratic capitalist countries because it has never had a strong party of the Left. This phenomenon, often called "American Exceptionalism," has meant that business in the United States has had more power than in other countries. Workers' interests have not been as strongly represented in the halls of national government as they have been elsewhere. Labor unions, which can act as a countervailing power to business, are also weaker in the United States. Politicians, such as Barack Obama, John Kerry, Al Gore, and Bill Clinton, who are regarded as being on the "left" in the United States, take positions on issues that would mark them as conservatives in most European countries. The fact that John Kerry was not in favor of government-sponsored or -mandated health insurance for every citizen would have made him unelectable as a conservative party candidate in many European countries.[12]

Despite the comparatively narrow range of ideological structures of the two major American political parties, there are some significant policy outcome differences between Democratic and Republican presidents. Political scientist Larry Bartels studied the economic record of every president since the end of World War II and found that income inequality increased under Republican presidents, and in four of five cases, decreased under Democratic. Bartels found that in the second year a president is in office, when the policies of the president's initial or "honeymoon year" have had an opportunity to impact the economy, families at the bottom of the income scale experienced the greatest growth of any income quintile when Democrats were in office. Republican presidents actually produced a decline in real income for these same families in their second year in office.[13] Bartels also found that real income for all groups grew more under Democratic than Republican presidents between 1948 and 2005.

A study of the rise of conservatism in the Republican Party indicates that the political and policy differences between the two parties have increased substantially in recent years. Republicans have increasingly embraced tax cuts above all other budget priorities and neglected government programs that would aid the middle- and lower classes.[14] The Democrats may not have shifted very far to the Left, but the Republicans have certainly tilted strongly to the Right in recent decades as the party has become more anchored in the South.

The Bush tax policies are indicative of this trend. Bush's tax reductions gave the bulk of the income tax cuts to those at the upper end of the income scale. Bush proposed, and a Republican Congress enacted, a phaseout of the inheritance or estate tax, even though just 2 percent of Americans die with enough wealth that their heirs are subject to federal estate tax. (The election of Barack Obama virtually ensures that there will be a federal estate tax in the United States for some time to come.) Republicans have also been staunch defenders of the notion that income earned from investments such as stock dividends or capital gains from the sale of assets like stocks should be taxed at lower rates than income attained through work. Since almost 90 percent of the stock in the United States is owned by the wealthiest 20 percent of taxpayers, these lower rates on investment income inevitably benefit the wealthy far more than those further down the economic ladder. Democrats, while not proposing steep tax increases on the wealthy, have generally opposed tax cuts that largely benefit the wealthiest citizens.

Despite the relatively small differences between the two major American political parties, there is much at stake in American elections. Democrats retain a commitment to government as a mechanism for providing vital services such as health care and retirement income. In recent decades, Republicans have believed that large tax cuts would deprive government of the revenues necessary to maintain its commitments to citizens, a strategy some have labeled "starving the beast."[15] The GOP has advocated tax incentives and private sector solutions to problems such as health care access for all citizens and also as a mechanism to provide retirement income. The Republicans' ideological commitment to such an agenda is unshaken by public reluctance to support some key components of their agenda. George Bush's 2005 proposal to at least consider allowing taxpayers to invest a portion of their Social Security taxes in private accounts was never brought to a vote in the Republican-controlled Senate due to strong constituent opposition. It is easy to be cynical about American politics, but those who argue that there is no difference between the parties are guilty of considerable exaggeration. As Bartels notes, politics does matter with respect to the economic fortunes of different segments of the population.

Which Side Are You On? Taxes in the 2008 Election

A major issue in the presidential campaign was how to deal with the tax cuts enacted at the behest of George Bush, which are scheduled to expire in 2011. The two major presidential candidates offered very different policies on federal taxation and each was consistent with his party's general ideological orientation over the past several elections. McCain proposed retaining nearly all of Bush's tax cuts, which Democrats condemned as favoring the wealthy, and also favored added tax cuts for families and corporations. Obama proposed to repeal the Bush tax cuts for families making more than $250,000 a year.

Still, each candidate deviated from the past in an interesting way. John McCain had opposed the Bush tax cuts as a presidential candidate and voted against them as a member of the U.S. Senate. As he sought the White House in 2008, McCain embraced Bush's tax policy and even proposed some additional tax cuts. Obama, on the other hand, deviated from his party's general opposition to tax cuts, by promising to keep the Bush tax cuts for all but the richest 5 percent of taxpayers.

Though he had voted against the major Bush tax cuts of 2001 and 2003, in his 2008 presidential campaign John McCain proposed to make permanent nearly all of George W. Bush's tax cuts that were scheduled to expire in 2011. McCain also stated he would reduce the rate of corporate taxation from 35 to 25 percent. Obama would often attack this plan, which McCain claimed would aid American business, as assisting the richest corporations including the quite unpopular oil companies. To offset the cost of tax reduction, McCain called for the elimination of the infamous earmarks, or special projects that members of Congress add to spending bills that mandate projects such as roads, bridges, federal buildings, and a host of other goodies for their constituencies. McCain's focus on the infamous earmarks gained him much positive attention, but such spending accounted for only 0.5 percent of the federal budget. Simply eliminating earmarks would not do much to reduce federal spending. *The Economist* called McCain's plans, "half a fiscal policy, and the easy half at that."[16]

Barack Obama said that he would repeal the Bush tax cuts only for those with family incomes above $250,000 a year. Families earning less than that would receive a tax cut under the Democratic nominee's proposals. He was the first major party presidential nominee to propose rebating a portion of the Social Security payroll tax to low-wage workers and granting a tax credit for up to $800 in mortgage interest paid to "non-itemizers." Non-itemizers are almost exclusively in the bottom half of American income earners. Since those in the bottom third of income do not pay federal income taxes, but do pay Social Security and Medicare taxes, Obama was the rare presidential candidate offering cuts for low-wage workers. Like McCain, Obama offered few credible spending cuts that would offset his proposed tax reductions.

In August 2008, tax analysts at the nonpartisan Urban Institute summarized the distributional impact of the two candidates' tax plans.

> The two candidates' tax plans would have sharply different distributional effects. Senator McCain's tax cuts would primarily benefit those with very high incomes,

almost all of whom would receive large tax cuts that would, on average, raise their after-tax incomes by more than twice the average for all households. Many fewer households at the bottom of the income distribution would get tax cuts and those tax cuts would be small as a share of after-tax income. In marked contrast, Senator Obama offers much larger tax breaks to low- and middle-income taxpayers and would increase taxes on high-income taxpayers. The largest tax cuts, as a share of income, would go to those at the bottom of the income distribution, while taxpayers with the highest income would see their taxes rise significantly.[17]

A September 2008 *Washington Post* poll found that 51 percent of Americans thought their taxes would go up under an Obama administration. The newspaper reported that this finding was a source of frustration for the Obama campaign whose tax proposals called for tax cuts for 95 percent of Americans and tax increases for families making more than $250,000 per year.[18] Republican political strategist Scott Reed attributed the widespread belief that Obama was proposing tax increases to the McCain campaign's repeated assertions that the Illinois senator was for raising taxes on all American families. One-third of poll respondents believed that their taxes would go up under Senator McCain, even though he proposed tax cuts for the upper two-thirds of American income earners and no tax increases of any kind.[19]

While campaigning in a working-class neighborhood in Toledo, Ohio, Barack Obama was confronted by Samuel J. Wurzelbacher, a local resident. Wurzelbacher asked Obama whether he believed in a flat tax, a policy that would require all income to be taxed at the same rate rather than at the progressive rate that has existed in the United States for many decades. Obama stated that he supported a progressive income tax and thus did not support a flat tax. Wurzelbacher claimed that he was planning to buy a plumbing business with revenue of $250,000–280,000 a year and that Obama's plan would tax him more.[20] Obama responded by acknowledging that the prospective business owner would be taxed at 39 percent on income from the business that was above $250,000. (As the "facts" were presented by Wurzelbacher, since the revenue for the business was only in the $250,000–$280,000 range it is unlikely that the net income from the business would have exceeded $250,000 a year and thus, his taxes would not have increased at all under Obama's plan.) Obama responded by saying,

> It's not that I want to punish your success. I just want to make sure that everybody who is behind you, that they've got a chance at success, too.... My attitude is that if the economy's good for folks from the bottom up, it's gonna be good for everybody. If you've got a plumbing business, you're gonna be better off [...] if you've got a whole bunch of customers who can afford to hire you, and right now everybody's so pinched that business is bad for everybody and I think when you spread the wealth around, it's good for everybody.[21]

While much of Wurzelbacher's statement to Obama proved to be false (he was not in a position to buy the small company where he worked and his income was about $40,000 a year), John McCain took up his cause in the third debate and for the rest of the campaign. Dubbing Wurzelbacher, "Joe the Plumber," McCain presented him as the proto-typical American whose dreams of wealth would be taxed away by the redistributionist policies of Obama. (Joe the Plumber admitted that he had a modest income and stated that he feared Obama was a socialist who would eventually increase taxes on people such as himself who earned modest incomes.) McCain and his running mate Sarah Palin often focused on Obama's remarks to Joe the Plumber by labeling him as a socialist or a redistributor of the wealth whose repeal of the Bush tax cuts for the wealthiest Americans would deprive citizens of their hard-earned wealth. Obama responded by noting that McCain had opposed the Bush tax cuts when they were originally passed and asked whether McCain was a socialist when he opposed the tax cuts in 2001 and 2003.[22] Still, Joe the Plumber offered McCain a chance to present Republicans as populist champions of the regular people against big government liberals. Ohio political scientist Melissa Miller summed the issue up by saying, "Even if we agree that Joe the Plumber would be better off under Obama, McCain is saying I'm looking out for the little guy. It's not about comparing ten-point plans."[23]

The U.S. government does less to redistribute wealth than other capitalist democracies.[24] Socialist parties and politicians have gained less traction in electoral politics in the United States than in Europe where socialist parties have often held power. Still, when many Americans faced the prospect of unemployment, home foreclosures, or major reductions in the value of their retirement accounts, they have been less frightened than Joe Wurzelbacher was by the prospect of some minor redistribution of wealth.

McCain also attacked Obama's plan to rebate portions of the payroll tax for Social Security and Medicare for individuals who did not pay income tax. The Republican nominee argued that Obama wanted to turn the IRS into a welfare agency. Obama acknowledged that some recipients of his tax cuts paid no income tax but they did pay payroll taxes and that it was fair to cut payroll tax as a mechanism to provide tax relief to the lowest-paid working Americans. Speaking of Obama's tax plans, McCain said that, "Since you can't reduce taxes on those who pay zero, the government will write them all checks called a tax credit. And the Treasury will have to cover those checks by taxing other people, including a lot of folks just like Joe."[25] Speaking in St. Louis, Obama responded directly to McCain's attacks, "That's right, Missouri—John McCain is so out of touch with the struggles you are facing that he must be the first politician in history to call a tax cut for working people "'welfare.'"[26]

In the end, the arguments over taxes did not appear to benefit either candidate because a majority of voters fully expected their taxes to go up no matter which candidate won the elections. Sixty-one percent of voters thought that their taxes would increase under John McCain and 36 percent of these voters supported McCain. An even higher 71 percent of voters thought their taxes would increase if Barack Obama was elected and 40 percent of these voters supported Obama.[27] The electorate was treated to a full and vigorous debate on two distinctly different approaches to tax policy. Interestingly, a majority concluded that neither candidate would cut their taxes.

The Fall Financial Meltdown

Few prognosticators would have guessed that the eight weeks preceding the election of 2008 would be dominated by a grave financial crisis. In 2003 and 2004, prominent economists argued that the business cycle could be managed by fiscal and monetary policy in a manner that would cause relatively minor disruptions in American life.[28] By 2007 these predictions seemed justified. That summer the Dow Jones industrial average exceeded 14,000 for the first time and Treasury Secretary Henry Paulson proclaimed that the economy was in good shape.[29] Indeed, in the summer of 2007 it appeared as though the Iraq War might be the major issue in the 2008 presidential election. It was the war, rather than any major differences on economic policy, that helped Barack Obama in his primary campaign against Hillary Rodham Clinton.

While officially declared by the federal government in late November 2008, the United States had been in a recession since December of 2007. In the summer of 2008, the American economy was hampered by high gas prices that made commuting to work more expensive and caused some Americans to reconsider vacation plans. Unemployment was slowly edging up as each month brought a net loss of jobs in the economy. In July 2008, Labor Department statistics indicated that the wages of rank-and-file employees (those in nonsupervisory or managerial roles) were failing to keep pace with inflation. The cost of living had increased by 5.6 percent from July 2007. Energy prices were the most conspicuous contributor to the higher cost of living, but food, beverage, and transportation costs all increased significantly. The average worker's wages decreased 3.1 percent from July 2007 to July 2008 when inflation was considered against wage increases.[30] Any pain felt in the country by the summer of 2008 would seem mild by comparison to what was to follow.

Before proceeding to a consideration of the political impact of the economic meltdown of 2008, it is worth considering the overall well-being of American workers during the preceding years—several of which saw considerable economic growth. Entry-level wages for high school and college graduates fell in real terms from 2001 through 2007.[31] Even more striking was the fact that median family income was lower in inflation-adjusted dollars at the end of the latest period of growth (late 2007) than it was at the end of the previous period of expansion in 2000. In 2007, the real dollar income of the median American family was $60,500 as opposed to $61,000 in 2000. The first six years of the Bush administration were the first period of economic expansion since the end of World War II in which a rising economy did not coincide with an increase in the real wages of American workers.[32] The benefits of economic growth in the first years of the twenty-first century were concentrated in the upper 10 percent of wage earners, and especially the top 1 percent. Many citizens maintained their lifestyles with borrowing, often against the rising values of their homes or on credit cards.[33] A large majority of American workers were not thriving before the fall of 2008, though this income and wage stagnation received relatively little press attention. Many American families entered the fall of 2008 in fragile economic states, even if their precarious circumstances were not entirely visible to the national media.

In the first two weeks of September the focus of media attention was on Sarah Palin, McCain's intriguing, if controversial, vice presidential running mate. McCain gained in the polls as the plain-spoken governor added a measure of star power and celebrity that had seemed to be the monopoly of the Obama campaign. In mid-September, economic shock waves would consign the charismatic governor of Alaska to a considerably reduced, but by no means negligible, role in the coverage of the campaign.

In the months preceding the election, major American financial institutions went bankrupt or required major infusions of cash from federal institutions to survive. On September 15, Lehman Brothers, the 158-year-old Wall Street investment bank collapsed as a result of bad investments in risky mortgage-backed securities and filed for bankruptcy. Lehman Brothers' collapse represented the largest bankruptcy in American history. Just a week earlier, the primary institutions in the American secondary mortgage markets, Fannie MAE and Freddie MAC, were seized by the Federal Housing Finance agency and their shareholders' stock value was wiped out in return for a $200 billion commitment of public money from the Treasury Department. The largest insurance company in the world, American International Group (AIG), faced a severe financial crisis and was rescued by loan guarantees from the Federal Reserve that permitted the government to purchase up to 79.2 percent of the bank's holdings. Over the next three weeks AIG received $122 billion in loans from the Fed as its stock lost more than 95 percent of the value it had had a year before. Just ten days after Lehman Brothers collapsed, Seattle-based Washington Mutual, the nation's sixth largest bank, filed for bankruptcy and was absorbed into J. P. Morgan Chase. Other venerable financial institutions were absorbed by rivals after losing most of their market value due to very poor business judgments. Merrill Lynch, most famous for its commercials that bragged of its faith in the stock market with the symbol of a bull, was absorbed by Bank of America. Wachovia, the financial services firm based in Charlotte, North Carolina, was purchased at a steep discount by Wells Fargo after suffering major financial losses.[34]

The fiscal crisis was rooted, in large part, in the loose mortgage-lending practices that had been encouraged by the emphasis on government deregulation of businesses in the preceding 30 years. As the journalist William Greider noted, both major political parties had largely subscribed to the notion that business, including the financial services industry, would serve the country if they were not hampered by regulations first imposed in the New Deal era.[35] Many mortgages were "sub-prime" or loans to borrowers with poor credit ratings who were charged higher interest rates. Other loans had low "teaser" interest rates that increased after a period of time and increased mortgage payments well beyond what the borrower could possibly pay. In many cases, no real proof was required that mortgage borrowers held jobs or that their incomes were what they stated to their prospective lender. In one case, Washington Mutual received a mortgage application from a borrower who claimed to earn a six-figure income as mariachi singer. Unable to verify the singer's income, a WAMU agent took a picture of the applicant in a mariachi outfit and submitted the photo into his file. The loan was granted. In another WAMU case, a gardener offered, without any evidence, the claim that he earned $12,000 a month. A photo of the gardener in front of his truck with the name of his business on it was submitted and the mortgage loan was approved.[36] These WAMU cases may not have been typical, but they indicate the degree to which financial institutions were free to make risky loans.

The severity of the crisis was underscored at a meeting of key senators and representatives with Federal Reserve Chair Ben Bernanke and Treasury Secretary Henry Paulson on September 18, 2008. Paulson and Bernanke warned the group of legislators that without drastic action the nation was headed for financial devastation.[37] Senator Christopher Dodd, a Democrat from Connecticut and chair of the Senate Banking Committee, said that the assembled group of senators and representatives were warned, "That we're literally maybe days away from a complete meltdown of our financial system, with all the implications here at home and globally."[38] In the face of predictions of the dire consequences of inaction from the country's leading economic officials, both McCain and Obama voted for the unpopular $700 billion bailout package for financial institutions that was passed by Congress and signed by President Bush. Despite the skepticism of the electorate that, according to exit polls, opposed the $700 billion bailout by a 56–39 percent margin, neither candidate opted to vote against the measure.

The setbacks for these firms caused a credit crunch that threatened the business and consumer credit that allowed the American economy to function. It also caused a major plunge in the stock market and, to a lesser extent, in bond markets, resulting in the loss of over $2.4 trillion to Americans' holdings in mutual funds. Individual investors, financial institutions, college endowments, public and private pension funds, and charitable foundations all saw major losses in the value of their holdings. For individuals, the loss in retirement funds was especially frightening because in the preceding decades most Americans with any pension coverage no longer held defined benefit plans, under which their employer was responsible for paying them a specific pension amount. Rather, as part of what political scientist Jacob Hacker has called the *Great Risk Shift*, most Americans participate in defined contribution retirement plans in which their retirement income is determined by the performance of investment choices they made.[39] It has long been common wisdom in the United States that a substantial portion of one's pension savings should be held in funds that were invested in the stock market. For those who had followed the experts' advice, October 2008 was a frightening month.

The economic pain that swept across the country was not confined to financial markets. There was a net loss of jobs in the economy in every month from January through August of 2008. These job losses accelerated in the two months preceding the election as the economy shed 403,000 jobs in September and an additional 320,000 jobs in October.[40] Despite John McCain's insistence, many Americans probably did not think that the fundamentals of the economy were sound. In fact, exit polling indicated that just 7 percent of those who cast ballots in the presidential election rated the state of the economy as excellent or good, while 93 percent classified the economy as being not so good or poor.

Faced with a perplexing financial and economic crisis that seemed to befuddle the nation's economic officials, neither candidate ever offered a specific plan to deal with the rapidly evolving financial crisis. In the context of an eight-week general election campaign and a very complex situation, it was not likely that either candidate would produce such a major policy proposal on the financial crisis.

The economic difficulties that spread fear across the country seemed to harm the McCain campaign. In the last six weeks of the election there was little attention paid to foreign policy, which McCain saw as his strong suit and where he hoped to benefit from his long years of service in the Senate. However, as they watched their pensions and savings diminish, it is likely that few Americans were seriously concerned about which candidate was best prepared to resolve the potential crisis related to Georgia and Russia's competing claims to South Ossetia and Abkhazia. Iraq, where McCain believed that diminished American casualties and increased political stability had vindicated his long support for the war and the 2007 increase in American troop levels ("the Surge"), was not discussed much in the campaign. Nothing symbolizes the enhanced importance of domestic policy more than the fact that in the first of the three presidential debates, held on September 26 in Oxford Mississippi, about half the time was allocated to discussion of the economy even though this was to be the foreign policy debate.

Statements about the economy from McCain and his associates also created an impression that he was perhaps out of touch with the realities of everyday life. In July, with gas prices high and monthly job losses continuing, Phil Gramm, the former Texas Republican senator and co-chair of McCain's campaign, stated that the United States was only in a "mental recession" and that the country had become a "nation of whiners."[41] Gramm stepped aside from an official role in the McCain campaign after his initial remarks, but Gramm renewed his sentiments in September when he told banking lobbyists that because they were not whiners he knew they would be supporting Senator McCain.[42] Barack Obama used the whiner remarks on several occasions, including his acceptance speech at the Democratic Convention in Denver, in an attempt to portray McCain as out of touch with average Americans.

The Arizona senator did not help his campaign when he included a reference to the strength of the economy in remarks delivered in Jacksonville, Florida, on September 15. The Obama campaign and the media gave great attention to the remarks about the vitality of the economy, even though when examined in their entirety they are more modulated than some in the media and the Democrats depicted them at the time. McCain stated, "Our economy, I think still, the fundamentals of our economy are strong. But these are very, very difficult times."[43] The very same day Joe Biden, Obama's running mate, campaigning in St. Clair Shore, Michigan, ridiculed McCain, "I could walk from here to Lansing and I wouldn't run into a single person who thought our economy was doing well, unless I ran into John McCain."[44]

Whether all claims about McCain being out of touch were fair or not the Republican nominee seemed hurt by some voters' perception that, though he had the right experience to be president (59 percent of voters thought McCain had the right experience to be president, while 50 percent said that Obama had the appropriate experience), he was not able to empathize with average citizens. In the network exit polls 57 percent of voters said Obama was in touch with people like them, while just 39 percent stated that McCain was similarly in touch with the average voter. Obama also held a 59–50 edge in the number of voters who believed he exercised good judgment.[45]

There is no way to know whether McCain was hurt by the news coverage that erupted when he could not recall the number of homes he and his wife owned.[46] In economic hard times the revelation that they had seven residences may not have been helpful to his cause, even though his opponent's one home had cost well over a million dollars. McCain's lack of information about his homes may have further contributed to the notion that he was not in touch with most Americans, who surely do know the number of homes they own.

McCain also appeared to hurt his candidacy when, just three days before the first presidential debate, he announced that he would suspend his campaign and return to Washington to work to craft a financial bailout package for major financial institutions. McCain indicated that he might not actually appear at the debate. Obama argued that presidents had to be able to handle many tasks simultaneously and announced that he would attend the debate in Oxford, Mississippi, irrespective of McCain's decision. After Senate negotiations that involved both McCain and Obama did not produce a bipartisan deal, the Arizona senator returned to the campaign trail and attended the first debate. Some commentators argued that by suspending and then resuming his campaign in a 72-hour period, even though no progress had been made on the financial bailout, McCain appeared erratic and did not project the image of the experienced statesman that he cherished.

Republicans and McCain were further hurt by the crisis as it seemed to undermine the Republicans' long-held view that the economy did not need much government regulation. Ronald Reagan had famously proclaimed that government was the problem rather than the solution to economic ills. Since the 1980s, there had been a much greater shift to reduced regulation of financial markets in particular, and the economy in general. This policy championed by Republicans was also supported by many Democrats.[47] As leading Republican economic authorities such as Bernanke and Paulson warned of economic collapse brought on by risky financial deals, it was hard for McCain and Palin to convince voters that Obama and Biden would enact crippling regulations on an economy that would do just fine if left to its own devices.

McCain had long been a Republican who deviated from orthodox Republican views on issues such as the environment, campaign finance reform, the torture of detainees captured after September 11, 2001, and immigration. While opposing gay marriage, McCain said that that matter should be left up to each state to decide. Such a view would leave gay marriage legal in Connecticut and Massachusetts, a position that outraged some religious conservatives. McCain's embrace of the maverick label in the campaign was mostly accurate. However, on issues such as deregulation of business and financial markets, McCain had long been in general agreement with the laissez-faire economic policies of the Republican Party.[48] Also, to prevail in the Republican primaries, McCain had been forced to defend his Republican credentials and embrace the Bush legacy that was still popular among a substantial portion of the Republican primary electorate. McCain had gone so far as to say that he supported the president 90 percent of the time. The year 2008 was simply a difficult year to be a defender of unregulated markets when some of the major institutional actors in these markets had brought the nation to the brink of financial disaster. John McCain was not, by political history or by his focus on foreign policy, well positioned to deal with the economic circumstances that he faced in the fall of 2008.

The near-total focus on the economy in the last seven weeks of the campaign made it more difficult for Republicans to gain traction with a campaign of cultural populism that they had employed successfully against Democrats in many prior presidential elections. Since the 1930s, Democrats have engaged in economic populism by accusing Republicans of enacting tax- and spending policies that favored the wealthiest Americans. Beginning in the 1960s Republicans have practiced cultural populism as they argued that Democrats are opponents of mainstream moral values, are not genuinely patriotic, are allied with the Hollywood elites, and hold average Americans in contempt.[49] In the 2008 Democratic primaries, Barack Obama was accused of elitism by the Clinton campaign after he was recorded at a fund-raiser in San Francisco (a center of cultural elitism according to conservatives) as saying that working-class whites in industrial areas and rural parts of the country cling to their guns and religion out of bitterness at their economic plight.[50]

Michael Massing claims that the most vicious attacks on Obama came not from the McCain-Palin campaign, but from conservative talk radio hosts, Internet bloggers, and Fox News commentators. Massing says that these attacks were supplemented by emails, direct mail, and robocalls that accused Obama of a host of alleged sins including being a Muslim, a black racist, and the Anti-Christ.[51] The Republican presidential ticket attempted to discredit Obama directly when it questioned his past associations with University of Illinois Education Professor William Ayers, who had been an active member of the militant and violent Weather Underground organization in the late 1960s. The Ayers connection was raised most evocatively by Sarah Palin when she said that Obama had so little regard for his country that he was "palling around with terrorists."[52]

There is no way to actually know whether or to what extent Obama was harmed by the many allegations about his lack of patriotism, cultural elitism, or propensity to hang out with radicals. There is also no way to determine how such issues might have played out in a political environment that did not feature what was routinely termed as the worst financial panic since the Great Depression. In visits to three counties in northwest Ohio, Massing found that there were serious reservations about Obama in a corner of the key battleground state, but there was a pervasive anger about the job losses that had afflicted the area for several years.[53] As the economic outlook grew dimmer, the activities of Bill Ayers in 1969 and his present attitude about those activities, however repugnant to many Americans, probably seemed irrelevant to many swing voters.

Barack Obama had in many ways the easier task in the face of the financial crisis in the weeks preceding the November election. As a newcomer to national politics he had no long record of ties to the financial services industry, as did even many of his fellow Democrats in the Senate.[54] Until McCain picked Alaska Governor Sarah Palin as his running mate, the GOP often attacked Obama as inexperienced in national politics. The lack of a long career in the Senate or any other high-profile office allowed Obama to portray himself as an agent of change in a year when 75 percent of the voters told exit pollsters that the country was heading in the wrong direction. McCain could claim 26 years of experience in the Congress, including service as chairman of the Commerce Committee, but in 2008 a long association with the ways of Washington was not the best of credentials in a country where a majority had concluded that the system was badly broken.

Obama had to simply be perceived as a credible agent of change and a plausible potential president in the midst of crisis. Obama staff advised that the key to success in the debates was to be poised and unruffled by McCain's attacks on him.[55] Their specific advice to Obama was to write the phrase "command and control" on a sheet of paper. By appearing calm and knowledgeable, Obama was perceived as a credible candidate for president even as voters were aware that he was still in his first term in the Senate.

Adam Nagourney summed up the Obama campaign's view of the impact of the financial turmoil on the outcome of the November election: "In the general election, David Axelrod, a senior adviser for Mr. Obama, said that while he thought that the fundamentals of the race always favored Mr. Obama, he believed the candidate sealed the deal with voters between Sept. 15, when the economic meltdown began, and the first debate on Sept. 26."[56]

Domestic Policy and the Election

Exit polls recorded voter responses to the question of what they regarded as the most important issue in the election and how they cast their ballots for president. The choices available in the 2008 election polls were limited to economic and foreign policy issues. Only 19 percent of voters chose foreign policy or national security issues. McCain won voters most concerned about terrorism by a 73 percent margin, but these voters constituted just 9 percent of the electorate.

Sixty-three percent of voters chose the economy as the most important issue and Obama won these voters by a nine-point margin. Obama also carried the nine percent of voters who thought health care was the most important issue by a margin of 73–26 percent. He won the 7 percent of voters who thought that energy was the most important issue by a narrow 4 percent margin. The Democrat gained a margin of 10.2 percent of the total electorate among the 80 percent of voters who picked domestic issues as most important to them. John McCain won by a landslide 73 percent margin among the 9 percent of voters who rated terrorism as the most important issue. The predominance of domestic issues clearly worked to Obama's advantage.

Exit polls of voters also asked them whether they were worried about the economy. Those voters who described themselves as very worried about the economy voted for Obama by a 22 percent margin. The 13 percent of the electorate that was not worried about the economy provided McCain with 65 percent of their votes. Unfortunately for the Republican candidate, half of the electorate described themselves as very worried about the economy.[57]

Was It Only the Stupid Economy?

James Carville, one of Bill Clinton's strategists in 1992, summed up his campaign's main message with the slogan "It's the Economy, Stupid." The sluggish recovery that bedeviled and helped doom George H. W. Bush's reelection campaign was not nearly as threatening as the economy that Republicans had to run with as the incumbent party in presidential politics in 2008. It is obvious that the economy played an important role in the 2008 presidential campaign. Still, it would be a mistake to reduce the results of the 2008 election just to the economy and the financial meltdown that loomed over the nation.

John McCain was attempting to gain a third consecutive four-year term in the Oval Office for his party. This feat has been attempted by five candidates in the years since World War II. Only the first President Bush, running for what some have called Reagan's third term, succeeded. The electorate has shown an inclination to vote for change in the White House after eight years. McCain or any other Republican nominee was facing unfavorable odds in 2008.

In explaining the outcome of the 2008 election, it would also be a mistake to neglect the changing ethnic composition of the electorate. When Bill Clinton was elected president in 1992, the electorate was 87 percent white. When George W. Bush and Al Gore battled in the famously close election of 2000, 82 percent of the voters were white. The white portion of the electorate dropped to 77 percent in 2004 and further declined to 74 percent in 2008. John Kerry lost the white vote by 17 percent in 2004. Obama lost the white vote to McCain by the same 12 percent margin that Al Gore lost the white vote to George W. Bush by in 2000. Gore, of course, scored a half-point win in the popular vote and suffered a narrow defeat in the electoral college.

Obama scored a decisive win because of the more diverse electorate in 2008. African-Americans who gave Gore 90 percent of their votes and Obama 95 percent, increased from 10 to 13 percent of the electorate from 2000 to 2008. Exit polls indicated that Gore and Obama each won the Hispanic vote by 67–31 percent.[58] In 2000, Hispanics were 4 percent of the electorate, while in 2008 they constituted 9 percent. Asians were listed as 2 percent of the vote in 2000 and 2008, but they gave Obama 62 percent as opposed to Gore's 54 percent. In 2004, a new category of Other was added to the choice of options when voters were asked to select their ethnicity for the exit polls. Perhaps this question is meant to reflect small groups such as Native-Americans and the growing number of Americans who regarded themselves as multiracial.[59] Three percent of voters classified themselves as other and two-thirds of them voted for Obama. The Other voters gave Obama a one-point margin of the national electorate or more than one-seventh of his 7.25 percent margin in the national popular vote. In 2004, John Judis and Ruy Teixeira published a book called *The Emerging Democratic Majority* in which they argued that the Democrats would gain as the electorate was composed of more voters disposed to vote for them.[60] Nonwhite voters were a key group in Judis and Teixeira's prospective Democratic majority. Given the trends over the past eight years and the results of the 2008 election Judis and Teixeira seem, at least for the moment, to have been prophetic.

Obama won voters 18–29 years old by a margin of 66–32 percent of the vote. Since the media exit polls began in 1976, no Democrat had gained more than 54 percent of the youth vote nor had won them by more than the 19 percent margin that Bill Clinton carried them by in the three-way presidential race of 1996.[61] Barack Obama had shown an ability to attract exceptional support among young voters beginning with the first contest of the Democratic nominating process where Obama also demonstrated his potential appeal to white voters. In the Iowa caucuses, Obama gained 57 percent of the young caucus goers and defeated Hillary Clinton by a 5–1 margin among this demographic group. Obama's extraordinary appeal among the young also contributed to his victory in the general election.

The economy was not irrelevant to Obama's strong showing among minority voters. The perilous state of the economy almost certainly contributed to his improvement over Kerry's performance among all ethnic groups. The considerations raised in the preceding paragraphs are not intended to gainsay the importance of the economy in the 2008 presidential election. The economy was the overriding issue in 2008. Still, it is important to recall that the explanation for the outcome of an event as complex as a presidential election can rarely be reduced to a single cause.

Notes

1. The results of Iowa and subsequent caucuses and primaries can be found at http://www.cnn.com/ELECTION/2008/primaries/results.
2. Julie Rovner, "The Candidates' Health Care Plans: Private vs. Public," NPR, Morning Edition, August 13, 2008; http://www.npr.org/templates/story/story.php?storyId=93445861.
3. Ibid.
4. Charles Lindblom, *Politics and Markets: The World's Political Economic Systems* (New York: Harper Collins, 1980).
5. *World Almanac and Book of Facts, 2004.*
6. Central Intelligence Agency, *The 2008 World Factbook* (Washington, DC: U.S. Government, 2008).
7. "A Safety Net in Need of Repair," *The Economist*, January 3, 2009, p. 22.
8. Ibid.
9. Ira Katznelson, Mark Kesselman, and Alan Draper, *The Politics of Power: A Critical Introduction to American Government*, Fifth Edition (New York: Wadsworth, 2006).
10. Andrew Hacker, *Money: Who Has How Much and Why?* (New York: Scribner, 1997).
11. Ibid.

12. The literature on American Exceptionalism is vast. For one particularly good explanatory essay, see, Martin Shefter, "Trade Unions and Political Machines: The Organization and Disorganization of the Working Class in the 19th Century," in Martin Shefter, *Political Parties and the State: The American Historical Experience* (Princeton, NJ: Princeton University Press, 1993).

13. Larry M. Bartels, *Unequal Democracy: The Political Economy of the New Gilded Age* (Princeton, NJ: Princeton University Press, 2007).

14. Jacob S. Hacker and Paul Pierson, *Off Center: The Republican Revolution and the Erosion of American Democracy* (New Haven: Yale University Press, 2005).

15. Ibid.

16. "The Man with Half a Plan," *The Economist*, April 19, 2008, pp. 40–41.

17. Leonard E. Burman, Surachai Khitatrakun, Greg Leiserson, Jeff Rohaly, Eric Toder, and Roherton Williams, "An Updated Analysis of the 2008 Presidential Candidates Tax Plans," Revised, August 15, 2008; http://www.taxpolicycenter.org/publications/url.cfm?ID=411749. Accessed September 12, 2008.

18. Lori Montgomery and Jennifer Agiesta, "Mixed Perceptions on Taxes," *The Washington Post*, September 11, 2008, p. A08.

19. Unlike Obama, McCain proposed no tax relief for the one-third of American workers who because of their low incomes pay no federal income tax, but do pay payroll tax. See the comparison of the two tax plans provided by the Tax Policy Center at http://www.taxpolicycenter.org/taxtopics/election_issues_matrix.cfm.

20. Larry Rohter, "Real Deal on Joe the Plumber," *The New York Times*, October 16, 2008. nytimes.com.

21. Mark Murray, "Joe the Plumber," *First Read*, MSNBC.com, October 15, 2008.

22. Michael Cooper, "Spreading the Wealth as Both Accusation and Prescription," *The New York Times*, October 19, 2008.

23. Michael Massing, "Obama in the Divided Heartland," *The New York Review of Books*, December 18, 2008; www.nybooks.com/articles22156.

24. Jonas Pontusson, *Prosperity and Inequality, Social Europe vs. Liberal America* (Ithaca, NY: Cornell University Press, 2005).

25. Michael Powell, "The Candidates Debate Tax Cuts and Welfare," *The New York Times*, October 18, 2008; http://the caucus.blogs.nytimes.com/2008/10/18/the-candidates-debate-tax-cuts-and-welfare.

26. Ibid.

27. The tax increase totals for the candidates are much higher than 100% because 49% of voters said their taxes would rise irrespective of the outcome of the election.

28. Paul Krugman, *The Return of Depression Economics and the Crisis of 2008* (New York: W.W. Norton, 2009).

29. Ibid.

30. Michael M. Grynbaum, "Living Costs Are Rising Fast and Wages Are Falling," *The New York Times*, August 15, 2007, p. C1.

31. Steven Greenhouse, *The Big Squeeze: Tough Times for the American Worker* (New York: Alfred A. Knopf, 2008).

32. David Leonhardt, "For Many, a Boom That Wasn't," *The New York Times*, April 9, 2008; nytimes.com.

33. Greenhouse, *The Big Squeeze*.

34. For an interesting and relatively concise analysis of the crisis, see John Cassidy, "Anatomy of a Meltdown: Ben Bernanke and the Financial Crisis," *The New Yorker*, December 1, 2008; www.newyorker.com/reporting/2008/12/01/081201fa_fact_cassidy.

35. William Greider, "Economic Free Fall?" *The Nation*, August 18–25, 2008, pp. 18–21.

36. Peter S. Goodman and Gretchen Morgenson, "By Saying Yes, WAMU Built Empire on Shaky Loans," *The New York Times*, December 28, 2008.

37. David Herzenhorn, "Congressional Leaders Stunned by Warnings," *The New York Times*, September 19, 2008; http://www.nytimes.com.

38. Ibid.

39. Jacob S. Hacker, *The Great Risk Shift: The Assault on American Jobs, Families, Health Care, and Retirement, and How You Can Fight Back* (New York: Oxford University Press, 2008).

40. Bureau of Labor Statistics, "Employment Situation Summary," December 5, 2008; BLS. Gov. Accessed December 13, 2008.

41. Michael Cooper, "McCain Adviser Refers to Nation of Whiners," *The New York Times*, July 11, 2008; nytimes.com.

42. Jackie Calmes, "The Whining Continues," *The New York Times*, September 9, 2008; nytimes.com.

43. Jeff Zeleny, "Candidates on Wall Street Turmoil," *The New York Times*, September 15, 2008; nytimes.com.

44. Ibid.

45. All exit polls cited in this chapter may be found at http://www.cnn.com/ELECTION/2008/results/polls.

46. Jonathan Martin and Mike Allen, "McCain Unsure How Many Houses He Owns," *Politico*, August 21, 2008; politico.com.

47. Donald Critchlow, *The Conservative Ascendancy: How the GOP Right Made Political History* (Cambridge, MA: Harvard University Press, 2007); David Vogel, *Fluctuating Fortunes: The Political Power of Business in America* (New York: Beard Books, 2003).

48. McCain's record is reviewed in Michael Barone and Richard Cohen, *The Almanac of American Politics*, 2008, Washington Journal, 2007.

49. Both skeins of populism are covered in Michael Kazin, *The Populist Persuasion: An American History* (Ithaca, NY: Cornell University Press, 1998). For concise and cogent analyses of the early years of this strategy see, Jefferson Cowie, "Nixon's Class Struggle: Romancing the New Right Worker, 1969–1973," *Labor History* 43:3 (2002): 257–283 and Jonathan Rieder, "The Rise of the Silent Majority," in Steve Fraser and Gary Gerstle, eds., *The Rise and Fall of the New Deal Order* (Princeton, NJ: Princeton University Press, 1989).

50. Jeff Zeleny, "Opponents Call Obama Remarks Out of Touch," *The New York Times*, April 12, 2008; nytimes.com.

51. Michael Massing, "Obama: In a Divided Heartland," *The New York Review of Books*, December 18, 2008; nybooks.com.

52. Kate Phillips, "Palin: Obama Is Palling Around with Terrorists," *The New York Times*, October 4, 2008; nytimes.com.

53. Massing, "Obama: In a Divided Heartland."

54. For a detailed exposé of the many mutually beneficial connections between powerful New York Democratic Senator Charles Schumer and the financial services industry, see, Eric Lipton and Raymond Hernandez, "A Champion of Wall Street Reaps Benefits," *The New York Times*, December 13, 2008; nytimes.com.

55. Newsweek Election Issue, *Newsweek*, November 17, 2008, p. 102.

56. Adam Nagourney, "From Obama Camp, a What If?" *The New York Times*, December 11, 2008; nytimes.com.

57. Thirty-six percent of voters described themselves as somewhat worried about the economy. They gave 53% of their votes to McCain.

58. In 2004, exit polls gave Kerry only a 53–44% margin over Bush among Latino voters.
59. In 2004, Other voters were 2% of the electorate and supported Kerry by a margin of 54–40%.
60. John Judis and Ruy Teixeira, *The Emerging Democratic Majority* (New York: Scribner, 2004).
61. John Kerry won the youth vote by 54–45% margin in 2004. This was a good showing among young voters for a candidate who lost the popular vote.

3

The Foreign Policy Election That Wasn't

John Kenneth White

The 2008 presidential election was supposed to be all about Iraq; it was not. It was supposed to be about Afghanistan; it was not. It was supposed to be about terrorism; it was not. It was supposed to be about foreign policy; it was not. In fact, the 2008 election was eerily reminiscent of the Great Depression–dominated election of 1932 that saw Franklin D. Roosevelt's ascension to the White House. The financial crisis that blossomed in October 2008 served to seal John McCain's fate in a year when voters were already tired of the Republicans and were eager to dispatch George W. Bush to Texas. That month, the Dow Jones Industrial Average experienced a massive 6,000-point fall from its 14,000-peak a year earlier. More than *8 trillion dollars* in stock value was lost in just a few short weeks. On a single day, October 10, 2008, the stock market had a 1,000-point swing, a first. And in the ensuing days, the market was extremely jittery—rising 900 points one day; losing 700 points the next. To insure financial stability, George W. Bush proposed a massive $700 billion Wall Street rescue plan—the largest government intervention in the private markets since Franklin D. Roosevelt's National Recovery Administration efforts of the 1930s.

Despite rapid congressional passage of the federal bailout (after an initial false start), Wall Street's financial crisis hit Main Street. October unemployment figures rose to 6.5 percent (with 2 million described as being "long-term unemployed"—i.e., not having a job for twenty-seven months or more).[1] In the succeeding months after Barack Obama's victory, unemployment continued its steady upward climb and the annual federal deficit reached $1.2 trillion, a record.[2]

These were not the only bad economic tidings. Millions of otherwise employed citizens, who joined what pollster John Zogby once called the "investor class" (and had been staunch supporters of George W. Bush), were shocked to open their 401K statements that dismal October and discover that their retirement savings had been sharply reduced.[3] Home foreclosures also reached record levels, as the combination of unemployment and bad credit meant that millions had to surrender their personal palaces to the banks. In the three-month period from July to September 2008, foreclosures totaled 765,000, and six states (Nevada, California, Florida, Ohio, Michigan, and Arizona) accounted for 60 percent of the lost homes.[4] (Barack Obama won five of these six states, losing only in John McCain's adopted home state of Arizona.) Finally, the American automobile makers hit the skids. Absent available credit and lacking consumer confidence, few would-be shoppers traipsed to the showrooms, prompting the executives of Ford, General Motors, and Chrysler to ask for their own federal bailout—a request denied by Congress. In December George W. Bush ordered his treasury secretary to make available some of the existing bailout monies to General Motors and Chrysler, saving these companies from bankruptcy, but only until March 2009.

The gloomy financial headlines led to a consumer crisis of confidence. In October, retail sales fell 2.8 percent, as other would-be customers seriously scaled back their spending.[5] The prevailing mood was captured in the Consumer Confidence Index, as it fell from 61.4 in September 2008 to just 38.0 one month later—the lowest number since 1967.[6] Jerry Mills, an Ohio welder and former Bush supporter, was among those fearing foreclosure and he blamed Bush: "I voted for Bush, and I can't believe it. I don't want to admit to it, I'm not happy with where he put us."[7] Mills backed Obama, as did 51 percent of his fellow Ohioans.

Barack Obama's victory represented just how desperate voters were for change. Indeed, their collective willingness to choose someone from the back benches to be the forty-fourth President demonstrated just how eager voters were for some financial security. This, too, was eerily reminiscent of 1932 when Franklin D. Roosevelt, having been governor of New York State for just four years, was chosen to be the new president. Herbert Hoover was viewed by most Americans as inept in dealing with the gargantuan problems facing the nation and his reputation suffered accordingly; a similar fate that awaited George W. Bush 68 years later. Following the chaos that gripped Iraq in the aftermath of the U.S. invasion, and Hurricane Katrina that devastated New Orleans, just 25 percent of Bush's fellow Americans concluded that he was someone who manages the government effectively.[8] By contrast, 75 percent of Americans rated Ronald Reagan as either a "very competent" or a "somewhat competent" president.[9]

It was not supposed to be this way. Ever since Franklin D. Roosevelt's reelection in 1940, most presidential contests were dominated by foreign policy issues (with the sole exception of Bill Clinton's reelection in 1996). The preeminence presidents and voters gave to foreign policy made sense. The end of World War II gave way to a 50-year-long Cold War, and voters looked to their commanders in chiefs to lead the struggle of the Free World against the communists positioned behind the Iron Curtain. Many congresses enhanced the president's ability to determine U.S. foreign policy. As George W. Bush himself recalled, the world was divided between the Free World and those who were enslaved behind an Iron Curtain: "When I was coming up, it was a dangerous world. And we knew exactly who the 'they' were. It was us versus them, and it was clear who 'them' was."[10]

Thus, voters frequently cast their ballots based on foreign policy issues, an agenda that hardly mattered in congressional elections where domestic issues and constituent service were all that mattered. In 1984, to cite just one example, only 1 percent of voters mentioned foreign policy as the most important factor in casting their congressional vote.[11] No wonder Democrats were able to keep control of Congress (especially the House) for so long, while Republicans were able to win the presidency nearly all the time. MSNBC commentator Chris Matthews once famously likened the Republican Party to the "Daddy Party"—a stern, no-nonsense party that would keep you safe, while Democrats were the "Mommy Party"—a compassionate party willing to use government to help others.[12]

Clearly, the emphasis on foreign policy that the Cold War provided favored Republicans in most presidential contests. From 1952 to 1988, there were ten presidential elections and the GOP won seven of them—the exceptions being John F. Kennedy's narrow win in 1960; Lyndon B. Johnson's landslide in 1964; and Jimmy Carter's smallish victory in 1976.[13] Each of these Democratic victories happened because of unusual circumstances surrounding each of these contests: 1960 was marred by Fidel Castro's takeover of Cuba a year earlier, along with a prevailing sense that the United States was losing ground to Nikita Khrushchev's Soviet Union; 1964 was a year in which Americans desired continuity following the Kennedy assassination; 1976 was dominated by Watergate as issues took a backseat to the character of the next president, a role Jimmy Carter understood and fulfilled.

Otherwise, it was the Republicans who, more often than not, won the White House, though not much else. As table 3.1 shows, from 1960 to 1988, Republican candidates were preferred by substantial margins when it came to dealing with the Soviet Union and its allies. Handling foreign policy, maintaining a strong national defense, and creating an economy that was sustained by what Dwight D. Eisenhower famously termed a "military-industrial complex" gave Republicans an enormous advantage over the Democrats.[14] Voters came to see Republican candidates as patriots who would stick up for America, even as they were relatively cautious when it came to actually deploying U.S. troops into combat. Simply put, for most of the Cold War era and the years that followed, voters chose Republican presidents in times of danger and Democratic ones in times of relative calm.[15]

The demise of the Soviet Union in 1991 gave the Democratic Party an opening. Political parties experience moments of great peril either when they *fail* to deliver on the promises they make or when they are *successful* in keeping their promises. The collapse of the Berlin Wall in 1989, and the fall of the Soviet Union two years later, was an unqualified success for U.S. foreign policymakers and the Republican Party that had made defeating communism its top priority. Ronald Reagan, in particular, was given credit as the president who had done the most to end the Cold War. Many who had once ridiculed Reagan when he forecast in 1983 that communism's "last pages even now are being written" were forced to admit that the Great Communicator was right.[16] Indeed, with each passing year since leaving office, Reagan's standing both among historians and the public has risen.[17] In 2008, for example, 62 percent considered Reagan to be a great

Table 3.1 Perceptions of presidential candidates' ability to handle foreign affairs

Text of question	Public response
"Which of these two men, Nixon or Kennedy, if elected president do you think would do the most effective job of dealing with Russia's leaders?" (1960)	67% Nixon 39% Johnson
"How much trust and confidence would you have in the way Barry Goldwater [Lyndon Johnson] would handle Khrushchev and relations with Russia?" (1964)	34% Goldwater 67% Johnson
"Agree/Disagree. Richard Nixon knows how to stand up to communists." (1968)	53% agreed
"If he were president, who do you think would be better able to negotiate with the Russians and Chinese—Nixon or McGovern?" (1972)	70% Nixon 11% McGovern
"Now if you had to choose, who do you think could do a better job as president on handling relations with Russia—Gerald Ford or Jimmy Carter?" (1976)	41% Ford 30% Carter
"I'm going to mention some problems facing the nation today and as I mention each one I would like you to tell me who you thought would do the best job of handling that problem—Gerald Ford or Jimmy Carter. …Maintaining a strong national defense." (1976)	49% Ford 29% Carter
"How would you rate the specific job President Carter has done while in office on handling relations with Russia?" (1980)	26% excellent/good 70% fair/poor
"Does the following phrase apply more to Ronald Reagan or to Walter Mondale?…More capable of handling relations with the Soviet Union." (1984)	69% Reagan 20% Mondale
"Based on what you know about Walter Mondale and Ronald Reagan as a whole, which of the two presidential candidates is likely to maintain our military strength relative to the Soviet Union?" (1984)	69% Reagan 20% Mondale
"Please tell me whether you feel George Bush or Michael Dukakis would do a better job of guarding against Soviet aggression." (1988)	62% Bush 24% Dukakis
"Please tell me whether you feel George Bush or Michael Dukakis would do a better job of handling relations with the Soviet Union." (1988)	67% Bush 22% Dukakis

Sources: Gallup poll, October 18–23, 1960; Gallup poll, October 1964; Louis Harris and Associates, poll, September 11–13, 1968; Opinion Research Corporation, poll, October 20–22, 1972; Louis Harris and Associates, poll, September 1976; Robert M. Teeter, national surveys, November 1976; ABC News/Louis Harris and Associates, poll, November 7–10, 1980; Gallup poll, October 21, 1984; Gordon Black survey for *USA Today*, September 25–26, 1984; Daniel Yankelovich Group, poll, November 4–7, 1988; Daniel Yankelovich Group, poll, November 4–7, 1988.

president—just behind the 69 percent and 67 percent that gave that same designations to Franklin D. Roosevelt (FDR) and John F. Kennedy, respectively.[18] But Reagan's success as a modern-day Republican equivalent of FDR proved to be a moment of peril for his fellow Republicans. When the Soviet Union breathed its last on Christmas Night 1991, George H. W. Bush suddenly found himself to be a Cold War president without the Cold War. And he was defeated for reelection in 1992.

The complete victory of the United States over the Soviet Union and its allies left many Americans restless. At the conclusion of the Cold War, Richard

M. Nixon, that astute observer of American politics, wrote that the demise of the Soviet Union had several unintended consequences: "Historically there is always a period of exhaustion after a military victory. Victory in the Cold War was not just military. It was a complex ideological, political, and economic triumph. Our exhaustion is therefore felt in all these dimensions simultaneously."[19] This combination of restlessness and exhaustion created the conditions for Bill Clinton's 1992 victory. Moreover, the economic dislocations created by a military-industrial complex that had no Cold War to sustain it added to the voters' collective distress. As a shipyard worker in Groton, Connecticut, so memorably put it, "We won the Cold War, and now they're saying here's a pink slip."[20]

Yet even as Americans awarded Clinton the presidency he had so long sought they retained a healthy skepticism of both Clinton and the Democrats, giving Clinton less than 50 percent of the vote in 1992 and 1996 and putting the Republicans in charge of Congress in 1994. One reason for the voters' skepticism was that they continued to see the Democrats as weak representatives of U.S. interests overseas, or, as Republicans so frequently put it, soft-minded. Jimmy Carter, in particular, gave the Republicans lots of ammunition to use against his fellow Democrats. During his tenure, American hostages were held in Iran and Afghanistan fell to the Soviet Union. In 1997, Carter derided the Republicans for their "inordinate fear of communism," a line that Republicans used against Carter and his fellow Democrats in the years since.[21]

Even so, the disappearance of any immediate foreign policy dangers to the safety and security of the American citizenry meant that the Republican presidential party would continue to be deprived of their most important issue. In 1996, Bill Clinton emphasized Medicare, Medicaid, education, and the environment to win an easy victory over Bob Dole (though still short of 50 percent of the vote). In 2000, Republicans still could not use foreign policy to propel their presidential hopes—a situation that contributed to the stalemate that made *Bush v. Gore* such an anomaly in U.S. history.

The terrorist attacks of September 11, 2001 put foreign policy back at the forefront of American politics. A new enemy, Islamic extremism personified in the person of Osama bin Laden, reared itself in the collapse of the World Trade Center, the scarred Pentagon building, and the wreckage of United Airlines Flight 93 in rural Pennsylvania. In the aftermath of the attacks, George W. Bush revived the stark rhetoric of the Cold War, telling Congress and the world: "Every nation, in every region, now has a decision to make. Either you are with us, or you are with the terrorists."[22] Three weeks after 9/11, Bush's approval scores jumped to an astounding 90 percent.[23] MSNBC commentator Chris Matthews depicted Bush prior to September 11 as "an easy-going Prince Hal" who, thanks to the terrorist attacks, was "transformed by instinct and circumstance into a warrior King Henry."[24] This image was both consoling and comforting to many Americans. All the controversy surrounding Bush's election in 2000, and the Supreme Court's subsequent actions in *Bush v. Gore*, disappeared, and few felt little, if any, buyer's remorse. A Zogby poll taken shortly after the 9/11 attacks found 67 percent did not believe the country would be better off if Al Gore had been president.[25] Similar percentages were happy that Bill Clinton was no longer in the White House, and that Dick Cheney, rather than Joe Lieberman, was vice president.[26]

The return of foreign policy to the forefront of political issues was a boon to the Republican Party. In 2002, Republicans captured eight additional seats in the House and added two more in the Senate, restoring them to majority status in both houses of Congress.[27] In many respects the votes Republicans captured in 2002 were "belated ballots," as Americans rallied behind George W. Bush as their commander in chief. Commenting on the Democratic Party's defeat that year, Bill Clinton, that other astute observer of American politics, declared, "When people feel uncertain, they'd rather have somebody who's strong and wrong than somebody who's weak and right."[28]

For most of the Bush years, Democrats tried unsuccessfully to get Americans to think about something else—indeed, *anything else*—other than foreign policy. It did not work. In 2004, terrorism remained crucial in the voters' minds, as 19 percent named it the most important issue. Of these voters, 86 percent backed Bush. So-called security moms likewise were worried about another attack. Thus, 48 percent of women and 59 percent of voters who were married and had children living with them supported Bush's reelection.[29] George W. Bush and Dick Cheney did nothing to quell voter concerns. In an advertisement, the Republican ticket likened the terrorists to bands of roaming wolves and offered themselves as the only ones who could keep the country secure.[30] In a candid moment, former Deputy Secretary of State Richard Armitage said, "Since 9/11, our principal export to the world has been our fear."[31]

One could argue that fear became our principal import as well. In 2004, a group of Republicans disparaged Democratic candidate John Kerry as a quisling Vietnam veteran who disparaged his fellow soldiers in their infamous Swift Boat advertisements. Karl Rove, the person whom George W. Bush credited as the "architect" of his 2004 victory,[32] said of Kerry and his fellow Democrats: "Liberals saw the savagery of the 9/11 attacks and wanted to prepare indictments and offer therapy and understanding for our attackers."[33] Even as they prepared to leave office, both Bush and Cheney continued to insist that they (and the Republican Party) deserved credit for preventing another terrorist attack similar to September 11 on U.S. soil. Addressing the U.S. Army War College in December 2008, Bush noted, "While there's room for honest and healthy debate about the decisions I've made—and there's plenty of debate—there can be no debate about the results in keeping America safe."[34] As Richard Nixon famously observed, "People react to fear, not love. They don't teach that in Sunday school, but it's true."[35]

Nixon's political maxim held true once more in 2008. But it was fear about an economic collapse, not some danger overseas, that prompted voters to pull the Democratic lever. Republicans tried to get voters to think about terrorism and the consequences of failures in Iraq and Afghanistan to no avail. At one town hall meeting, John McCain told voters that the selection they faced was a stark one: "It's a very clear choice, and whether it be on Iran, or whether it be on

Iraq, or whether it be on other national security issues, Senator Obama does not have the experience and the knowledge and clearly the judgment, my friends."[36] Charlie Black, a senior advisor to the McCain campaign, bluntly told reporters that another terrorist attack on U.S. soil "would be a big advantage" for McCain, a comment that caused McCain to disassociate himself from Black but revealed the thinking within the Republican Party.[37] McCain further undermined his foreign policy credentials by choosing Alaska Governor Sarah Palin to be his running mate. Palin had few, if any, foreign policy credentials, as she demonstrated in an interview with ABC News anchorman Charlie Gibson. When asked to define the Bush doctrine (which gives the United States the right to preemptively attack any country believed to be launching strikes against the United States), Palin was at a loss for words.[38] Quickly, her ineptitude became fodder for the late-night comedians and Saturday Night Live.

Even if McCain and Palin had been more effective candidates, their efforts probably would have still resulted in their defeat. By 2008, Americans had soured both on the Iraq War and George W. Bush.[39] Although Bush claimed that the surge in U.S. forces he commenced in 2007 ebbed the violence in Iraq, Americans concluded that the war had been a serious mistake. Whatever good news came from Iraq was marred by these facts: no weapons of mass destruction were ever found there; terrorists had not made Iraq a base until the U.S. invasion; and the war in Afghanistan suffered as additional U.S. resources were committed to securing Iraq at Afghanistan's expense. In June 2008, 46 Americans and allied forces died in Afghanistan, more than during any other month since the war began in 2001, and more than the 31 Americans who had died in Iraq that same month.[40] Leaving the polling places in November, 63 percent of voters said they disapproved of the war in Iraq, and 54 percent said history would judge U.S. involvement there to be a failure.[41] A December 2008 poll found 35 percent believing that undertaking the Iraq War was George W. Bush's biggest failure as president, his number one response in a long list.[42]

In 2003, Defense Secretary Donald Rumsfeld posed this test for judging U.S. success in the war on terror: "Are we capturing, killing, or deterring and dissuading more terrorists every day than the madrassas and the radical clerics are recruiting, training and deploying against us?"[43] Five years later, Americans concluded that the Iraq War had made the country less safe, and that Bush and Rumsfeld had failed to meet the standard they set for themselves despite their protestations to the contrary.[44] When ABC News correspondent Martha Raddatz pointed out that Iraq prior to the U.S. invasion had neither weapons of mass destruction nor a significant terrorist presence, George W. Bush memorably responded, "So what?"[45]

Unlike Ronald Reagan, what Republicans experienced most under George W. Bush was *failure*—that other scenario most dreaded by political parties. CNN senior political analyst William Schneider likened the Bush presidency to "a failed marriage," adding, "As President Bush prepares to leave office, the American public has a parting thought: Good riddance."[46] Indeed. On the eve of Barack Obama's inauguration, 75 percent said they were glad Bush was leaving the White House, and only a one-third wanted him to assume any future public role.[47] When the Pew Research Center asked respondents to use one or two words of their own choosing to describe their impressions of George W. Bush, the responses were especially devastating:

- Incompetent, 43 percent;
- Honest, 24 percent;
- Idiot, 21 percent;
- Arrogant, 18 percent;
- Good, 15 percent;
- Failure, 12 percent;
- Honorable, 12 percent;
- Stupid, 12 percent;
- Ignorant, 11 percent;
- Selfish, 10 percent;
- Mediocre, 9 percent;
- Ass, 7 percent;
- Ineffective, 7 percent;
- Inept, 7 percent;
- Integrity, 7 percent.[48]

Unable to punish George W. Bush (since he could not stand for election again), voters instead took out their wrath on the GOP—which had uncritically supported Bush for eight years. In 2006, the electorate gave the Republicans a "thumping" (Bush's words) when it returned Congress to Democratic control. It gave the Republicans yet another thumping in 2008, as Democrats won the White House and padded their congressional majorities. Foreign policy hardly mattered, as 63 percent of voters named the economy as the most important issue. Only 10 percent cited Iraq, and a mere 9 percent mentioned terrorism as crucial voting issues.[49]

Republicans had hoped to continue the contentious Democratic primary contest when Hillary Clinton charged that Barack Obama was naive when it came to foreign policy, noting his willingness to sit down with sworn U.S. enemies (including Iranian President Mahmoud Ahmadinejad and others) without preconditions. McCain continued to charge that Obama was naive on foreign policy issues, saying in their first presidential debate:

> Senator Obama twice said in debates he would sit down with [Iran's Mahmoud] Ahmadinejad, [Venezuela's Hugo] Chavez, and [Cuba's] Raul Castro without precondition. Without precondition. Here is Ahmadinejad...who is now in New York, talking about the extermination of the State of Israel, of wiping Israel off the map, and we're going to sit down, without precondition, across the table, to legitimize and give a propaganda platform to a person that is espousing the extermination of the State of Israel, and therefore then giving them more credence in the world arena and therefore saying, they've probably been doing the right thing, because you will sit down across the table from them and that will legitimize their illegal behavior.[50]

But Democrats were hardly in the mood to concede foreign policy dominance to John McCain and the Republicans. Vice presidential candidate Joe Biden captured the prevailing mood among his fellow Democrats:

> I refuse to sit back like we did in 2000 and 2004. This administration is the worst administration in American foreign policy in modern history—maybe ever. The idea that they are competent to continue to conduct our foreign policy, to make us more secure and make Israel secure, is preposterous.... Every single thing they've touched has been a near disaster.[51]

Despite the Democrats' protestations, John McCain still retained a sub-stantial advantage over Barack Obama when it came to foreign policy issues. McCain was seen as a better commander in chief by a 57–38 percent margin.[52] And on the question of handling terrorism, McCain also had a significant lead: 59–37 percent.[53] But what voters wanted more than anything else was an eco-nomic chief who would give them financial security, not the personal security they so craved in 2004. Even on the vaunted issue of handling foreign policy— once the province of the Republican Party, and should have been once more in 2008, given John McCain's long military service and heroism during the Vietnam War—voters were hardly in the mood to accord the GOP much credit. An October 2008 Pew Research Center poll found McCain with a *one-point* lead over Obama as the person who would make wise decisions about U.S. foreign policy.[54]

The Republican Party, too, retained some of their Cold War–era and post 9/11 advantages when it came to foreign policy issues. Democratic pollster Stan Greenberg found that when it came to ensuring a strong military, combating terrorism, national security, homeland security, and keeping America strong, Republicans enjoyed healthy, but hardly overwhelming, leads over the Democrats (see table 3.2). But when asked which party could reduce U.S. dependence

Table 3.2 Party-dominated foreign policy issues, 2008

Issue	Republicans much better/ somewhat better (%)	Democrats much better/ somewhat better (%)
GOP dominated		
Ensuring strong military	57	27
Combating terrorism	48	33
National security	49	35
Homeland security	43	36
Keeping the United States strong	43	38
Dem dominated		
Reducing dependence on foreign oil	35	32
Handling Iraq	47	36
Handling foreign policy	45	39

Source: Greenberg, Quinlan, Rosner Research, poll, July 21–24, 2008. Text of question: "I am going to read a list of issues and I want you to tell me whether, overall, you think the Democrats or the Republicans would do a better job with this issue. If you do not know, just tell me and we will move on to the next item."

on foreign oil, handle the situation in Iraq, or administer U.S. foreign policy, Democrats were preferred. In sum, foreign policy issues in 2008 no longer provided the fortress for the Republican Party that insulated it from Democratic attacks. This was crucial, as any would-be president, Republican or Democratic, must be seen as someone who can step into both the commander in chief and diplomat in chief roles of the presidency.

This partisan stalemate on foreign policy issues that existed in 2008 is in sharp contrast to the Cold War elections featured in table 3.1. Not since 1988 had the Republicans surrendered so much of their foreign policy portfolio to the Democrats. As Matthew Iglesias points out, this happened because George W. Bush and the Republicans made a fatal mistake when it came to implementing their foreign policy vision:

> Conservative Republicans have not merely made some mistakes on Iraq, and some other mistakes on Iran, and some other mistakes on North Korea, plus some mistakes on Syria, while mishandling the Israeli-Palestinian conflict and, by coincidence, damaging our relationships with formerly close allies. Rather, they are making *one big mistake* in seeking to transform the United States' role in the world...to that of an imperial superpower that seeks to use its national strength to dominate the world and needlessly heighten conflicts.[55]

It is these mistakes that have given Barack Obama and the Democrats an historic opportunity. In December 2008, an ABC News/*Washington Post* poll found 56 percent believing that Democrats would do a better job in coping with the main problems the nation faces over the next few years; only 23 percent chose the Republicans.[56] Barack Obama is also enjoying a significant and potentially prolonged honeymoon with the voters. In December 2008, 76 percent said he is a strong and decisive leader; 82 percent thought he inspires confidence, and 80 percent said Obama is tough enough to be president. These numbers are better than George W. Bush's following the September 11 attacks, and even on a par with Ronald Reagan in 1981.[57] If Obama continues to keep company with Reagan in this way, he could be in the pantheon of great Democratic presidents.

For the foreseeable future, however, economic problems will dominate the national agenda. Obama's first test (and maybe his only one) will be how he handles the financial crisis. But to the extent that President Obama and the Democrats also prove themselves to be effective stewards of the nation's defenses and foreign policy, they will have a decent chance of keeping power for years to come. If they accomplish this, Republicans could find themselves in the wilderness for some time—a situation that they actually found themselves in from the 1930s until Dwight D. Eisenhower ended 20 years of Democratic rule in 1952. The onset of the Cold War together with a stalemate in Korea gave the Republicans a chance to seize the presidency. It may be that it will take yet some other unknown foreign policy crisis to put the Republicans back in charge at the White House. Time will tell.

Notes

1. Bureau of Labor Statistics, "Employment Situation Summary," press release, October 3, 2008.
2. See Mark Murray, "The Bush Years—Then and Now," First Read, MSNBC.com, January 7, 2009. The deficit is projected for 2009 by the Congressional Budget Office.
3. John Zogby, "Investors for Bush," *Wall Street Journal*, March 15, 2005.
4. See Patrick O'Connor, "U.S. Layoffs Mount, Home Foreclosures Rise," Inteldaily. com, October 24, 2008.
5. Jack Healy, "A Record Decline in October's Retail Sales," *New York Times*, November 15, 2008.
6. See Michael M. Grynbaum, "Rattled by Housing Slide, Consumers See Worse to Come," *New York Times*, October 29, 2008. According to this survey, a reading of 100 represents the consumer outlook on the economy in 1985.
7. Quoted in Peter Wallsten and Janet Hook, "Four Big Questions of the Presidential Election," *Los Angeles Times*, November 2, 2008.
8. CNN/Opinion Research Corporation, poll, December 19–21, 2008. See also Paul Steinhauser, "Poll: 75% Glad Bush Is Done," CNN.com, December 26, 2008.
9. Gordon Black/*USA Today*, poll, January 27, 1987. Text of question: "Overall, how would you rate (Ronald) Reagan as President. Is he very competent, somewhat competent, not very competent, or not competent at all?" Very competent, 30%; somewhat competent, 45%; not very competent, 15%; not competent at all, 8%; don't know, 2%.
10. Quoted in Samantha Power, "The Democrats and National Security," *New York Review of Books*, August 14, 2008, p. 68.
11. CBS News/*New York Times*, poll, November 4, 1984. Text of question: "What is the single most important reason you are for the (Republican/Democratic) candidate for the U.S. House of Representatives in your district? (open-ended)" Ideology, 35%; party affiliation, 25%; Reagan/Mondale, 4%; experience/done a good job, 19%; just like him/her, 6%; economy, 9%; domestic issues, 15%; foreign policy, 1%; other, 3%; don't know/no answer, 15%.
12. See Chris Sollentrop, "For the Archive: *Radar* Essay on Hillary Clinton," sollentrop. com, October 21, 2005.
13. For much more on this see John Kenneth White, *Still Seeing Red: How the Cold War Shapes the New American Politics* (Boulder, CO: Westview Press, 1997).
14. Dwight D. Eisenhower, Farewell Address, Washington, DC, January 17, 1961.
15. For more on this see Power, "The Democrats and National Security," p. 66.
16. Ronald Reagan, speech to the National Association of Evangelicals, Orlando, Florida, March 3, 1983.
17. See, e.g., Sean Wilentz, *The Age of Reagan: A History: 1974–2008* (New York: HarperCollins, 2008).
18. Zogby International, "Roosevelt Holds Top Ranking on Presidential Greatness Scale," press release, February 28, 2008.
19. Richard Nixon, *Beyond Peace* (New York: Random House, 1994), p. 8.
20. NBC News, *Sunday Today*, broadcast, March 29, 1992.
21. Jimmy Carter, Commencement Address at Notre Dame University, South Bend, Indiana, May 22, 1977.
22. George W. Bush, Address to a Joint Session of Congress, Washington, DC, September 20, 2001.

23. Gallup poll, September 21–22, 2001. Text of question: "Do you approve or disapprove of the way George W. Bush is handling his job as president?" Approve, 90%; disapprove, 6%; no opinion, 4%.

24. Chris Matthews, *Now Let Me Tell You What I Really Think* (New York: Free Press, 2001), p. 37.

25. Zogby International, survey, September 17–18, 2001. Text of question: "Do you believe that the United States would be better off if Al Gore were president instead of George W. Bush?" Yes, believe, 17%; no, do not believe, 67%; not sure, 16%.

26. Zogby International poll, October 8–10, 2001. Text of first question: "Who would you rather have sitting in the White House during this time of crisis—George W. Bush or Bill Clinton?" Bush, 72%; Clinton, 20%; neither/not sure, 8%. Text of second question: "Who would you rather have as Vice President of the United States during this time of crisis—Dick Cheney or Joseph Lieberman?" Cheney, 70%; Lieberman, 17%; not sure, 13%.

27. Republicans won a majority in the House in 1994 and kept it until 2006. In the Senate, a one-seat Republican majority ended in May 2001, when Vermont Senator James Jeffords left the GOP to become an independent.

28. Quoted in Power, "The Democrats and National Security," p. 66.

29. Voter News Service, exit poll, November 2, 2004.

30. In the 2004 advertisement, a female announcer says: "In an increasingly dangerous world, even after the first terrorist attack on America, John Kerry and the liberals in Congress voted to slash America's intelligence operations by six billion dollars. Cuts so deep they would have weakened America's defenses. And weakness attracts those who are waiting to do America harm."

31. Quoted in Power, "The Democrats and National Security," p. 71.

32. George W. Bush, Victory Speech, Washington, DC, November 3, 2004.

33. Power, "The Democrats and National Security," p. 70.

34. George W. Bush, Speech to the U.S. Army War College, Carlisle, Pennsylvania, December 17, 2008.

35. Quoted on PBS broadcast, "Nixon: The American Experience," September 24, 1992.

36. Quoted in Power, "The Democrats and National Security," p. 70.

37. Ibid.

38. Charlie Gibson, Interview with Governor Sarah Palin, *World News Tonight*, broadcast, September 11, 2008.

39. Bush's reputation was also permanently damaged by the inadequate and inept federal response to Hurricane Katrina.

40. See Power, "The Democrats and National Security," p. 66.

41. Edison Media Research and Mitofsky International, exit poll, November 4, 2008. Text of question: "How do you feel about the U.S. war in Iraq?" Approve, 36%; disapprove, 63%. Gallup/*USA Today*, poll, February 21–24, 2008. Text of question: "In the long run, how do you think history will judge the U.S. invasion and subsequent involvement in Iraq—as a total success for the United States, mostly successful, mostly a failure, or as a total failure for the United States?" Total success, 4%; mostly successful, 38%; mostly a failure, 36%; total failure, 18%; no opinion, 4%.

42. NBC News/*Wall Street Journal*, poll, December 4–8, 2008. Text of question: "Which one of the following things do you think will be remembered as being George W. Bush's biggest failure as president?…Undertaking the war in Iraq, not preventing the current economic recession, producing the largest federal deficit in history, having an inadequate response to Hurricane Katrina, promoting policies that do more to help the wealthy than the middle class, having policies that hurt the environment."

Undertaking the war in Iraq, 35%; not preventing the current economic recession, 21%; producing the largest federal deficit in history, 21%; having an inadequate response to Hurricane Katrina, 9%; promoting policies that do more to help the wealthy than the middle class, 8%; having policies that hurt the environment, 1%; other (volunteered), 1%; none (volunteered), 2%; not sure, 1%.

43. Quoted in Power, "Democrats and National Security," p. 68.

44. A CBS News poll taken in March 2008 found 62% believing that the Iraq War had either made the country less safe from terrorism or had no effect. CBS News, poll, March 15–18, 2008. Text of question: "As a result of the United States's military action against Iraq, do you think the United States is more safe from terrorism, less safe from terrorism, or hasn't it made any difference?" More safe, 36%; less safe, 24%; no difference, 38%; don't know/no answer, 2%.

45. ABC News, Interview, December 15, 2008.

46. CNN broadcast, December 26, 2008.

47. CNN/Opinion Research Corporation, poll, December 19–21, 2008. Text of question: "Which comes closest to your view of President Bush as he prepares to leave the White House? Glad he is going or will miss him." Glad he is going, 75%; will miss him, 23%; not sure/no opinion, 2%.

48. Pew Research Center, poll, December 3–7, 2008. Text of question: "Please tell me what one word best describes your impression of George W. Bush. Tell me just the one best word that describes him." Open-ended question and up to two responses were accepted.

49. Edison Media Research and Mitofsky International, exit poll, November 4, 2008. Text of question: "Which one of these five issues is the most important facing the country?" Economy, 63%; the war in Iraq, 10%; terrorism, 9%; health care, 9%; energy policy, 7%.

50. "Transcript of the First Presidential Debate," *New York Times*, September 26, 2008.

51. Quoted in Power, "Democrats and National Security," p. 68.

52. ABC News/*Washington Post*, poll, October 18–21, 2008. Text of question: "Regardless of who you may support (for president in 2008), who do you think would be a better commander in chief of the military—(Barack) Obama or (John) McCain?" Obama, 38%; McCain, 57%; both (volunteered), 1%; neither (volunteered), 1%; no opinion, 3%.

53. Gallup Poll, October 23–26, 2008. Text of question: "Regardless of which presidential candidate you support, please tell me if you think Barack Obama or John McCain would better handle each of the following issues. How about terrorism?" McCain, 59%; Obama, 37%; same (volunteered), 2%; don't know, 2%; refused, 1%.

54. Pew Research Center, poll, October 16–19, 2008. Text of question: "Regardless of who you support, which one of the presidential candidates—John McCain or Barack Obama—do you think would do the best job of making wise decisions about foreign policy?" McCain, 45%; Obama, 44%; neither (volunteered), 1%; don't know/refused, 10%.

55. Quoted in Power, "Democrats and National Security," p. 70.

56. ABC News/*Washington Post*, poll, December 11–14, 2008. Text of question: "Overall, which party, the Democrats or the Republicans, do you trust to do a better job in coping with the main problems the nation faces over the next few years?" Democrats, 56%; Republicans, 23%; both (volunteered), 3%; neither (volunteered), 15%; no opinion, 3%.

57. See Paul Steinhauser, "Poll: Obama's Leadership Rates High as Bush's after 9/11," CNN.com, December 31, 2008.

4

Searching for the Social Issue

Kevin J. McMahon

In many ways, it was an issue that was missing. For a generation of presidential campaigns, some type of social issue—whether "law and order," or welfare reform, or abortion—had typically emerged as a significant electoral concern to the voters; often linked as James Sundquist has written, "by a common thread: the breakdown of family and social discipline, of order, of concepts of duty, of respect for law, of public and private morality."[1] Indeed, just four short years ago, quick analyses of the exit polls and voting results led commentators to dub the 2004 race as the "moral values" election. But in 2008, those who designed the exit poll did not even think to include "moral values"—or any other concern typically defined as a "social issue"—as a possible choice when asking voters about the most important issue of the election. With the economy so central to the race, it is easy to understand why they decided to exclude that option. Their decision to leave out a question on abortion, which had been part of many past exit surveys, is a little more perplexing. At the same time, it is quite telling, for it reveals the extent to which any social issue was seemingly absent from the presidential campaign of 2008. Still, I suggest that initial appearances are somewhat misleading; that upon closer inspection, there were at least four areas where social issues made an appearance and were somewhat significant to the final outcome; namely, the race for the Republican nomination, the future makeup of the Supreme Court, Republican John McCain's selection of Alaska Governor Sarah Palin as his running mate, and the ballot measures being considered in various states across the county. In this chapter, I explore these areas. Before doing so, I briefly revisit the electoral events from four years ago.

"Moral Values" and the Reelection of George W. Bush

As noted earlier, in the immediate wake of the 2004 presidential election, commentators focused on "moral values" as the deciding factor in President George W. Bush's popular and electoral vote victories over Democratic challenger John

F. Kerry.[2] Three factors primarily drove this conclusion. First, when answering which issue was the most important of the election, 22 percent of respondents selected "moral values," more than any other of the possible choices. And significantly, 80 percent of those "value voters" supported President Bush. Second, religiously conservative voters reportedly turned out in unprecedented numbers to support the president's reelection. This turnout was a significant change from four years earlier. Then, according to chief Bush political strategist Karl Rove, approximately 15 million evangelic Christians came out to support his candidate, instead of the expected 19 million.[3] The exit polls of 2004 told another story, suggesting that approximately 22 million white evangelical Christians turned out for Bush.[4] Specifically, of the 23 percent of voters who described themselves as white born-again or evangelical Christians, 78 percent voted for the president. Those numbers virtually mirrored those of the "values voters." Moreover, "the percentage of voters who said they attend church more than once a week grew from 14 to 16 percent, a significant difference in an election decided by [2.4] percentage points." Of that group, Bush increased his 2000 numbers by 1 percent, from 63 to 64 percent. "Without question," Alan Cooperman and Thomas Edsall wrote just after the 2004 election, "Bush's conservative Christian base was essential to his victory."[5] Bush's conservative appeal, however, was not limited to evangelical Christians. With the aid of some staunchly conservative church leaders he also won the Catholic vote (27 percent of voters), besting the Catholic Kerry 52–47 percent.[6]

The third values factor centered on the 11-state referenda banning same-sex marriage that passed by wide margins on Election Day. According to those advancing the "moral values" story of the election these 11 referenda inspired religious conservative voters to go to the polls, feeding the huge evangelical turnout. John Kerry won just 2 of these 11 states, both by narrow margins.[7] And in Ohio, where a constitutional amendment banning same-sex marriages and civil unions passed by a 24-point margin, Kerry lost by approximately 118,000 votes. Significantly, if Kerry had won Ohio, he would have won the presidency.

To be sure, many quickly dismissed the importance of "values voters" in Bush's reelection equation. For example, conservative *New York Times* columnist David Brooks thought this "official story" of the election—"that throngs of homophobic, Red America values-voters surged to the polls to put George Bush over the top"—was plainly wrong. Instead, according to Brooks, Bush's victory was the result of a "diverse but stable Republican coalition.... Social issues are important, but they don't come close to telling the whole story." Conservative columnist Charles Krauthammer thought the "moral values" story of the election was based on a misreading of exit polls. After combining some possible choices with others to create three main issues: war issues, economic issues, and moral values, he concluded, "If you pit group against group, moral values comes in dead last: war issues at 34 percent, economic issues at 33 percent and moral values at 22 percent. And we know that this is the real ranking."

Brooks and Krauthammer both blamed "liberals" and "the media" for advancing this myth of the "redneck vote."[8] In targeting liberals, each might have had Thomas Frank in mind. In his 2004 bestseller, *What's the Matter with Kansas?*

How Conservatives Won the Heart of America, Frank argued that Republicans have repeatedly won elections by convincing working-class Americans to vote against their economic interests by stressing cultural concerns such as abortion and Hollywood smut.[9] However, others have suggested that the religious Right had the most to gain by advancing this line of electoral analysis, noting that by doing so its leaders would have more influence during Bush's second term. And indeed, many religious conservative leaders did emphasize the "moral values" story of the election in an effort to persuade the Bush administration to pursue their agenda, particularly when it came time to select new justices for the Supreme Court. As former Governor Christine Todd Whitman of New Jersey, a moderate Republican, complained,

> Just hours after the president declared victory, one longtime conservative activist, Richard Viguerie, wrote, "Now comes the revolution...Make no mistake—conservative Christians and 'values voters' won this election for George W. Bush and Republicans in Congress. It's crucial that the Republican leadership not forget this—as much as some will try." James Dobson, the head of the conservative group Focus on the Family, asserted that President Bush must now move to pass a constitutional amendment regulating marriage, to overturn *Roe v. Wade*, and also to prohibit all embryonic stem cell research. "I believe that the Bush administration now needs to be more aggressive in pursuing these values," he said, "and if they don't do it I believe they will pay a price in four years." Christian conservative organizer Phil Burress boldly proclaimed, "The president rode our coattails," while another, Austin Ruse, said that his pro-life group has essentially "earned" the right to name the next chief justice of the Supreme Court.[10]

As Whitman's criticism of her fellow Republicans suggests, on the most relevant social issues of the day the most significant debate has recently occurred within the GOP. In 2008, it did again. And the nature of this debate revealed clear tensions within the Republican Party and likely influenced the behavior of "value voters" at the polls.

John McCain, Evangelical Christians, and the Republican Nomination

To evangelical Christian leaders, John McCain was no George W. Bush. There are many reasons why these leaders did not view the two men in the same terms. But perhaps the best way to display their differences is to recount a moment from an event that occurred nearly a decade ago. The moment came in response to a question near the end of debate among Republican presidential contenders in Des Moines, Iowa, in mid-December 1999. The question was a seemingly simply one: "What political philosopher or thinker do you most identify with and why?" Steve Forbes was the first to answer, saying John Locke "because he set the stage for what became a revolution." Next, Alan Keyes answered that it was the founders because they established "instruments of government that have preserved our liberty now for over 200 years." George W. Bush was third in line. His answer surprised many: "Christ, because he changed my heart." The questioner wanted more, asking how "he's changed your heart." Bush responded with details that surely pleased born-again evangelical Christians, who according to one poll would make up 40 percent of Republican Iowa caucus participants the following month, "Well, if they don't know, it's going to be hard to explain. When you turn your heart and your life over to Christ, when you accept Christ as the savior, it changes your heart. It changes your life. And that's what happened to me." Bush's answer not only drew loud applause from the audience, but it also seemed to alter the answers of two of the last three candidates to respond. After Bush, Senator Orrin Hatch of Utah answered Abraham Lincoln and Ronald Reagan, but added, "I bear witness to Christ, too. I really know him to be the savior of the world. And that means more to me than almost anything else I know." Gary Bauer, an evangelical Christian leader in his own right, was last to answer. In naming Christ as well he quoted Scripture before concluding, "If America's in trouble in the next century, it will be because we forgot what he taught us." In between Hatch and Bauer, John McCain answered. Despite the clear tone of the room, McCain said nothing about Jesus Christ. His philosopher was Theodore Roosevelt.[11]

Aside from his general resistance to invoke religion in his first campaign for the presidency, McCain had also recently taken a position on abortion that was in clear conflict with evangelical Christian leaders. While he had a consistent pro-life voting record in the Senate, in 1999 he told the *San Francisco Chronicle*, "[C]ertainly in the short term, or even the long term, I would not support repeal of *Roe v. Wade*, which would then force X number of women in America to [undergo] illegal and dangerous operations."[12] Later in the 2000 primary season, McCain, showcasing his "maverick" qualities that he emphasized during his most recent race for the White House, famously took on two of the early and important leaders of the Christian Right, first referring to Jerry Falwell and Pat Robertson, as "agents of intolerance" and then—in a comment he would quickly retract—denouncing them for "the evil influence that they exercise over the Republican Party."[13] McCain's disagreements with Falwell and Robertson stemmed mainly from his advocacy of campaign finance reform,[14] but at the time he made those comments he was still reeling from his loss in the South Carolina primary to George W. Bush; and was still very upset by the campaign tactics used by his critics (but not necessarily by the Bush campaign itself.)[15] McCain was apparently particularly perturbed at Robertson, who had made phone calls during the South Carolina primary that used portions of a passage from a book written by former New Hampshire Senator and McCain campaign Cochairman Warren Rudman. In his book, *Combat: 12 Years in the U.S. Senate*, Rudman had written, "Politically speaking, the Republican Party is making a terrible mistake if it appears to ally itself with the Christian right. There are some fine, sincere people in its ranks, but there are also enough anti-abortion zealots, would-be censors, homophobes, bigots and latter-day Elmer Gantrys to discredit any party that is unwise enough to embrace such a group." Selectively quoting from the passage, Robertson told potential South Carolina primary voters that Rudman was an "anti-religious bigot."[16] Robertson was supporting Bush and, when the then Texas governor was elected president, he got his wish.

As he began his second race for the presidency, McCain sought to make amends with members of the Christian Right leadership. In an event that attracted a great deal of attention, he traveled to Jerry Falwell's Liberty University to deliver the commencement address in May 2006. He also amended his views on *Roe*, noting in February 2007, "I do not support Roe versus Wade. It should be overturned."[17] McCain still had more work to do on this issue. He also had upset social conservatives when in 2005 he led the so-called Gang of 14, a bipartisan group of senators committed to "reducing the rancor" that had increasingly become part of the judicial confirmation process.[18] In agreeing to block Republican Majority Leader Bill Frist's threats to use the "nuclear option"— which would have changed Senate rules to prevent the Democratic minority from filibustering judicial nominees—conservatives believed McCain had helped prevent President Bush from securing judicial posts for the most ideological conservative jurists (i.e., those most likely to reject *Roe*). In 2008, McCain took steps to signal that he was on board with the Republican judicial strategy by proclaiming, "I am a Republican because I believe the judges we appoint to the federal bench must understand that enforcing our laws, not making them, is their only responsibility."[19] McCain elaborated on these commitments in a widely noted speech at Wake Forest University in May 2008, objecting to "the common and systematic abuse of our federal courts by the people we entrust with judicial power." After a lengthy rehashing of long-standing conservative complaints about liberal judicial activism, McCain promised to "look for accomplished men and women with a proven record of excellence in the law, and a proven commitment to judicial restraint. I will look for people in the cast of John Roberts, Samuel Alito, and my friend the late William Rehnquist—jurists of the highest caliber who know their own minds, and know the law, and know the difference."[20] Finally, he suggested that he would reconsider his views on a constitutional amendment banning gay marriage. McCain still believed that the question of same-sex marriage belonged in the states. But he reportedly told Falwell that "he would support a federal constitutional amendment defining marriage as the union of one man and one woman if a federal court were to strike down state constitutional bans on gay marriage."[21] Not all of the leaders of the Christian Right were as forgiving as Falwell, even one of those McCain praised in his 2000 "agents of intolerance" speech. Specifically, James Dobson told a radio talk show host in early 2008, "Speaking as a private individual, I would not vote for John McCain under any circumstances." He added, "I pray that we won't get stuck with him."[22] And McCain made no effort to reach out to Pat Robertson, who, as detailed later, endorsed a different candidate for the Republican nomination.

Despite continued difficulties with Dobson and Robertson, McCain benefitted from the fact that he was not the only leading contender for the nomination who had difficulties with his previous positions on the most important social issues of the day. For example, on the issue of discarding *Roe*, other leading contenders had an unclear record as well. Indeed, before former Arkansas Governor Mike Huckabee rose from the obscurity of single-point showings in the polls, pro-life Republican primary voters had difficulty identifying a viable candidate to trust on overturning *Roe*. Along with McCain, Mitt Romney, Rudy Giuliani, and Fred Thompson had expressed support for abortion rights in the past. As with McCain, Romney and Thompson disavowed their past support, each seeking to reassure the GOP's base that he was solidly opposed to abortion rights.[23] In contrast, Rudy Giuliani chose—after some awkward initial missteps—to be forthright about his long-standing and continued support for legal abortion. In doing so Giuliani tested conventional wisdom, which held that no pro-choice candidate could win the Republican nomination.[24] In a speech at Houston Baptist College on May 11, 2007, Giuliani declared that "[u]ltimately, there has to be a right to choose" and urged the party faithful to overlook their disagreement on this issue. Drawing attention to the trade-off between ideological purity and electoral success, the former New York City mayor, called on his party to sacrifice its principles in order to win: "If we don't unite, if we don't find a way of uniting around broad principles that will appeal to a large segment of this country, if we can't figure that out, we are going to lose this election."[25]

In part, Giuliani was betting that the revised primary calendar for 2008, in which California, New York, and several other blue states moved their primaries up to February 5, 2008 (so-called Super Tuesday), would allow him to capture the nomination without winning—or even performing well—in primary contests in the nation's most conservative states. He also tried to navigate these waters by issuing pledges on the matter of judicial appointments that were substantially at odds with his pledges regarding legal abortion, suggesting a willingness to appoint individuals intent on overturning *Roe v. Wade*.[26] While most leaders of the Christian Right remained skeptical of Giuliani's balancing act, he did attract the support of one of McCain's "agents of intolerance." To the surprise of many, Pat Robertson endorsed the former mayor. Understanding that "uppermost in the minds of social conservatives is the selection of future Supreme Court justices and lower court judges," Robertson explained that Giuliani "understands the need for a conservative judiciary and...has assured the American people that his choices for judicial appointments will be men and women who share the judicial philosophy of John Roberts and Antonin Scalia."[27] Robertson's endorsement was particularly problematic to Mitt Romney who was working had to secure the backing of leaders of the Christian Right. But, as David D. Kirkpatrick and Michael Cooper reported, "many former Christian conservative allies dismissed the endorsement as an inexplicable stunt." The ultimate victor of the Republican nomination, John McCain, did not know how to respond, saying, "Every once in a while, I am left speechless. This is one of those times."[28] In the end, Robertson's endorsement did not make any difference. Giuliani did not even make it to Super Tuesday, despite spending more than 60 million dollars in the race. In short, conventional wisdom won out. The Republican nominee would have to be pro-life, even if his name was John McCain.

Toward a More Socially Conservative Supreme Court

During the general election campaign, the abortion issue never attracted the type of attention it had in the past, and even the Republican nominee's wife,

Cindy McCain, appeared to be confused about her husband's (or her own) current position on *Roe v. Wade*. When asked by CBS anchor Katie Couric about her position, the senator's wife said that she agreed with her husband, that *Roe* should stand. As the *New York Times* reported, when Couric noted that that was not in fact his position, "Mrs. McCain, looking a bit confused, then said she, too, wanted the legality of abortion to be determined by individual states." At the end of the segment, Couric noted that the campaign later clarified Mrs. McCain's position: "They told us that, like Laura Bush, Mrs. McCain does not favor overturning *Roe v. Wade*, which guarantees the legal right to an abortion."[29] A few days later, when both the McCains appeared on "The View," the candidate sought to clarify his own position once again. To some groans from the audience, he stressed that he believed "*Roe v. Wade* was a very bad decision." Later, he added, "I believe that if *Roe v. Wade* were overturned then the states would make these decisions."[30] While many viewers may not have grasped the significance of that line, McCain was laying out a position that was in clear conflict with that of the most socially conservative members of his party. More specifically, rather than offering up a constitutional amendment banning abortion across the land, he was signaling a willingness to allow the states to decide, fully aware that some would outlaw the procedure and others would legislate a "right to choose" fully in line with the dictates of *Roe*.

But in speaking of his distaste for *Roe* so directly, McCain was actually forced to do something George W. Bush had successfully avoided during both his races for the White House. As the *New York Times* described it, Bush preferred to discuss abortion "with gentle euphemisms to avoid turning off more moderate voters."[31] And he preferred not to discuss *Roe v. Wade* at all. In fact, in the eight years of his presidency he never publicly used the word *Roe* once.[32] His strategy of speaking to the conservative base on abortion but doing so in a fashion that did not offend "swing" voters actually originated in his father's bid for reelection in 1992. Recall, in the midst of that race, a sharply split Supreme Court announced its opinion in the abortion case of *Planned Parenthood v. Casey*. And to the surprise of many, the Court chose not to eradicate *Roe v. Wade*, deciding instead to endorse some portions of the Pennsylvania's anti-abortion law while still maintaining the principle that women had a right to choose to terminate an unwanted pregnancy.[33]

To social conservatives, the *Casey* decision still stands as one of the most disappointing in recent memory.[34] Beyond the ruling itself, the makeup of the 5–4 *Casey* majority was deeply disturbing to those hoping for the decimation of *Roe*. After all, at that time, eight of the Court's nine justices were Republican appointees. And the sole Democratic appointee was Justice White, who was one of *Roe*'s two dissenters. In reaching this mixed result, moreover, Justices O'Connor, Souter, and Kennedy—all appointed by the two most recent Republican presidents—had joined forces. Significantly, each of those three had raised some alarm among conservatives when either Ronald Reagan or George H. W. Bush announced their nominations to the nation. In other words, conservative willingness to "trust" these Republican presidents had apparently limited the Court's conservatism. President Bush's reaction to the high bench's decision in *Casey* furthered that unease.

Despite the long GOP-led drive to reverse *Roe*, the president did not denounce the ruling by any means. Rather, Bush stressed that he "was pleased with the Supreme Court's decision upholding most of Pennsylvania's reasonable restrictions on abortion." He then articulated his position on abortion, which unlike many social conservatives in his party, allowed for the procedure in cases of "rape or incest or where the life of the mother is at stake."[35] Bush continued to emphasize this stance when asked about his position on abortion on the campaign trail. Strikingly it was a position in clear conflict with the Republican Party's platform, which proclaimed "that the unborn child has a fundamental individual right to life which cannot be infringed," and endorsed "legislation to make clear that the Fourteenth Amendment's protections apply to the unborn children."[36] But Bush did not seem to care, noting during one question-and-answer session with voters: "I'm not going to necessarily be bound [by the Republican platform]. I'm the President. I'll say what I'm for and what I'm against."[37] To be sure, the president also made sure to emphasize his more conservative position at times. For example, addressing the Knights of Columbus a few weeks before the Republican Convention, he called attention to the "national tragedy [represented by] more than a half a million abortions in this country every year."[38] But still, the message seemed clear. While Bush considered himself a pro-life president, if he was elected to a second term, overturning *Roe v. Wade* would not be at the top of his agenda. The reason was also clear. Polls suggested in strong terms that Americans were uninterested in seeing the decision discarded.[39]

George W. Bush pursued a similar—more refined—strategy on abortion; avoiding talk of the *Roe* decision while highlighting his commitment to a "culture of life." Here is how he answered a question on abortion in the final debate during the 2004 election:

> I think it's important to promote a culture of life. I think a hospitable society is a society where every being counts and every person matters. I believe the ideal world is one in which every child is protected in law and welcomed to life. I understand there's great differences on this issue of abortion, but I believe reasonable people can come together and put good law in place that will help reduce the number of abortions.... What I'm saying is, is that as we promote life and promote a culture of life, surely there are ways we can work together to reduce the number of abortions: Continue to promote adoption laws—that's a great alternative to abortion; continue to fund and promote maternity group homes. I will continue to promote abstinence programs.... All of us ought to be involved with programs that provide a viable alternative to abortion.

In a follow-up question, moderator Bob Schieffer asked Bush directly about the *Roe v. Wade* decision: "[Senator Kerry earlier] said that you had never said whether you would like to overturn *Roe v. Wade*. So I'd ask you directly, would you like to?" In response, Bush refused to take the bait, telling Schieffer: "What he's asking me is will I have a litmus test for my judges, and the answer is no, I will not have a litmus test. I will pick judges who will interpret the Constitution, but I'll have no litmus test." As suggested earlier, just like his father's campaign in 1992, the Bush team was apparently concerned that advocating the overturn of *Roe*—or even discussing the decision—would be destructive to their candidate's electoral chances, as pro-choice women (in particular) would be much less inclined to vote for him. In the end, this strategy seemingly paid off. In his study of the 2004 election results, political scientist Barry C. Burden found "tentative support for the popular 'security mom' thesis." In other words, Bush did particularly well with white women concerned about security but seemingly less concerned about the end of *Roe v. Wade*.[40]

Of course, to please his conservative base, Bush could not avoid discussing abortion altogether. Along with highlighting "culture of life" themes, he emphasized his support of the popular ban on partial-birth abortion. For example, his response to the abortion question in the final debate included: "Take, for example, the ban on partial-birth abortion. It's a brutal practice. People from both political parties came together in the Halls of Congress and voted overwhelmingly to ban that practice. It made a lot of sense. My opponent, in that he's out of the mainstream, voted against that law."[41] On the campaign trail, Bush consistently referred to the partial-birth ban in similar fashion.[42]

Bush also made a very strong statement on *Roe* during the second debate without mentioning the ruling by name. In response to a question on selecting Supreme Court justices, he said in part:

> I would pick somebody who would not allow their personal opinion to get in the way of the law. I would pick somebody who would strictly interpret the Constitution of the United States. Let me give you a couple of examples.... Another example would be the *Dred Scott* case, which is where judges years ago said that the Constitution allowed slavery because of personal property rights. That's personal opinion. That's not what the Constitution says. The Constitution of the United States says we're all—it doesn't say that. It doesn't speak to the equality of America. And so I would pick people that would be strict constructionists. We've got plenty of lawmakers in Washington, DC. Legislators make law. Judges interpret the Constitution.[43]

Although most in the audience likely missed the significance of Bush's words, they certainly attracted the attention of ardent social conservatives who have long viewed *Roe* as the twentieth century's *Dred Scott*. In fact, Associate Justice Antonin Scalia—the justice President Bush once noted as the type of jurist he would select for the Court if presented with the opportunity—has repeatedly made this comparison in his opinions on abortion cases.[44] And following the debate, noted conservatives expressed their pleasure with the president's reference to the 1857 decision. For example, the Reverend Louis P. Sheldon, chairman of the conservative Traditional Values Coalition, called Bush's answer "a very poignant moment, a very special gourmet, filet mignon dinner." "Everyone knows the *Dred Scott* decision and you don't have to stretch your mind at all. When he said that, it made it very clear that the [*Roe*] decision was faulty because what it said was that unborn persons in a legal sense have no civil rights."[45] Bush's strategy seemingly worked as pro-life voters turned out at the polls in strong numbers for his reelection, although some of these "value voters" might have been motivated more by other "moral" issues such as same-sex marriage and stem cell research.

But even George W. Bush would ultimately have his difficulties with social conservatives with regard to the makeup of the Supreme Court. Surprisingly, they originated in the summer of 2005 when the near-20-year reign of the Rehnquist Court came to an end. Unchanged since 1994, the first vacancy on the Court occurred when Sandra Day O'Connor announced her retirement from the bench in early July. Two months later Chief Justice William Rehnquist, who had hoped to serve another year in the center chair, lost his battle with illness and age, creating a second vacancy for President Bush to fill.

In considering his options, Bush understood the importance of his choices to the social conservatives at the core of the Republican Party. After all, although Republicans had chosen seven members of this Court (including O'Connor and Rehnquist), its biggest critics had consistently come from the ideological right of American politics. Indeed, many conservatives were profoundly displeased with their inability—despite successes at the ballot box—to produce a thoroughly conservative Supreme Court during Rehnquist's time as chief. None other than Robert Bork, appointed by Ronald Reagan to the Court in 1987 but rejected by a Democratic Senate, had been one of its sharpest critics. For example, writing in 2002, Bork noted, "The Court as a whole lists heavily to the cultural left." To him, "no matter how many Justices are appointed by Republican presidents, the works of the Warren Court and the victories of the ACLU are not reversed." Instead, the Court is the most "elite institution in America," in that it is most often "ahead of the general public in approving, and to a degree enforcing, the vulgarization or proletarianization of our culture."[46] Other conservatives had been as equally vocal in expressing their distaste for the Rehnquist Court, especially for those justices who were appointed by Republican presidents but who failed to live up to the expectations of social conservatives. For example, in 2006, longtime conservative activist Phyllis Schlafly told a conference on "Confronting the Judicial War on Faith," that the record of Justice Anthony Kennedy, the fourth most conservative justice on the Rehnquist Court, was so poor that "Congress ought to talk about impeachment."[47]

To some on the Left, the nature of this Court's doctrine actually proved to be beneficial to the electoral interests of the Republican Party. Indeed, one of Thomas Frank's complaints about the Republicans' use of culture war issues to attract voters is that its party leaders—despite attaining power—often fail to deliver on the promises they make during the election season. As he writes: "Abortion is never halted. Affirmative action is never abolished. The culture industry is never forced to clean up its act."[48] In one of the debates during the 2000 Republican primary, Gary Bauer made a similar point to Frank's. In attacking George Bush for "refusing to apply an anti-abortion 'litmus test' to federal court nominees," Bauer criticized Bush's father's selection of David Souter for the Supreme Court. "I not only think that President Bush made a colossal mistake by putting a justice on the court that is a reliable vote for Clinton and Gore, I believe we can never afford to make another mistake like that." Bauer added, "Look, seven of the current nine Supreme Court justices were appointed by Republican presidents. Abortion should be over." When asked to respond, Bush stayed on message, avoiding any commitment to a "litmus test" and emphasizing his intent "to put people on the bench that strictly interpret the Constitution and do not use the bench as a place from which to legislate." On Souter, he simply said, "My dad can defend himself."[49]

With O'Connor's retirement and Rehnquist's death, however, things were set to be different on a whole range of issues. (On the specific issue of abortion, even with two additional anti-*Roe* justices, social conservatives would still come up short in overturning the decision. However, O'Connor's departure did open up the possibility that the Court would uphold the federal ban on partial-birth abortion.[50]) After all, in 2005, with Republicans in control of the Senate and a conservative in the White House, most assumed it would be easy to find two ideologically reliable conservatives who would be confirmed without too much difficulty. With his first choice for the Court, Bush, by virtually all accounts, selected the type of jurist conservatives were hoping for. John Roberts was smart, experienced, and most importantly, a committed conservative. Roberts was originally selected to fill O'Connor's seat, but with the death of Rehnquist the president withdrew that nomination and named Roberts to the center chair. In searching for a new nominee, Bush was reportedly still committed to finding the most conservative jurist who was confirmable, but he also seemed concerned about one of the few criticisms of the Roberts selection. As Justice O'Connor herself put it, "He's good in every way, expect he's not a woman."[51] It was a position that First Lady Laura Bush reportedly agreed with.[52] And after searching long and hard to find the right person for the spot the president settled on Harriet Miers, the White House legal counsel. To Bush, Miers, who was a friend, was just the person to deliver the conservative decisions he expected. As he explained in introducing her to the nation, "I know her heart, I know her character....I'm confident [she] will add to the wisdom and character of our judiciary." But to social conservatives, she was simply unacceptable. And after trusting the president's father in 1990 (and receiving Justice Souter), they were unwilling to risk such an important vacancy on another Bush hunch. As legal journalist Jeffrey Toobin explains, "Although the right tried to phrase its complaints about Miers as a matter of qualifications...the problem...[was] their own lack of certainty that she would follow their agenda on the Court." Commenting on the level of confidence among conservatives at the time, Toobin adds that in 1987 "Bork couldn't be confirmed *because* he opposed *Roe v. Wade*; in 2005, a nominee couldn't be selected *unless* he or she opposed *Roe v. Wade*."[53] And since influential social conservatives were uncertain about Miers's position on the decision, the president was ultimately forced to withdraw her nomination. In her place, he named Samuel Alito, a nominee who was considered even more conservative than the new chief justice.[54]

As described earlier, with Miers's withdrawal and the conservative approval of Roberts and Alito fresh in their minds, John McCain and other leading contenders for the GOP nomination made it clear that they would find similar jurists to fill any vacancies on the Court. Specifically, apparently missing the irony of social conservative distaste for the science, McCain pledged "to find clones of

Alito and Roberts."[55] Moreover, during the general election, his campaign made sure to emphasize what the Court might become if Barack Obama was elected to the presidency. As former Tennessee Senator Fred Thompson told the delegates at the Republican Convention, a Democratic victory might result in a Supreme Court "lost to liberalism for a generation."[56]

For his part, when it came to the Supreme Court, Barack Obama followed a path well worn by previous Democratic nominees, promising to protect already-won rights rather than articulating a new set of goals. Indeed, one of the main reasons why a chapter on social issues focuses so heavily on the Republican Party is due to the fact that Democrats have largely been playing defense in this part of the electoral arena. For example, during the three most recent presidential campaigns, the Democratic candidate offered no major criticisms of the Supreme Court or any of its decisions.[57] Instead, when these Democratic candidates discussed the Court, they tended to emphasize the future rather than the past, suggesting that conservative justices were close to attaining the necessary votes to discard landmark rulings such as *Roe v. Wade*. This has forced them to use some highly speculative language—likely to little avail—or to virtually ignore the Court on the campaign trial. In 2008, Barack Obama followed suit. In fact, he attracted the most attention with regard to the Court when he noted his *support* of a June 2008 decision that struck down a strict Washington D.C. gun law and established for the first time an individual right to bear arms.[58] And when Obama did criticize one of the Court's decisions—in a case that ruled out the death penalty for child rape—John McCain gave him credit for doing so. But McCain had more to say. Although Republican presidents have appointed 13 of the last 15 justices, he added, "My opponent may not care for this particular decision, but it was exactly the kind of opinion we could expect from an Obama Court."[59]

In the end, however, the social issues at the center of the debate over the makeup of the Supreme Court did not take up much space in the campaign. As Cindy McCain, seeking to avoid discussing the issue once again, explained at one point during the race, abortion is "not what's foremost in the voters' minds right now, at all."[60] With the economy absorbing most of the attention, she was indeed correct. But given the importance of religious voters to past Republican victories, she might have hoped it had been.

Sarah Palin: A Savior to the Base

The video is over a decade old. It shows a proud wife thrilled with her husband's victory in the "Iron Dog Race." Smiling wide and with a bundled-up baby in her arms, a thirtyish Sarah Palin responds to a reporter's question about whether she was happy about the victory, "Yes, I'm very happy. I'm very thankful. We thank God. That's who we thank."[61] The answer was simple enough, and one commonly heard in interviews following athletic events. But it reveals much about why evangelical Christians were so pleased with John McCain's selection of Palin as his running mate. Before her days as a politician in the city of Wasilla, Alaska, or amidst the bright lights of a presidential campaign, this self-described "hockey mom" spoke in clear evangelical terms in discussing her emotions. Given McCain's difficulties with the social conservatives in the past, the choice of Palin was sure to please the Republican Party's base.

According to press accounts, Palin was not McCain's first choice. He apparently wanted an individual who already had experience running for the vice presidency of the United States. Specifically, he wanted Senator Joe Lieberman of Connecticut; the Democrat-turned "Independent Democrat" who had been Al Gore's running mate in 2000. The choice of Lieberman would no doubt have been stunning, even from the "maverick" McCain. But ultimately the candidate's advisors convinced him that it would afflict a body blow to his candidacy. After all, Lieberman was a strong supporter of abortion rights, and McCain's pollster reportedly thought, "[A] pro-choice running mate had the potential to cause a 20-point drop in support among McCain's core voters. A small uptick in independent voters or crossover Democrats wouldn't begin to make up the difference."[62]

The others on the short list were apparently uninspiring to the candidate. He wanted someone who, as he would later describe his choice, would "ignite a spark in America."[63] Sarah Palin was the right person for the task. She was viewed by a key member of the McCain team as potentially a "conservative populist, the kind of throw-'em-red-meat, bash-the-elites politician who thrilled the Republican base." Some in the campaign were reportedly "a little nervous about the Hail Mary quality" of the choice but, given the state of the economy and the unpopularity of the Republican incumbent, that may have been McCain's only option.[64]

The selection of Sarah Palin certainly stirred up the race for the White House. Social conservatives, still uncertain about a McCain candidacy, were thrilled. As the New York Times reported, as "a committed conservative, she had been a hero to the anti-abortion movement since she gave birth to a child with Down syndrome" in the spring of 2008.[65] And with Palin by his side, McCain's once small crowds "suddenly swelled to Obama-size numbers—5,000, 10,000, 15,000 people." Democrats at first were taken aback a bit, concerned about the level of attention and excitement Palin was receiving but also confident that her selection would ultimately amount to "message suicide" for the McCain campaign.[66] More specifically, given that McCain had been seeking to undermine Obama's message of change for months by questioning his experience for the job, to the Obama team it seemed unwise to select someone as inexperienced as Palin. And as press attention toward Palin reached unprecedented levels for a vice presidential nominee, the candidate showed the signs of someone unfamiliar with the spotlight of the national press core. In particular, in interviews with Charlie Gibson of ABC News and then (and more significantly) with Katie Couric of CBS News, she struggled to answer some seemingly easy questions. Perhaps worst of all for the candidate was the performance of Tina Fey (as Sarah Palin) on NBC's Saturday Night Live. In her first of several skits Fey (as Palin) stood next to Amy Poehler (who played Hillary Clinton). After Poehler (as Clinton) articulated a line on foreign policy intended to convey the real New York senator's knowledge and experience, Fey (as Palin) said, "And I can see Russia from my house." The audience roared with delight.[67] But it certainly was not helpful for a candidate hoping to be a "heartbeat away from the presidency."

On Election Day, the selection of Sarah Palin likely both helped and harmed the Republican ticket.[68] On the one hand, according to exit polls, only 38 percent of respondents thought she was qualified enough to be president. On the other hand, of the 60 percent of respondents who said her selection was a factor in determining their vote, 56 percent supported the Republican ticket. Some of them were no doubt white evangelical born-again Christians. And according to the exit polls, more voters defining themselves in those terms turned out for John McCain in 2008 than for George W. Bush in 2004. More specifically, white evangelical born-again Christians made up 26 percent of the electorate in 2008 (compared to 23 percent in 2004). And while they were slightly less supportive of McCain in percentages than Bush (74–78 percent), in real numbers more than 25 million white evangelical born-again Christians voted for McCain—approximately 3.3 million more than Bush four years earlier. On the other hand, as table 4.1 displays, of the most religious voters (defined in terms of church attendance), McCain did not fare well in comparison to his partisan predecessor. As table 4.1 shows, his percentage of those voters who attend religious services more than once a week fell from 16 to 12 percent and McCain only won 55 percent of that vote (compared to Bush's 64 percent in 2004).

In turn the exit polls suggest that Barack Obama made some inroads with some of the most religious voters in America, particularly Catholics. In some ways, this is odd since the revelation that Obama's minister, Reverend Jeremiah Wright, had made harsh comments about the United States soon after the 9/11 attacks threatened to derail his campaign during the Democratic primary

Table 4.1   Religion and the vote, 2004 and 2008

Question	2008	D	R	2004	D	R
Attend religious service?	Total %	Obama	McCain	Total %	Kerry	Bush
More than once a week	12	43	55	16	35	64
Once a week	27	43	55	26	41	58
A few times a month	15	53	46	14	49	50
A few times a year	28	59	39	28	54	45
Never	16	67	30	15	62	36
Which Religion?						
Protestant	54	45	54	54	40	59
Catholic	27	54	45	27	47	52
Jewish	2	78	21	3	74	25
Something else	6	73	22	7	74	23
None	12	75	23	10	67	31
White evangelical born-again Christian?						
Yes	26	24	74	23	21	78
No	74	62	36	77	56	43

Source: Figures from National Election Pool exit poll.

season.[69] And in one of his few verbal blunders during the campaign, he suggested that white working-class voters at times "cling...to religion."[70] At the same time, Obama usually speaks with a certain ease when discussing the role of religion in his life and in America—in a way McCain doesn't. Recall one of the most memorable lines of his speech at the 2004 Democratic Convention, designed to respond to what was deemed a media-generated red/blue divide in America, centered on the importance of religion. It was a simple line, but it said much: "We worship an 'awesome God' in the Blue States, and we don't like federal agents poking around in our libraries in the Red States." And a bit later in the speech, in speaking of "the audacity of hope," he stressed, "In the end, that is God's greatest gift to us, the bedrock of this nation. A belief in things not seen. A belief that there are better days ahead."[71]

The Ballot Measures: Liberal Defeats, Liberal Victories

Given the role that ballot measures banning gay marriage had reportedly played in increasing turnout and reelecting George W. Bush in 2004, Democrats had a right to be wary about the possible effects of similar bans on the ballots of three states in 2008, two of them large electoral prizes (California with 55 electoral votes and Florida with 27; the other was Arizona with 10 electoral votes). But Barack Obama won California easily and turned the previously red Florida blue with a 3-percentage point margin victory. As expected Arizona supported its own senator, John McCain. But to liberal advocates of same-sex marriage, the news was not all good on election night. As table 4.2 displays, in all three states, bans on gay marriage passed. In addition, an Arkansas measure designed to bar gays and lesbians from adopting children easily succeeded as well.

The outcome was particularly upsetting to advocates of same-sex marriage in California, where they had been performed since June following a decision by the

Table 4.2   Results of state ballot measures involving social issues (by percentage)

States	Ballot measure	Yes	No
Arizona	Ban on same-sex marriage	56	44
Arkansas	Ban on gay couples adopting children	57	43
California	Ban on same-sex marriage	52	48
	Abortion limits	48	52
Colorado	End affirmative action	49	51
	Human life from moment of conception	27	73
Florida	Ban on same-sex marriage	62	38
Michigan	Allow medical marijuana	63	37
	Allow stem cell research	53	47
Nebraska	End affirmative action	58	42
South Dakota	Abortion limits	45	55
Washington	Allow physician-assisted suicide	58	42

Source: Based on the final election figures from the individual states.

state's highest court. The reason for the ban's passage is fairly straightforward. The coalition Barack Obama built to win the state with 61 percent of the vote split on the issue. Specifically, 70 percent of African-American and 53 percent of Latino voters supported the ban while 51 percent of white voters opposed it. Arizona's vote was also significant because the state had rejected a similar ban two years earlier. These results meant that after Election Day 30 states had bans against gay marriage. Only two, Connecticut and Massachusetts, allowed same-sex marriages. And notably, in both, gay marriage became a legal right as a result of a court decision, not success at the polls. In expressing his reasons for backing the ban, Reverend Joel Hunter, a prominent evangelical pastor in Florida who gave the benediction at the Democratic National Convention, spoke in terms that evoked social issue themes that had aided conservatives in past elections. "There is enough of the population that is alarmed at the general breakdown of the family, that has been so inundated with images of homosexual relationships in all of the media. It's almost like it's obligatory these days to have a homosexual couple in every TV show or every movie."[72]

But the extent of conservative success on ballot measures involving social issues was largely limited to bans on same-sex marriage. Specifically, in three states, South Dakota, California, and Colorado, voters rejected ballot measures designed to restrict abortion. Michigan voters supported a measure allowing the medical use of marijuana and another to permit human embryonic stem cell research. In Washington, voters supported a measure that would allow physician-assisted suicide. On the issue of affirmative action, Nebraska voters did support a ban. But in Colorado, voters rejected a similar measure. To be sure most of the states that rejected conservative measures on social issues also supported Barack Obama for the presidency, some by large margins. But nevertheless, outside of the issue of gay marriage, the results suggest that Republicans may need to find new concerns to connect with voters; that GOP-friendly social issues may be missing from the electoral equation for some time to come.

Notes

1. James Sundquist, *Dynamics of the Party System: Alignment and Realignment of Political Parties in the United States* (Washington, DC: Brookings Institution Press, 1983), p. 383.
2. For a discussion of the recent politics of values generally, see, James Davison Hunter, *Culture Wars: The Struggle to Define America* (New York: Basic Books, 1991); and John Kenneth White, *The Values Divide: American Politics and Culture in Transition* (New York: Chatham House, 2003). See also, Gertrude Himmelfarb, *One Nation, Two Cultures: A Searching Examination of American Society in the Aftermath of Our Cultural Revolution* (New York: Vintage, 2001); John Micklethwait and Adrian Wooldridge, *The Right Nation: Conservative Power in America* (New York: Penguin Press, 2004); and John C. Green, Mark J. Rozell, and Clyde Wilcox, eds., *The Values Campaign?: The Christian Right and the 2004 Elections* (Washington, DC: Georgetown University Press, 2006).
3. Jeffrey Toobin, "Ashcroft's Ascent: How Far Will the Attorney General Go?" *New Yorker*, April 15, 2002, pp. 50–63, 63.

4. Although different exit poll wording makes it difficult to tell whether evangelical Christians made up a greater share of the electorate than in 2000, political scientist John Green's polling showed that President Bush increased his share of the evangelical vote by 5% from 2000, from 71 to 76%; Green cited in Laurie Goodstein and William Yardley, "Bush Benefits from Efforts to Build a Coalition of the Faithful," *New York Times*, November, 5 2004; See also, John C. Green, "The American Religious Landscape and Political Attitudes: A Baseline for 2004," available at pewforum.org.

5. Thomas B. Edsall, "Exit Poll Data Inconclusive on Increase in Evangelical Voters"; and Alan Cooperman and Thomas B. Edsall, "Evangelicals Say They Led Charge for the GOP," *Washington Post*, November 8, 2004.

6. David D. Kirkpatrick and Laurie Goodstein, "Group of Bishops Using Influence to Oppose Kerry," *New York Times*, October 12, 2004.

7. Moreover, the two Kerry states (Michigan and Oregon) were the only ones where the same-sex ban did not pass by more than 20% of the vote.

8. David Brooks, "The Values-Vote Myth," *New York Times*, November 6, 2004; Charles Krauthammer, "'Redneck Vote' Is a Liberal Myth," *New York Daily News*, November 12, 2004. On the "moral values" nature of the election generally, see also, Green, Rozell, and Wilcox, *The Values Campaign?*

9. Thomas Frank, *What's the Matter with Kansas?: How Conservatives Won the Heart of America* (New York: Metropolitan Books/Henry Holt & Company, 2004).

10. Christine Todd Whitman, *It's My Party, Too: Taking Back the Republican Party and Bringing the Country Together Again* (New York: Penguin, 2005, 2006), pp. 2–3.

11. The details of this portion of the debate are recounted in David Domke and Kevin Coe's *The God Strategy: How Religion Became a Political Weapon in America* (New York: Oxford University Press, 2008), pp. 29–30; Additional quotes from Stephen Buttry, "Candidates Focus on Christian Beliefs," *Des Moines Register*, December 15, 1999.

12. Terry M. Neal, "McCain Softens Abortion Stand," *Washington Post*, August 24, 1999.

13. Byron York, "John McCain: Can He Be a Falwell Republican?" *Washington Post*, May 7, 2006.

14. Dan Balz, "McCain Reconnects with Liberty University," *Washington Post*, May 14, 2006.

15. To be sure, some in the McCain camp did blame the Bush campaign. As Evan Thomas writes, Cindy McCain "personally blamed Karl Rove, Bush's political guru, for unleashing the old Lee Atwater attack machine, using anonymous smear artists to spread around leaflets suggesting that her adopted daughter, Bridget, was the love child of John McCain and a black prostitute." Thomas adds, "Rove always vigorously denied any such thing, and the link was never proved." But Cindy McCain still harbors deep-seated resentment toward Rove. For example, when asked in 2007 whether she would stab Rove in the back if she saw him, she answered, "No. I'd stab him in the front"; Evan Thomas, "Going into Battle," from *Newsweek's* "How He Did It," published November 5, 2008 for magazine issue November 17, 2008. Available at http://www.newsweek.com/id/167582.

16. Carey Goldberg, "Advising McCain, Rudman Is Happily Back in the Fray," *New York Times*, February 26, 2000. See also, Warren Rudman, *Combat: 12 Years in the U.S. Senate* (New York: Random House, 1996).

17. Jim Davenport, "McCain: Roe v. Wade Should be Overturned," *Washington Post*, February 18, 2007.

18. Memorandum of Understanding on Judicial Nominations.

19. Carl Tobias, "On Judges, Don't Doubt McCain's Conservatism," *Christian Science Monitor*, February 11, 2008.

20. Remarks by John McCain at Wake Forest University, May 6, 2008, available online, http://www.johnmccain.com/Informing/News/Speeches/5385B2DD-FC8F-4BC9-9FB0-DA2E2F1D9F98.htm.

21. Teddy Davis, "McCain Woos the Right, Makes Peace with Falwell," ABCNews.com, March 28, 2006; see also, David Grann, "The Fall: John McCain's Choices," *The New Yorker*, November 17, 2008, pp. 56–66.

22. Bob Unruh, "Dobson Says 'No Way to McCain Candidacy,'" WorldNetDaily.com, January 13, 2007.

23. Robin Toner, "Anti-Abortion Leaders Size Up G.O.P. Candidates," *New York Times*, July 30, 2007. On Romney, see also Michael Luo, "Romney Works to Put Skeptics' Doubts to Rest," *New York Times,* May 11, 2007. On Thompson, see also Jo Becker and David D. Kirkpatrick, "Group Says it Hired Fred Thompson in Abortion Rights Bid," *New York Times*, July 7, 2007; Jo Becker, "Records Show Ex-Senator's Work for Family Planning Unit," *New York Times*, July 19, 2007.

24. Adam Nagourney and Marc Santora, "Embracing Abortion Rights, Giuliani Treads a New Path," *New York Times*, May 10, 2007.

25. "In His Own Words," *New York Times*, May 12, 2007.

26. For more on this point, see Kevin J. McMahon and Thomas Keck, "Rudy of Two Minds on Abortion," *The Hartford Courant*, October 11, 2007.

27. Excerpt available at http://thecaucus.blogs.nytimes.com/2007/11/07/pat-robertson-endorses-giuliani/?ref=politics.

28. David D. Kirkpatrick and Michael Cooper, "In a Surprise, Pat Robertson Backs Giuliani," *New York Times*, November 8, 2007.

29. Alessandra Stanley, "Obama Steps into O'Reilly's 'No Spin Zone,'" *New York Times*, September 5, 2008.

30. Video available at http://www.youtube.com/watch?v=BoQ_G6eMJAQ&feature=related.

31. David D. Kirkpatrick, "Firing Up the Faithful with Echoes of Culture War Rhetoric," *New York Times*, September 5, 2008.

32. Search of the *Weekly Compilation of Presidential Documents*.

33. *Planned Parenthood v. Casey*, 505 U.S. 833 (1992).

34. Conservatives found some solace with the three dissenting justices. For example, Justice Scalia spoke in clear terms on what he thought the Court should have done with *Roe:* "We should get out of this area, where we have no right to be, and where we do neither ourselves nor the country any good by remaining," *Planned Parenthood v. Casey*, 833, 1002.

35. Bush, "Statement on the Supreme Court Decision on Abortion," June 29, 1992, *Weekly Compilation of Presidential Documents*.

36. 1988 Republican Party platform.

37. Bush, "Question-and-Answer Session in Secaucus, New Jersey," October 22, 1992, *Weekly Compilation of Presidential Documents*.

38. "Remarks to the Knights of Columbus Supreme Council Convention in New York City," August 5, 1992, *Public Papers of George Bush*.

39. For example, a Gallup Poll taken right before the 1992 Republican Convention showed that far more voters supported maintaining *Roe* (60%) than did those who wanted to see it overturned (33.6%); Gallup Poll taken from August 13, 1992 to August 14, 1992.

40. Barry C. Burden, "An Alternative Account of the 2004 Presidential Election," *The Forum* 2:4 (2004).

41. George W. Bush, "Presidential Debate in Tempe, Arizona," *Weekly Compilation of Presidential Documents*, October 13, 2004, pp. 2377–2378, p. 2371.

42. See, e.g., George W. Bush, "Remarks in Vienna, Ohio," *Weekly Compilation of Presidential Documents*, October 27, 2004, pp. 2628–2634, p. 2634.

43. George W. Bush, "Presidential Debate in St. Louis, Missouri," *Weekly Compilation of Presidential Documents*, October 8, 2004, p. 2307.

44. Most recently, he opened his 2000 dissent in a Nebraska partial-birth abortion case with:

> I am optimistic enough to believe that, one day, *Stenberg v. Carhart* will be assigned its rightful place in the history of this Court's jurisprudence beside *Korematsu* and *Dred Scott*. The method of killing a human child—one cannot even accurately say an entirely unborn human child—proscribed by this statute is so horrible that the most clinical description of it evokes a shudder of revulsion. (*Stenberg v. Carhart, 530 U.S. 914*)

45. Conservative constitutional scholar Douglas Kmiec and Eleanor Smeal, president of the liberal Feminist Majority, both agreed that Bush was attempting to reach out to his conservative base with his reference to *Dred Scott* (although the Bush campaign denied any abortion-related significance); Peter Wallsten, "Abortion Foes Call Bush's Dred Scott Reference Perfectly Clear," *Los Angeles Times*, October 14, 2004.

46. Robert H. Bork, "Adversary Jurisprudence," in Hilton Kramer and Roger Kimball, eds., *The Survival of Culture: Permanent Values in a Virtual Age* (Chicago, IL: Ivan R. Dee, 2002), pp. 196, 217, and 221.

47. Dana Milbank, "And the Verdict on Justice Kennedy Is: Guilty," *Washington Post*, April 20, 2006. See also, Phyllis Schlafly, *The Supremacists: The Tyranny of Judges and How to Stop It* (Dallas, TX: Spence Publishing Company, 2004).

48. Frank, *What's the Matter with Kansas?* pp. 6–7.

49. Jill Zuckerman and Michael Kranish, "Bush, McCain Dominate GOP Debate," *Boston Globe*, January 7, 2000. This does not mean that the Rehnquist Court did not limit the extent of the "right to choose" originally outlined in *Roe*. It did. For example, the majority opinion in *Planned Parenthood v. Casey* did reject *Roe*'s trimester system, replacing it with the vaguer "undue burden" test and allowing states to enact more restrictive legislation. Nevertheless, abortion remained legal across the United States. For some women, however, access is quite limited. For a discussion of the recent politics of abortion, see, William Saletan, *Bearing Right: How Conservatives Won the Abortion War* (Berkeley, CA: University of California Press, 2003).

50. *Gonzales v. Carhart*, 550 U.S. 124 (2007).

51. Jan Crawford Greenburg, *Supreme Conflict: The Inside Story of the Struggle for Control of the United States Supreme Court* (New York: Penguin, 2007), p. 213.

52. Elisabeth Bumiller, "Pillow-Talk Call for a Woman to Fill O'Connor Seat," *New York Times*, July 18, 2005.

53. Jeffrey Toobin, *The Nine: Inside the Secret World of the Supreme Court* (New York: Doubleday, 2007), pp. 289–290, 292–293, and 266. See also, Kevin J. McMahon, "Explaining the Selection and Rejection of Harriet Miers: George W. Bush, Political Symbolism, and the Highpoint of Conservatism," *American Review of Politics* 29:2 (Fall 2008): 253–270.

54. In the often-used perceived ideological scores calculated by political scientist Jeffrey Segal, which range from 0 (most conservative) to 1 (most liberal), Miers received a .270, more moderate than both Roberts (.120) and Alito (.100). In addition, Miers did not fare well in comparison to Roberts and Alito with Segal's perceived qualifications scores. For these three, the perceived qualifications scores—ranging from 0 (least qualified) to 1 (most qualified)—were as follows: Roberts (.970), Miers (.360), and

Alito (.810). Segal's scores are available at http://ws.cc.stonybrook.edu/polsci/jsegal/qualtable.pdf.

55. Tobias, "On Judges, Don't Doubt McCain's Conservatism."

56. Kirkpatrick, "Firing Up the Faithful with Echoes of Culture War Rhetoric."

57. According to a search of the *New York Times*.

58. Lisa Tozzi, "Candidates React to Supreme Court's Gun Ruling," *New York Times*, June 26, 2008; *District of Columbia v. Heller* (2008). During one of the debates, Obama also said he disagreed with a recent equal protection decision of the Court dealing involving pay discrimination.

59. Elisabeth Bumiller, "McCain Warns of an Obama Court," *New York Times*, July 1, 2008.

60. Video available at http://www.youtube.com/watch?v=ZHNG6Zvgt44.

61. Available at http://www.youtube.com/watch?v=20E7KZuOb6s. The child in her arms is presumably one of her children but is unidentified in the video.

62. Thomas, "Center Stage," from *Newsweek's* "How He Did It." See also, Jane Mayer, "The Insiders: How John McCain Came to Pick Sarah Palin," *New Yorker*, October 27, 2008, pp. 38–42.

63. Video available at http://www.youtube.com/watch?v=xyQpmN-nH64.

64. Thomas, "Center Stage," from *Newsweek's* "How He Did It."

65. Kirkpatrick, "Firing Up the Faithful with Echoes of Culture War Rhetoric.".

66. Thomas, "Center Stage," and "The Final Days," from *Newsweek's* "How He Did It."

67. Video available at http://www.nbc.com/Saturday_Night_Live/video/clips/palin-hillary-open/656281/.

68. Thomas writes, "Palin, the polls showed, had succeeded in rallying the Republican base. But she, or the simmering anger around her, helped make Obama supporters out of countless independent voters," "The Great Debates," from *Newsweek's* "How He Did It."

69. Obama was likely aided by John McCain's decision not to use the Wright video—and other potentially inflammatory items related to social issues—during the general election. As Evan Thomas explains,

> McCain had set firm boundaries: no Jeremiah Wright; no attacking Michelle Obama; no attacking Obama for not serving in the military…[McCain advisor Steve] Schmidt vetoed ads suggesting Obama was soft on crime (no Willie Hortons); and before word even got to McCain, Schmidt and [Mark] Salter scuttled a "celebrity" ad of Obama dancing with talk-show host Ellen DeGeneres (the sight of a black man dancing with a lesbian was deemed too provocative). (ibid.)

70. Audio available at http://www.huffingtonpost.com/mayhill-fowler/obama-no-surprise-that-ha_b_96188.html.

71. Speech available at http://www.americanrhetoric.com/speeches/convention2004/barackobama2004dnc.htm.

72. Jesse McKinley and Laurie Goodstein, "Bans in 3 States on Gay Marriage," *New York Times*, November 6, 2008.

Part III

The Regions

5

The Northeast

Blue, Deep Blue

Kevin J. McMahon

Election Day was only minutes old, and the news from the Northeast was already bad for John McCain. In New Hampshire's Dixville Notch, a little town in the far North of the state with the distinct tradition of being first in the nation to vote on Election Day, the tallies were announced. Barack Obama, 15; John McCain, 6. It was the first time in 40 years that the good voters of Dixville Notch had supported the Democratic ticket, which in 1968 included their popular neighbor Maine Senator Edmund Muskie as the vice presidential candidate. Indeed, in most of the elections since the town's voters agreed to stay up late to vote together so that their ballots could be counted quickly, the race had not been close. And the Democratic nominee had not fared well. For example, in 1960, John F. Kennedy did not win a vote. Four years later, Lyndon Johnson (LBJ) won just one. But on this Election Day, Barack Obama sailed to an easy victory. And it was barely past midnight.

The voters of Dixville Notch represent more than a small group of committed citizens willing to stay up past their bedtime to cast their votes. They represent an image of small-town New England democracy for sure but, in 2008, their voting pattern also symbolized the clear shift throughout vast swaths of the Northeast to the Democratic Party. In 2008, as in the recent past, these 12 states plus the District of Columbia provided the Democratic nominee with his base of support.[1] But Barack Obama did even better than his partisan predecessors, performing at a higher level in the region than Bill Clinton, Al Gore, or even Northeast native John Kerry. Indeed, when all the votes were tallied, the story was one of near-domination. Losing only West Virginia—an odd fit for the region—Obama racked up wins in the rest of the Northeast by margins not seen for a Democrat since LBJ's historic electoral wipeout of Barry Goldwater in 1964. More specifically, Obama captured 7 of the 12 states with more than 60 percent of the vote. And even the closest race in the region was not all that close. With the aid of

15 of Dixville Notch's 21 voters, Obama beat John McCain in New Hampshire by just under 10 percent. For a state that had given McCain two significant victories in the Republican primaries of 2000 and 2008 and where Obama had suffered a surprising and stinging defeat at the hands of Hillary Clinton in the Democratic primary just 10 months earlier, the margin was somewhat astounding.

Of course, it was not always this way. In fact, the Northeast's development as a Democratic stronghold represents a dramatic turnaround for the region, long regarded as the most Republican in the country. This chapter analyzes both the politics of the Northeast and its political transformation within the context of the 2008 presidential election. In doing so, it explores how and why the Northeast has emerged as the nation's bluest region. More specifically, it offers two intertwined explanations, centered on the electoral and ideological focus of the Republican Party and the region's own political independence.

As Maine Goes, so Goes? The Bluing of the Northeast

In the 1980s and early 1990s, trivia buffs had an easy time stumping all but the keenest observers of the political scene with a version of the following question: "Excluding the presidential election of 1964, which state has not voted for the Democratic Party's presidential nominee since 1824?" While most would-be responders would instinctively target their attention toward the fire engine Red states of Middle America, the answer actually lay in the middle of Blue America. More specifically, it lay in Vermont. By the early 1990s, Vermont may have had Howard Dean as its governor and Democratic Socialist Bernie Sanders as its congressman, but in more than a century and a half of voting it had only supported the Democratic presidential candidate once. Even in the Democratic Party's headiest years, Vermont had remained true to its Republican roots. For example, in Franklin Roosevelt's (FDR) historic landslide victory in 1936, only Vermont—along with Maine—voted for Republican Alf Landon. And Vermont, by virtue of giving Landon 56.4 percent of its vote, was the more Republican of the two New England neighbors. If FDR's sweeping victory surprised any, it surprised those in Maine. "Until 1958, Maine held state elections in September ... [and] the results [there] were taken as a gauge of national partisan movement—hence the saying, 'As Maine goes, so goes the nation.'" Thus, when GOP Governor Lewis Barrows captured 56 percent of the vote to win reelection in September 1936, Republicans held out hope that their presidential candidate might defeat the popular FDR. Two months later, when only Vermont joined Maine in support of Landon, Democratic Party Chairman James Farley updated the old saying by quipping, "As Maine goes, so goes Vermont."[2]

Maine and Vermont's support for Landon highlight a simple fact: for much of its existence, the foundation of the Republican Party has been in the Northeast. Indeed, from the GOP's formation in 1854 until the election of 1936, its presidential candidate won a majority of the Northeast's twelve states every election save one. The exception was the election of 1912, which pitted Democrat Woodrow Wilson against the two candidates of a divided GOP (President Howard Taft and former President Theodore Roosevelt). Four years later, with the Republican Party united behind Charles Evans Hughes, Wilson won only two Northeastern states. In his four races for the White House, FDR did make inroads in the Northeast. But they were not as enduring as he would have hoped. In the ten presidential elections after his death (from 1948 to 1988), the Republican candidate won a majority of the Northeast's states seven times.

All the evidence suggests, however, that Republican control of the Northeast at the presidential level ended in 1992. In that year, Arkansas Governor Bill Clinton won Vermont (easily) and every other state in the region (plus the District of Columbia). In fact, by virtue of both states' substantial support for third-party candidate Ross Perot, Vermont and Maine were two of the least Republican states in the nation that election year (forty-seventh and forty-eighth, respectively). In contrast, South Carolina and Mississippi—the two most Democratic states in 1936 (with FDR winning 98.6 percent and 97.0 percent, respectively)—were the two most Republican states (with George H. W. Bush capturing 48.0 percent and 49.7 percent, respectively). In 1996, Clinton swept the Northeast again. And symbolically he and his wife Hillary moved to New York following their years in the White House, with the president setting up his office in Harlem and the first lady winning one of the Empire State's Senate seats in 2000. In that year's presidential race, Al Gore suffered defeats in only two of the Northeast's twelve states. He lost the traditionally Democratic but culturally conservative West Virginia and the traditionally Republican but socially moderate New Hampshire, the latter by a mere 7,000 votes (with Ralph Nader capturing 22,000 votes). If he had won either state, he would have won the presidency. In 2004, John Kerry lost just West Virginia. Moreover, he piled up his biggest victories in his blue backyard, winning his home state of Massachusetts with 62 percent of the vote, and both Rhode Island and Vermont with 59 percent. In 2008, Barack Obama scored victories in the same places as Kerry, but exceeded his popular vote total by nearly 4 percentage points (59.1 percent compared to Kerry's 55.5 percent). Obama's domination was perhaps best displayed in New England where he won every county in the six states save one, which he lost by a mere 355 votes.[3] As the next sections show, this Democratic supremacy in the Northeast in presidential elections has been both evolutionary and dramatic. And, as noted earlier, it was partially—indeed largely—tied to the electoral strategies and ideological commitments of the Republican Party.

The Importance of Past Elections: The Path to the Present

In one sense, the Republican Party has displayed a remarkable amount of consistency since World War II. With only one exception, in the fifteen presidential elections between 1948 and 2004, four familial names have appeared as either the party's presidential or vice presidential candidate (Dewey, 1944, 1948; Nixon, 1952, 1956, 1960, 1968, 1972; Dole 1976, 1996; and Bush, 1980, 1984, 1988, 1992, 2000, and 2004).[4] On the other hand, in the course of those 60 years, the party's electoral base has undergone a radical restructuring. Two of the most important elections driving that change occurred during the transformative decade of the 1960s; specifically, 1964 and 1968.

In July 1969, with those two elections fresh in his mind, political analyst Kevin Phillips published a book laying out the forthcoming political fortunes of the GOP. It was a book *Newsweek* called "the political bible of the Nixon era." Entitled *The Emerging Republican Majority*, Phillips offered extensive evidence for why the title would tell the tale of the GOP's future. Beyond Phillips' many maps and charts, the story was a simple one. If the GOP could capture the vast majority of those 1968 voters who cast their ballots for Alabama Governor George Wallace, it would emerge as America's majority party. As Phillips understood it, this electoral strategy—commonly known as the "southern strategy"—would require some sacrifice, particularly in the Northeast. But this type of sacrifice was to be expected. As political scientist Robert Speel writes: "[W]hen a party attempts to expand its base with new groups of voters, it inevitably loses voters from its old base. That the North and the South voted along opposite partisan lines in the presidential elections of 1860, 1896, and 1996 is not merely a coincidence."[5]

Writing in the late 1960s, Phillips thought a "successful moderate conservatism" on the part of the Nixon administration "and the lack of a Wallace candidacy would greatly swell the 1972 Republican vote in the South, West, Border and the Catholic North." Thus, "the upcoming cycle of American politics" was destined to pit "a dominant Republican Party based in the Heartland, South and California against a minority Democratic Party based in the Northeast and the Pacific Northwest (and encompassing Southern as well as Northern Negroes)." Under these terms, Phillips thought the GOP could "easily afford to lose the states of Massachusetts, New York, and Michigan," and predicted that the Democratic Party would find the core of its strength in the ten most Democratic states of 1968 (seven of which were in the Northeast).[6] In fact, the 1964 Republican presidential candidate Senator Barry Goldwater even wryly suggested that the "country would be better off if we could just saw off the Eastern Seaboard and let it float out to sea."[7]

The basis of the GOP's geographical shift stemmed largely from its move to the right on social and cultural matters—particularly civil rights—and the Democratic Party's corresponding endorsement of "liberal" positions on these issues. As Phillips explains:

> Back in 1960 Richard Nixon had run for President as the candidate of a Republican Party still at least partly controlled, as Henry Cabot Lodge's vice-presidential nomination bore witness, by its traditional Yankee bastion. By 1968, however, things had changed. Not only had the civil rights revolution cut the South adrift from its Democratic moorings and drawn the Northeast towards the Democrats, but it had increased the Southern and Western bias of the GOP to a point—the 1964 Goldwater nomination—where the party had decided to break with its formative antecedents and make an ideological bid for the anti-civil rights South....By the dint of the 1964 election, the Republican Party shed the dominion of its Yankee and Northeastern Establishment creators, while the Democrats...sank the foundations of their future into the Northeast.[8]

Up until 2008, Phillips's forecast for the Republican alliance stood largely intact. Before that, the Democratic presidential candidates were usually able to secure more states than his analysis suggested—particularly California and heartland Illinois—but the battle lines had not changed much since 1968. For example, in 2004, of the 19 states that John Kerry won, all but 1 (Delaware) was a top 20 Democratic state in 1968.[9] Moreover, the Northeast supplied Kerry with 12 of his 20 victories (the District of Columbia included), nearly half of his electoral vote total.[10] In his much-celebrated effort to expand the field of play for Democrats, however, Barack Obama changed the terms of Phillips's now-dated formula by capturing three states in each of the other three regions that President Bush had won in 2004. Still, the Northeast remained significant for the Democratic nominee. After all, he was only able to pursue this path to the White House because he was able to rely on the region's support from the start.

The bluing of the Northeast at the presidential level has occurred gradually. In the five elections between 1972 and 1988, Republicans won a majority of the twelve states four times. And in 1976, Jimmy Carter only narrowly won the region, capturing seven states to Gerald Ford's five.[11] Nevertheless, the 1980 election was a turning point. Despite Ronald Reagan's Northeast success that year (winning nine of the twelve states), the strength of Republican Representative John Anderson's independent bid for the White House revealed in clear terms the region's direction in future presidential contests. Robert Speel explains the Anderson effect in Vermont:

> In 1980, John Anderson's presidential candidacy fit well with Vermont's moderate-to-liberal Republican tradition…Through his campaign [Anderson] emphasized his conservative positions on fiscal and budgetary matters, his liberal views favoring personal privacy on abortion and religion, and his opposition to hawkish defense and military views of the world. Anderson's call for discipline, responsibility, and avoidance of simple solutions for complex problems, combined with his ideological views, gained him much support among Yankee and well-education voters in Vermont, who for years had been voting for like-minded Republican candidates. As national Republican presidential candidates drifted away from such views, these voters increasingly switched to the Democrats, especially when alternatives like Anderson were not available.[12]

In other words, just as Democrat George Wallace served as a gateway for socially conservative Democrats (mainly from the South) to move into the Republican fold, John Anderson's defection from the GOP convinced many northeastern Republicans to support the Democratic Party.

Why So Blue?

This trend certainly made it difficult for Republicans to win in the Northeast. As Republican Vincent "Buddy" Cianci—the fallen "Prince of Providence," Rhode Island—put it in 1980 after losing his bid to become the Ocean State's governor, "Running in Rhode Island as a Republican is like being the Ayatolah Khomeini at the American Legion Convention."[13] But soon after Cianci made his statement, the fortunes of the GOP candidates seeking the governor's office in Rhode Island and most of the rest of the Northeast actually improved. In fact, for much of the 1980s and 1990s, Republican gubernatorial candidates often won in the Northeast even as it was becoming increasingly blue in presidential elections. As recently as 2004, Republicans held 7 of the Northeast's 12 gubernatorial offices.

Even George W. Bush had some notable experiences in the Northeast. Indeed, it is somewhat ironic that one of the most memorable moments of Bush's presidency took place in the city at the heart of Blue America. Recall, in the immediate wake of the 9/11 attacks on the United States, Bush at first seemed to struggle in his public appearances. By most accounts, however, he rose to the challenge the crisis presented when he visited the scene of the most tragic of those attacks, the remains of the Twin Towers of the World Trade Center (a.k.a., Ground Zero). As he stood atop a charred fire truck, Bush spoke to members of the rescue and recovery team. Someone in the group, straining to hear his words, shouted, "[W]e can't hear you." Through a megaphone, the president boomed: "I can hear you. The rest of the world hears you, and the people who knocked these buildings down will hear all of us soon."[14] While Bush would go on to make many more statements about the events of 9/11, few will be remembered more than this one.

Several weeks later, the president made another appearance in New York City. This time the occasion was a happier one and where he spoke not a word. It took place at Yankee Stadium in the Bronx, where Bush—a well-known fan of the game—had come to throw out the first pitch to open Game Three of the World Series between New York's Yankees and the Arizona Diamondbacks. Warned by the Yankees' star shortstop Derek Jeter that the crowd would boo if he either failed to throw the pitch from the rubber or failed to reach the catcher, the president walked to the top of the mound, reared back, and threw a perfect strike. Although he had not supported Bush in the 2000 election, one Yankee fan in the stadium that night later recalled that at that moment he was "my representative."[15] It was an emotion many Americans felt toward the president following the 9/11 attacks as his public approval rating soared above 90 percent.

Bush's response to those attacks was not surprisingly a centerpiece of his reelection campaign. And in the Northeast, he made inroads with that message. In comparison to his first race for the White House, as Alan Abramowitz writes, "Bush gained an average of 5.4 percentage points in the three states most directly affected by the September 11th terrorist attacks—New York, New Jersey, and Connecticut—compared with 2.5 percentage points in the rest of the country."[16] Indeed, of the 18 states where Bush saw his two-party vote percentage decline from 4 years earlier, 5 were in the Midwest and 8 in the West. In other words, as the president traveled farther away from New York City, he did less well in comparison to his performance in 2000. In the Blue Northeast, Bush improved his two-party vote percentage in nine of its twelve states. Still, he won only one (also losing the District of Columbia).

In 2008, George W. Bush remained an important player in the election, as Barack Obama worked to link John McCain to his policies and McCain sought to distinguish himself from the same. In the process, it became clear that any progress Bush made during his first term apparently vanished into the hustle and bustle of a New York City night as northeasterners' feelings of him as their "representative" faded with the memories of "The Pile" at Ground Zero and the Yankees in the World Series. Put bluntly, northeasterners did not believe Bush had governed as a president for all, least not for them. This fact clearly affected John McCain's chances in the region. While exit poll data is limited for the northeastern states, as table 5.1 shows, on the question of Bush's job performance, northeasterners were far more negative than Americans as a whole (78–71 percent).[17] (It is important to note here that the regional averages used throughout this chapter are not averages with respect to the population of each state but rather are the averages of the independent state figures. Unfortunately, the former figures were not available from the exit polls in 2008.) And those who held negative views toward Bush were more likely to vote for Obama than the national average (70–61 percent). As table 5.1 also displays, on the issue of the economy—which was by far the most important issue in the election[18]— northeasterners were much more likely to be "very worried" about the nation's economic conditions than the nation as a whole (59–50 percent). To them, Bush's stewardship of the economy had not served them well.

Bush's difficulty in the Northeast should not be much of a surprise. Republicans who win statewide office in the Northeast typically do so by holding positions clearly at odds with the national GOP. More specifically, successful Republicans in the Northeast usually prevail in statewide races by promising to keep the lid on spending, taxes, and crime while also proclaiming a liberal

Table 5.1   Attitudes on President Bush and economic conditions in Northeastern states, exit polls 2008

States	Disapprove of Bush (%)	Obama voters (%)	"Very worried" (%)	Obama voters (%)
Connecticut	82	74	64	65
Delaware	75	77	61	66
Maine	76	72	58	64
Maryland	76	70	56	65
Massachusetts	88	60	55	55
New Hampshire	78	68	57	62
New Jersey	74	68	57	61
New York	82	69	56	64
Pennsylvania	74	71	57	63
Rhode Island	82	71	65	66
Vermont	84	79	66	73
West Virginia	63	63	60	49
Northeast average*	**78**	**70**	**59**	**63**
National	**71**	**61**	**50**	**60**

Source: National Election Pool exit poll.

Note: *As noted in the text, the Northeast average is not a true average with regard to population but an average of the percentages from the individual states.

attitude on issues such as abortion and gay rights. One former northeastern governor summed up his successful philosophy in a single sentence: "I believe the government should stay out of your wallet, and out of your bedroom."[19] But in recent years, these views have been at odds with the core of conservative thought in the GOP. In her book, *It's My Party, Too: Taking Back the Republican Party and Bringing the Country Together Again*, another former northeastern governor, Christine Todd Whitman of New Jersey, sought to alter the terms of that arrangement. As she put it, she hoped her book would help in the effort to take back the GOP from "a group of ideological zealots whose rigid views on a variety of socials issues were driving the party farther away from its traditional roots." To Whitman, "Republican conservatism" had historically been tied to "restricting the size and scope of government, which traditionally meant keeping taxes down, balancing budgets, and controlling the growth of government." It has also been defined by respect for "the individual," which to her "meant limiting government's intrusion into people's everyday lives. Those beliefs, coupled with commitment to an engaged foreign policy, strong national defense, and security at home" were the reasons she considered herself "a traditional conservative Republican." But to her critics in the party, she was nothing but a RINO (Republican in Name Only).[20]

To Whitman, who served as Bush's EPA (Environmental Protection Agency) head during his first term, things only got worse after the president's reelection in 2004. As she writes in the 2006 preface to the paperback edition of her book, "[F]ar too many of those who are labeled conservatives in the Republican Party" are not practicing her style of Republican conservatism. Instead,

> federal spending is skyrocketing out of control, even when taking into account necessary increases for defense and homeland security. President Bush hasn't vetoed a single spending bill that the Republican-controlled Congress has been sending to his desk for five years.... At the same time, so-called conservative Republicans in Congress have been putting government's nose deeper and deeper into the private lives of individual Americans...making the Democrats' social engineering efforts of the sixties and seventies look like timid tinkering.[21]

Whitman's criticism of the GOP helps explain both why national Republicans struggle in the Northeast and why northeastern Republicans struggle when they attempt to move to the national stage, especially if they have their sights set on the presidency. So, for example, when former Massachusetts Governor Mitt Romney sought the Republican nomination in 2008, it was only after he transformed his views on the most important social issues so that they would be more in line with those of the core constituents of the Republican Party. The shift provoked strong criticism from his fellow contenders for the nomination, particularly when the former governor sought to sell himself as the most likely candidate to bring about change to Washington. In response, McCain spokeswoman Jill Hazelbacker told the Associated Press, "[I]t is laughable that Mitt Romney would think anyone buys his latest act as an agent of change. The only thing he's ever changed are his positions on nearly every important issue."[22] And after Romney told former Arkansas

Governor Mike Huckabee not to "try and characterize my position," during one of the debates, Huckabee asked sarcastically, "Which one?"[23] To some, the lack of authenticity in Romney's transformation doomed his campaign. Former New York City Mayor Rudy Giuliani tried a different approach, continuing, for example, to support abortion rights while also pledging to appoint judges who would likely decimate those rights.[24] That—somewhat inconsistent—strategy did not work either as Giuliani spent 57 million dollars to win just one delegate. As journalist Dan Morain explained (before the final dollar figure was tallied), "At that rate, it would have taken close to $60 billion in spending to capture the 1,191 delegates needed to win the nomination."[25]

Another former Massachusetts governor who had national aspirations, William F. Weld, is one more example of a Northeast Republican who did not travel well. Largely credited with reviving the Bay State's economy and amending its spendthrift ways Weld was a popular governor in the nation's most Democratic state during most of the 1990s, winning reelection by a record margin in 1994. After nearly two terms in the Massachusetts state house, however, Weld left office in April 1997 to accept President Bill Clinton's offer to become U.S. ambassador to Mexico. Weld reportedly agreed to this new challenge with a higher office in mind.[26] But in the end, Weld never made it to Mexico. He fell victim to an effort to block his Senate confirmation. Significantly, Weld's fiercest critics were not Democrats, but members of his own Republican Party. In short, his liberal views on social matters—which had been a basis for his popularity in Massachusetts— were his downfall in a Republican-controlled Congress. While Weld was pro-choice on abortion, supportive of gay rights, and an advocate of medicinal use of marijuana, conservative members of the GOP were not. Most importantly, North Carolina Senator Jesse Helms, chairman of the Senate Foreign Relations Committee, was not. And using his authority as chair Helms refused to convene a committee hearing on Weld's nomination, citing the governor's position on drugs as one of the chief reasons why he was not of "Ambassador quality."[27] After Weld withdrew from his battle with Senator Helms—which the governor once called a battle for "the future of the Republican Party"—he pledged to remain a strong voice in the GOP, defending the tradition of Abraham Lincoln and Theodore Roosevelt and reclaiming the party's commitment to "defending individual rights."[28] In 2006, he brought his message to the Republican voters of New York—where he was born and currently resides—in an effort to keep the governor's office in Republican hands. However, after difficulties on the campaign trial and rumors of scandal he gave up that fight, allowing the more conservative John Faso to take the nomination without serious challenge. It is unclear where Weld stands now. After backing Romney for the Republican nomination, he crossed party lines to support Barack Obama in the general election.[29]

In doing so Weld was part of a general trend in recent years, as more and more northeasterners moved toward supporting the Democratic Party. In turn, since 2004, Republican representation at the state level has diminished significantly. For example, in New York, the Republicans' 12-year hold over the governor's office ended in 2007 after Elliott Spitzer's landslide election victory the previous November. Before he was exposed as "Client #9" in a prostitution scandal that forced him from the governor's mansion, Spitzer swept nearly every county in the state en route to winning 69.6 percent of the vote. It was an unprecedented victory for a gubernatorial candidate who was not the incumbent. Despite Spitzer's downfall, Democrats continued to make gains in 2008 as Republicans lost control of the State Senate for the first time since the mid-1960s. And with just 41 out of 150 seats, Republican representation in the Assembly fell to an all-time low. Republicans had tried their mightiest to hold onto the Senate, which was "the party's last redoubt of power after Governor George Pataki left office." In recent years, they had succeeded in doing so in part by convincing aging lawmakers to run again and again. Indeed, by 2008, nearly half of the Republican senators "were at least 65." Significantly on election night 2008, two of those hoping to serve yet another term suffered sound defeats. One was 82 and another 75.[30] As Nelson Warfield, a Republican strategist, put it two years earlier, "It's like Dutch elm disease. The great Republican trees are dying."[31]

New York is not alone. As noted earlier, in 2004, Republicans held 7 of the region's 12 governor's offices. Today, they hold just three. (And conservatives in the party would most assuredly describe all three as RINOs.) In 2006, Republicans lost control of both houses of the New Hampshire legislature for the first time since 1911.[32] And currently, of the 24 state legislative houses in the Northeast, Republicans hold a majority in just one, the Pennsylvania Senate.

Ripe for the Picking: Why Barack Obama Won the Northeast

With the decline of Republican fortunes, most expected Barack Obama to do quite well in the Northeast. But to understand his success in the region, it is important to look beyond the geographical and ideological focus of the Republican Party for an explanation. It is also essential to understand the reasons why northeasterners were so receptive to Obama's message. To a large extent, the answer is simple. In the ideological terms, as table 5.2 displays, there are more liberals and moderates and fewer conservatives in the Northeast than in other parts of the country. Notably, the region's liberals were not more likely to vote for Obama than the national average. There were simply more of them. Added to this fact, northeastern moderates and conservatives were slightly more likely to vote for Obama than the national average. Not surprisingly, given the ideological nature of the two parties, the region's liberal bent has produced more voters defining themselves as Democrats and Independents compared to the national average. Similar to the region's liberals, they were no more likely to vote for Obama than the national average. There were just more of them.

In contrast there were far fewer white evangelical born-again Christians, a group historically attracted to the GOP's social conservative message, in the Northeast. As Mark Silk and Andrew Walsh write in their regional-based book on religion and politics in America, "only about 27 percent of [New England's] Protestants and 37 percent of its Protestant congregations are evangelical; in terms of people, that's 381,000 evangelical Protestants and 165,000 Pentecostal and Holiness adherents in the region's six states." In Silk and Walsh's other

Table 5.2 Ideology and party identification in Northeastern states

States	% Liberals	% Moderates	% Conservatives	% Democrats	% Republicans	% Independents
Connecticut	29	44	27	43	27	31
Delaware	23	50	27	48	31	21
Maine	27	44	29	35	26	39
Maryland	26	52	23	51	28	21
Massachusetts	32	46	21	43	17	40
New Hampshire	26	46	28	29	27	45
New Jersey	25	50	25	44	28	28
New York	29	44	27	50	26	25
Pennsylvania	23	50	27	44	37	18
Rhode Island	28	47	25	42	16	42
Vermont	32	44	24	37	23	39
West Virginia	18	48	34	48	34	19
Northeast average*	**27**	**47**	**26**	**43**	**27**	**31**
National	**22**	**44**	**34**	**39**	**32**	**29**

Source: National Election Pool exit poll.

Note: *As noted in the text, the Northeast average is not a true average with regard to population but an average of the percentages from the individual states.

Northeast region, the Middle Atlantic (which does not include West Virginia), evangelical Protestantism is somewhat more prevalent. But again, "mainliners, members of the denominations that first established themselves in the colonial era, outnumber evangelicals by better than two to one," a figure second only to New England where they "outnumber evangelicals by nearly three to one."[33]

The evidence suggests that the small number of white evangelicals in the Northeast was significant on Election Day. While full exit poll data on the percentage and voting patterns of white evangelical born-again Christians only exists for New York and West Virginia, the results confirm the expected. In the Empire State, only 9 percent of voters defined themselves as white evangelical born-again Christians (compared to 26 percent nationwide). And while New York's white evangelical born-again Christians were actually more likely to support John McCain than the national average of voters in their group (78 percent compared to 74 percent), their low numbers meant they were unable to make much of a difference on Election Day. In West Virginia, the story is a different one. With white evangelical born-again Christians making up 52 percent of the voters (66 percent of whom supported McCain), the Mountain State handed Barack Obama his only defeat in the Northeast (56–43 percent).

Another factor contributing to the Northeast's voting pattern in 2008 centers on its metropolitan nature, dominated by the cities—from Boston to New York to Washington, DC—and the suburbs making up the region's megalopolis. In 2004, according to exit polls, 21 percent of the region's voters lived in urban areas and a whopping 66 percent in the suburbs that surround cities. On the other hand, only 12 percent lived in rural communities. While these regional figures are not available from the 2008 exit poll, it is unlikely that these percentages changed dramatically in a four-year period. (Indeed, the national figures changed hardly at all.) Contrast these figures to national ones for 2008: urban, 30 percent; suburban, 49 percent; rural, 21 percent. In many ways, these figures define the divide between the Democrats and the Republicans nationally. In urban areas, Obama's support reached 63 percent. And significantly, he won the suburban vote by 2 percent. In rural areas, he lost by 7 percent. Given the urban/suburban nature of the Northeast, there was good reason to expect him to do well.

The size of his victory, however, was at least partially connected to the way northeastern voters viewed the status quo. As noted earlier, the region's voters were highly critical of President Bush's job performance generally and the economic conditions of the nation (see table 5.1). And while only voters in a few northeastern states were asked specific questions about specific issues, the results are quite telling with regard to their opposition to the war in Iraq, the position that most distinguished Barack Obama from Hillary Clinton in the Democratic primary season. While nationally, 63 percent of voters "disapproved" of the war and 41 percent "strongly disapproved," in those northeastern states where the exit poll included a question about the war, disapproval was typically higher; sometimes much higher. Specifically, in Delaware, 70 percent of respondents disapproved of the war, with 46 percent strongly disapproving; in Maryland, 75 percent disapproved, with 54 percent strongly disapproving; in Massachusetts, 79 percent disapproved, with 53 strongly disapproving; in New Hampshire,

66 percent disapproved, with 44 strongly disapproving; and in New York, 75 percent disapproved, with 51 strongly disapproving. Of the states where the question was asked, only Pennsylvania did not record a more negative assessment than the national figure. It actually matched that figure exactly.

The Hillary Factor

To be sure, during the battle over the nomination, there was some concern among Democrats about Barack Obama's ability to perform so well in the Northeast in the general election. After all, during the primary season, Hillary Clinton won 7 of the Northeast's 13 election contests (12 primaries and 1 caucus) in the region. And most importantly, as displayed in table 5.3, she won the region's four largest states, including New York and Pennsylvania. Put differently, Clinton won states that were set to award 92 electoral votes in November while Obama won states that would award just 30. In turn, many, including the New York senator herself, cautioned Democratic voters and super delegates that "Hillary voters" just might not return to the Democratic Party fold in November if Obama won the nomination. As Senator Clinton put it, "I have a much broader base to build a winning coalition on." To support the claim, she cited an Associated Press article "that found how Senator Obama's support among working, hard-working Americans, white Americans, is weakening again, and how whites in [Indiana and North Carolina] who had not completed college were supporting me." Adding to the analysis, Democratic strategist Paul Begala, a Clinton supporter, suggested, "[W]e cannot win with eggheads and African Americans, that's the

Table 5.3 Democratic primary results in the Northeast and the voting behavior of the region's white voters in the general election

States	Clinton primary vote (%)	Obama primary vote (%)	% White Obama voters	Change from 2004	% White Democrats for Obama	Overall change from 2004
Connecticut	47	51	51	0	86	+7
Delaware	42	53	53	+8	86	+9
DC	24	75	86	+6	97	+4
Maine Caucus	40	59	58	+5	89	+4
Maryland	36	61	47	+3	83	+6
Massachusetts	56	41	59	0	86	0
New Hampshire	39	37	54	+4	92	+4
New Jersey	54	44	49	+3	85	+4
New York	57	40	52	+3	85	+5
Pennsylvania	54	45	48	+3	85	+4
Rhode Island	58	40	58	+1	89	+4
Vermont	39	59	68	+10	96	+9
West Virginia	67	26	41	−1	69	0
National	**NA**	**NA**	**43**	**+2**	**85**	**+5**

Source: Based on the final primary and general election figures from the individual states and the National Election Pool exit poll.

Dukakis coalition which carried ten states and gave us four years of the first George Bush."[34] (To be sure, Barack Obama did not help things. In one of his rare—but widely reported—slipups during the campaign, Obama seemingly disparaged white working-class voters at a private fund-raiser in San Francisco. In answering a question about why he had difficultly attracting some of those struggling economically, he suggested that such voters were at times "bitter," and "they cling to guns or religion or antipathy to people who aren't like them, or anti-immigrant sentiment or anti-trade sentiment as a way to explain their frustrations."[35])

While Clinton's and Begala's comments came late in a campaign in which she was running out of options, some Democratic leaders continued to express concern about Senator Obama's ability to carry the white working-class vote. Most notably, in speaking about Barack Obama's chances to win his home state of Pennsylvania, Representative John Murtha told the *Pittsburgh Post Gazette*, "There is no question that western Pennsylvania is a racist area." He clarified these words by explaining that the area was no longer as "redneck" as it used to be. But he still felt there were "folks that have a problem voting for someone because they are black."[36] Of course, Murtha was not alone in thinking that Obama's race might make it more difficult for him to perform well in some areas of the Northeast than if Hillary Clinton had been the nominee. He was just more willing to say it publically.

In fact, political commentators speculated that the choice of Sarah Palin as John McCain's running mate might convince "Hillary voters" to abandon the Democratic ticket.[37] Obama's perceived weakness among "Joe Six-pack types,"

Table 5.4   The white "working-class" vote in Northeastern states (by education and income in percentages)

States	Whites—no college degree	Whites—college graduates	Whites— incomes < 50K	Whites— incomes > 50K
Connecticut	51	52	59	51
Delaware	52	55	56	51
Maine Caucus	56	61	62	55
Maryland	42	52	52	47
Massachusetts	57	62	68	57
New Hampshire	50	58	58	54
New Jersey	47	51	53	48
New York	44	58	60	50
Pennsylvania	42	52	49	48
Rhode Island	57	59	61	57
Vermont	61	73	70	66
West Virginia	41	42	51	35
Northeast average*	**50**	**56**	**58**	**52**
National	**40**	**47**	**47**	**43**

Source: National Election Pool exit poll.

Note: *As noted in the text, the Northeast average is not a true average with regard to population but an average of the percentages from the individual states.

also explains McCain's heavy emphasis on "Joe the Plumber" late in the campaign. But while Samuel Joseph Wurzelbacher (a.k.a. "Joe the Plumber") supported McCain, white working-class Democrats did not abandon their party's nominee in large numbers. As table 5.3 displays, white support in the region was consistent with the figures from 2004. So, for example, in Pennsylvania Obama garnered 4 more percentage points than John Kerry (55–51 percent) and he won the white vote by 3 percentage points more than Kerry (48–45 percent).[38] In addition, the regional average for white Democrats supporting Obama was 87 percent (two points above the national average). On the question of how Obama performed with white working-class voters, the answer depends largely on whether the emphasis is placed on the income or education of white voters.[39] As table 5.4 shows, Obama performed better in every state in the region among whites making less than $50,000 than he did with those making more than $50,000. At the same time, he did less well in every state in the region with voters who did not graduate from college as opposed to those who did. Both results were consistent with the national figures.

The Keystone State: Pennsylvania

In truth, there were no battleground states in the Northeast in 2008. But apparently no one told the McCain campaign, which pushed hard to win Pennsylvania. To some extent, the McCain campaign was simply working off the logic of the previous election. Then, in computing their Electoral College math, most political commentators set their sights on the three big battleground state prizes: Florida with 27 electoral votes, Pennsylvania with 21, and Ohio with 20. With that math in mind, it was common to hear commentators tell their audience members that whichever candidate won two of these three states would win the White House. And in the end, this prediction proved true as President Bush scored victories in Florida and Ohio. In 2008, the McCain campaign pursued Pennsylvania based in part on that same logic and with the hopes of picking up electoral votes in a previously blue state in order to offset expected losses of previously red states in other parts of the nation. In fact, in the last two weeks of the race, McCain visited the state 12 times and over the course of the campaign spent millions to get his message across the airwaves.[40] To say the least, it was destined to be an uphill battle. By Election Day, Pennsylvania state officials had processed more than 700,000 new voter applications in 2008 and the tide heavily favored the Democrats. Indeed, when the voters went to the polls, there were 1.2 million more registered Democrats than Republicans. And 54.5 percent of those voters supported Obama.

In winning Pennsylvania, Obama was able to improve significantly on John Kerry's performance four years earlier (winning by 10.3 percentage points as opposed to Kerry's 2.5 percentage point victory). In doing so, he pursued a somewhat different route. In 2004, Kerry narrowly won the Keystone State by performing well in its two largest metropolitan areas, Pittsburgh and Philadelphia, and by holding off Bush's dominance in the mainly rural counties in the middle of the state. To be sure, this red-blue division of the state was expected. As Democratic consultant James Carville once explained, Pennsylvania is divided into three sections: "Philadelphia in the east, Pittsburgh in the west, and 'Alabama in the middle.'"[41]

In 2008, Obama's path to a double-digit percentage victory was largely the result of his superb performance in the eastern part of the state. Not only did he win the City of Philadelphia by nearly a half a million votes, he captured all four of the surrounding suburban counties (Bucks, Chester, Delaware, and Montgomery) by margins that easily surpassed Kerry's figures four years earlier. In addition, he captured two more counties in the eastern part of the state that Bush had won four years earlier. At the same time, he did not perform as well as Kerry in western Pennsylvania. While he did win the Pittsburgh-dominated Allegheny County (by more than 100,000 votes), he lost all five of the surrounding suburban counties (Beaver, Butler, Fayette, Washington, and Westmoreland). Finally, he won four counties in the middle of the state that were red in 2004.

The Philadelphia region's support for Obama is actually a microcosm of the Northeast's political direction in recent years. In the early part of the twentieth century, Philadelphia was well known as one of the nation's most Republican big cities. The four counties surrounding Philadelphia, moreover, remained a bastion of northeastern Republicanism well into the 1980s. For example, while Democratic presidential candidate Michael Dukakis won 48.4 percent of the Pennsylvania vote in 1988, he won only 38.2 percent in the four suburban counties of Philadelphia (10.2 percent *less* than his statewide total). Although these counties were trending Democratic at the end of the last century, Bill Clinton did not win a majority of the vote in them in either of his three-man presidential races. In the strong Democratic year of 1996, he earned 47.7 percent in these four counties (1.5 percent *less* than his statewide percentage of 49.2 percent). In 2000, Al Gore did capture a majority of the vote in these four counties, winning 51.2 percent (0.6 *more* than his statewide total). In 2004, Kerry won 53.2 percent of the vote here (2.2 percent *more* than his statewide total).[42] And in 2008, Barack Obama continued this trend, capturing 57.3 percent of the vote in these four counties (2.7 percent *more* than his statewide total). Combining these counties together with the city of Philadelphia—which Obama won with 83.0 percent of the vote—the Democratic nominee won 66.4 percent of the vote in this section of the state, providing him with 41.1 percent of all his votes in Pennsylvania.

On the other hand, Obama did not do as well as his partisan predecessors in the Pittsburgh area.[43] In the six counties making up this section of the state—including Allegheny County—Obama barely won a majority of the vote (with 50.1 percent), which also reflects a trend for recent Democratic presidential candidates. In 1988, Dukakis won 59.1 percent of the vote in this part of the state. But by 2000, Gore was only able to win 52.9 percent. In 2004, the figure fell again as Kerry captured 52.2 percent. In fact, excluding the five Philadelphia counties, Kerry's percentage declined statewide in comparison to Dukakis in 1988, Clinton in 1996, and Gore in 2000. While Dukakis, Clinton, and Gore won 47.8, 45.5, and 45.4 percent (respectively) outside of the Philadelphia region, Kerry won

45.1 percent.[44] Significantly, Barack Obama was able to reverse that trend by winning 48.4 percent of the vote outside the five Philadelphia counties. His success overall in the state was no doubt aided by his running mate Joe Biden, who was born and partially raised in the Scranton area and represented neighboring Delaware in the U.S. Senate for 36 years.

Congressional Elections

It has never happened before. Since candidates started running under the party label, Republicans had always represented some part of the territory in the six New England states in the House of Representatives. Even in the midst of the dominance of Franklin Roosevelt's Democratic Party after the 1936 election—when the GOP held a scant 88 seats—New England Republicans could voice their concern on the floor of the House. They cannot anymore. With the defeat of Republican Christopher Shays in a district in the southwestern corner of Connecticut, there are no more Republicans representing the six New England states. Journalist Pam Belluck summed up what the House would be missing when it convened in 2009.

> It was a species as endemic to New England as craggy seascapes and creamy clam chowder: the moderate Yankee Republican. Dignified in demeanor, independent in ideology and frequently blue in blood, they were politicians in the mold of Roosevelt and Rockefeller: socially tolerant, environmentally enthusiastic, people who liked government to keep its wallet close to its vest and its hands out of social issues like abortion and, in recent years, same-sex marriage.[45]

Belluck actually wrote these words after the 2006 midterm elections, an election that was actually worse for moderate Republicans in New England than the 2008 election. Then, four New England Republicans lost their House seats, including New Hampshire's two congressmen, Charles Bass and Jeb Bradley. Bradley's defeat was especially surprising as he lost to "a virtual unknown with a virtually empty bank account."[46] The other two losses occurred in Connecticut as Nancy Johnson lost in devastating fashion and Rob Simmons lost by a whisker, a mere 91 votes. In the rest of the Northeast, the news was just as bad for the GOP as it lost a total of 11 House seats to Democrats. And in 2008, this trend continued as Democrats picked up a total of seven more seats in the House races. In doing so, Democrats not only collected all the House seats in New England but 26 of the 29 in neighboring New York. In total, as displayed in table 5.5, Democrats now hold 77 of the Northeast's 95 House seats (81 percent).

In the Senate, Republicans did not fare much better in the last two elections. In 2006, two northeastern senators lost their bids for reelection, conservative Rick Santorum of Pennsylvania and moderate Lincoln Chafee of Rhode Island. In Pennsylvania, the race was not even close as Santorum's brand of conservatism proved too unpopular for the voters in one of the Northeast's most conservative states (see table 5.2). He lost his race by nearly 20 percentage points to Democrat Bob Casey. Also, in 2006, Vermont's Democratic Socialist Congressman Bernie

Table 5.5 Partisan breakdown of House and Senate representation in Northeastern states

States	2005 Senate	2009 Senate	2005 House		2007 House		2009 House	
			D	R	D	R	D	R
Connecticut	2 D	2 D	2	3	4	1	5	
Delaware	2 D	2 D		1		1		1
Maine	2 R	2 R	2		2		2	
Maryland	2 D	2 D	6	2	6	2	7	1
Massachusetts	2 D	2 D	10		10		10	
New Hampshire	2 R	1 D 1R		2	2		2	
New Jersey	2 D	2 D	7	6	7	6	8	5
New York	2 D	2 D	20	9	23	6	26	3
Pennsylvania	2 R	1 D 1 R	7	12	11	8	12	7
Rhode Island	1 D 1 R	2 D	2		2		2	
Vermont	2 D	2 D	1		1		1	
West Virginia	2 D	2 D	2	1	2	1	2	1
Totals	**17 D**	**20 D**	**59**	**36**	**70**	**25**	**77**	**18**
	7 R	**4 R**						

Source: Based on the final election figures from the individual states.

Sanders moved over to the Senate to replace the Republican-turned Independent Jim Jeffords. In 2008, Republicans lost yet another Senate seat as John Sununu of New Hampshire lost by seven points in a rematch race against former Democratic Governor Jeanne Shaheen. With these victories, Democrats now hold 20 of the Northeast's 24 Senate seats (83 percent).

How did northeastern Republicans become such an endangered species in the U.S. Congress? Recall, when George W. Bush took the oath of office on January 20, 2001, Republicans held 40 of the Northeast's 100 House seats and 8 of its 24 Senate seats (40 and 33 percent, respectively). Five of those eight senators considered themselves moderates and some of those five have placed the blame squarely on the Bush administration for the sad state of the GOP in the Northeast. After all, six months into the president's first term, one of the five Senate moderates—Jim Jeffords of Vermont—declared his independence from the GOP.[47] His decision to caucus with the Democrats toppled the Republican majority in the Senate without an intervening election; an event unprecedented in American history. Another moderate Republican senator—Arlen Specter of Pennsylvania—made his way back to Washington in 2005 only after barely surviving a vigorous challenge from a member of his own party, who charged in a bitter primary fight that the incumbent was not conservative enough to represent either the state or the GOP in the Senate. A third, Lincoln Chafee, could not bring himself to cast his ballot for the incumbent when he voted for president in 2004. Instead, he symbolically wrote in the name of the president's father, George H. W. Bush. In 2006, after being bloodied and batted by a primary challenger from the right who was sponsored by the conservative Club for Growth, Chafee lost his bid for another term in the U.S. Senate. A year later, he announced that he was parting ways with the Republican Party by changing his registration to unaffiliated. According to Chafee, his path out of the Republican Party was driven by an administration bent on enacting a "radical agenda."[48] In 2008, Chafee chose not to support John McCain, who had campaigned for him in 2006, deciding instead to back Barack Obama, who had campaigned for his Democratic opponent. During the campaign, Chafee also made news when he described GOP vice presidential candidate Sarah Palin as a "cocky wacko." Defending his choice of words, Chafee said he objected to much of what she said during her speech at the Republican Convention, particularly her claim that while "Al-Qaida terrorists still plot to inflict catastrophic harm on America," Barack Obama is "worried that someone won't read them their rights." To Chafee, this single comment "got to the core of everything wrong with the last eight years." He added, "I consider that wacky, and certainly her tone was very, very cocky. So I thought they were appropriate words."[49]

All was not lost for the Northeast's Republican Senate moderates in 2008. Susan Collins of Maine easily beat back a challenge from a strong candidate, Representative Tom Allen. She explained her record of bipartisanship as a key reason to her victory. "The people in my state are sick and tired of the hyper-partisanship and the gridlock that has blocked action on so many important issues that affect their lives directly. The message from this campaign is a rebellion against excessive partisanship and a call for people to work together." She added, "What doesn't work is drawing a harsh ideological line in the sand."[50] It was a message that echoed the thoughts of other moderates such as Jeffords and Chafee.

Republicans also received somewhat of a boost from a surprising source. After losing the Democratic primary in 2006 to a more liberal candidate, Senator Joe Lieberman of Connecticut bolted from his party and declared himself an "Independent Democrat." In the general election, he won reelection for another six-year term. In 2008, driven largely by his steadfast support for the war in Iraq and his general hawkish foreign policy views, he decided that he was unable to support Barak Obama for presidency and instead backed Republican John McCain. While this decision was not all that surprising, especially given the close relationship of the two longtime senators, Lieberman's role in the campaign was. During the course of the race, Lieberman, who had been the Democratic Party's vice presidential nominee in 2000, became a constant presence on the campaign trial. And according to press accounts, he was even McCain's first choice to be his running mate.[51] In many ways, Lieberman's path out of the Democratic Party says much about the political trends of the Northeast. Motivated more by ideology than party, the voters in this region are willing to support candidates who offer visions consistent with their own. For those who do not, they have found little reason to stick with the partisan choices of their ancestors.

Notes

1. On the politics of Northeastern states, see generally: Duane Lockard, *New England State Politics* (Princeton, NJ: Princeton University Press, 1959); Josephine F. Milburn and William Doyle, *New England Political Parties* (Cambridge, MA: Schenkman,

1983); Robert W. Speel, *Changing Patterns of Voting in the Northern United States: Electoral Realignment, 1952–1996* (University Park, PA: The Pennsylvania State University Press, 1998); Jeffrey M. Stonecash, ed., *Governing New York State* (Albany, NY: State University of New York Press, 2001); John Kenneth White, *The Fractured Electorate: Political Parties and Social Change in Southern New England* (Hanover, NH: University Press of New England, 1983). See also, John Leonard, ed., *These United States* (New York: Thunder's Mouth Press/Nation Books, 2003); Alan Rosenthal and Maureen Moakley, eds., *The Political Life of the American States* (New York: Praeger, 1984).

2. Michael Barone and Richard E. Cohen, *The Almanac of American Politics* (Washington, DC: National Journal, 2004), p. 723.

3. Maine's Piscataquis County.

4. The lone exception is 1964 when Barry Goldwater and William E. Miller made up the GOP presidential ticket.

5. Kevin Phillips, *The Emerging Republican Majority* (Garden City, NY: Anchor Books, 1970; originally published by Arlington House in 1969); Speel, *Changing Patterns of Voting in the Northern United States*, p. 18.

6. Phillips, *The Emerging Republican Majority*, pp. 464–466, 29.

7. Goldwater quoted in Kathleen Hall Jamieson, *Packaging the Presidency: A History and Criticism of Presidential Campaign Advertising*, Third Edition (New York: Oxford University Press, 1996), p. 179.

8. Phillips, *The Emerging Republican Majority*, pp. 32–33.

9. Delaware was the twenty-fourth most Democratic state.

10. This figure also emphasizes the importance of California in the Democratic Party's election strategy. With 55 electoral votes, the Golden State supplied Kerry with nearly a quarter of his 252 total.

11. Carter also won Washington DC and, more importantly, took 108 of the region's 144 electoral votes.

12. Speel, *Changing Patterns of Voting in the Northern United States*, pp. 58–59.

13. Quoted in White, *The Fractured Electorate*, p. 72. For more on Cianci, see Mike Stanton, *The Prince of Providence: The Rise and Fall of Buddy Cianci, America's Most Notorious Mayor* (New York: Random House, 2003, 2004).

14. Bush quoted in Robert D. McFadden, "After the Attacks: The President," *New York Times*, September 15, 2001.

15. David Fisher quoted in HBO Films, *Nine Innings from Ground Zero*, 2004.

16. Alan Abramowitz, "Terrorism, Gay Marriage, and Incumbency: Explaining the Republican Victory in the 2004 Presidential Election," *The Forum* 2:4 (2004), article 3: 6.

17. The National Election Pool exit poll results are available at cnn.com.

18. According to exit polls, 63% of voters thought the economy was the most important issue from a list of five. The other issues (with percentages) were as follows: Energy Policy (7%); Iraq (10%); Terrorism (9%); and Health Care (9%).

19. Quote from then Massachusetts Governor William Weld at the 1992 Republican Convention.

20. Christie Todd Whitman, *It's My Party, Too: Taking Back the Republican Party and Bringing the Country Together Again* (New York: Penguin, 2005, 2006), pp. xi, xviii, and xvii. For more on the Republican Party, see Lewis L. Gould, *Grand Old Party: A History of the Republicans* (New York: Random House, 2003). See also, Nicol C. Rae, *The Decline and Fall of Liberal Republicans: From 1952 to the Present* (New York: Oxford University Press, 1989).

21. Whitman, *It's My Party, Too*, pp. xviii–xix.

22. Michael D. Shear, "Romney's New Role: Agent of Change," *Washington Post* (website), January 5, 2008.

23. Jill Zuckman and Rick Pearson, "McCain, Romney Clash at Republican Debate," *Chicago Tribune*, January 6, 2008.

24. See Thomas M. Keck and Kevin J. McMahon, "Rudy of Two Minds on Abortion," *The Hartford Courant*, October 11, 2007.

25. Dan Morain, "Guilani's 50-Million Dollar Delegate," *Los Angeles Times*, February 1, 2008. At the time of his writing, Morain thought the amount spent was $48.8 million (not the final total of 57 million).

26. According to a close Weld advisor, "By stepping out of elective politics and becoming a strong voice on Latin American drug trafficking and international trade, Weld could position himself as a national candidate after the year 2000 if a strong, independent movement emerges or if the GOP by then accepts a moderate on the ticket," Dale Russakoff, "From Its Apex, a Political Career Goes South," *Washington Post*, May 3, 1997.

27. Steven Lee Myers, "Helms to Oppose Weld as Nominee for Ambassador," *New York Times*, June 4, 1997; see also, Andrew Miga, "Rocky Road; GOP Reps Fighting to Derail Weld Post; Gov. Weld's Support of Medicinal Marijuana Use Has Some Conservative House Members Smoking Mad, Ready to Fight," *Boston Herald*, May 2, 1997.

28. Brian McGrory and Chris Black, "A Stymied Weld Gives Up Fight," *Boston Globe*, September 16, 1997.

29. Endorsement video available at http://www.boston.com/news/politics/politicalintelligence/2008/10/weld_backs_obam.html.

30. Danny Hakim, "Republicans Aim to Rebuild after a Bruising Election," *New York Times*, November 9, 2008.

31. Michael Cooper, "N.Y. Republicans Fear Waning Political Fortunes," *New York Times*, June 2, 2006.

32. Rinker Buck, "Senior Tsunami," *Hartford Courant*, November 9, 2007. See James M. Jeffords, *My Declaration of Independence* (New York: Simon & Schuster, 2001).

33. Mark Silk and Andrew Walsh, *One Nation, Divisible: How Regional Religious Differences Shape American Politics* (New York: Rowman & Littlefield, 2008), pp. 52, 3.

34. Kathy Kiely and Jill Lawrence, "Clinton Makes Case for Wide Appeal," *USA Today*, May 8, 2008; Kate Phillips, "Clinton Touts White Support," *New York Times* website, May 8, 2008. Article with Begala video available at http://thecaucus.blogs.nytimes.com/2008/05/08/clinton-touts-white-support/.

35. Audio available at http://www.huffingtonpost.com/mayhill-fowler/obama-no-surprise-that-ha_b_96188.html.

36. Ed Blazina, "Murtha Says Obama Will Win Pennsylvania Despite Racism," *Pittsburgh Post-Gazette*, October 16, 2008; additional "redneck" comments available on video at http://www.youtube.com/watch?v=DoPabBvVRpg.

37. See, e.g., Michael Duffy, "Will Women Vote for Palin?" *Time*, August 29, 2008.

38. The clear exception here is Connecticut. Obama won the state by 7 percentage points more than Kerry but did not improve among white voters.

39. For a discussion on defining white working-class voters, see Michael Tomasky, "How Historic a Victory?" *New York Review of Books*, December 18, 2008, pp. 44–47.

40. "Pennsylvania Deals Blow to McCain," November 5, 2008, BBC News. Available at http://news.bbc.co.uk/2/hi/americas/us_elections_2008/7709875.stm?ref=pickatrail.com. See also, Elisabeth Bumiller and Jeff Zeleny, "McCain Fights to Keep Crucial Blue State in Play," *New York Times*, October 22, 2008.

41. Quoted in Robert David Sullivan, "Beyond Red and Blue: The New Map of American Politics," *Commonwealth*, online only, 2003. Available at massinc.org/index.php?id=110&pub_id=1616.

42. Donald W. Beachler, "A New Democratic Era? Presidential Political in Pennsylvania, 1984–1996," *Commonwealth* 9 (1997–1998): 57–71, 60.

43. For possible reasons for this Democratic decline, see John B. Judis and Ruy Teixeira, *The Emerging Democratic Majority* (New York: Scribner, 2002), pp. 94–95.

44. Beachler, "A New Democratic Era?" pp. 60–61.

45. Pam Belluck, "A Republican Breed Loses Its Place in New England as Voters Seek Change," *New York Times*, November 26, 2006.

46. Ibid.

47. See James M. Jeffords, *My Declaration of Independence* (New York: Simon & Schuster, 2001).

48. Lincoln Chafee, *Against the Tide: How a Compliant Congress Empowered a Reckless President* (New York: Thomas Dunne Books, 2008), p. 54.

49. Transcript of Palin speech available at nytimes.com; "Chafee Defends Use of 'Cocky Wacko,'" Boston.com, September 12, 2008.

50. Carl Hulse, "3 Successful Republicans Caution against a Move to the Right," *New York Times*, November 13, 2008.

51. Evan Thomas, "Center Stage," from *Newsweek's* "How He Did It," published November 5, 2008 for magazine issue November 17, 2008. Available at http://www.newsweek.com/id/167582.

6

The South

Winking at Dixie

Donald W. Beachler

The South and Recent Elections

Democrats have long suffered from a severe disadvantage in presidential elections because of their inability to win electoral votes in the South. The once solid Democratic South has often been a solid Republican South in recent presidential elections.[1] From 1972 through 2004, only southern Democrats had been able to win states in the region (Al Gore of Tennessee was unable to win any southern states, including his home state.). Barack Obama was the first non-southern Democrat to win a southern state since Hubert Humphrey carried Texas with 41 percent of the vote in 1968.[2] Obama's victories in Florida, North Carolina, and Virginia represented a significant achievement as it was the best showing by a northern Democrat in the South in 48 years. Even more noteworthy was that these states were won by the first African-American to win the presidential nomination of a major political party in the United States.

Despite notable Democratic advances in 2008, the South remains a Republican stronghold in presidential and congressional politics. John McCain won 10 of 13 states in Dixie and took 113 of the region's 168 electoral votes. As the table at the front of the book illustrates, McCain won the popular vote in the 13 southern states by 3 million votes, or a 7 percent margin. The difference between 2008 and the two preceding presidential elections was that the Republican nominee was soundly defeated in other regions of the country.

After two bad election cycles for the GOP in 2006 and 2008, the South remains the Republicans' stronghold in congressional elections. In the Senate the Republicans hold 19 of the 26 southern seats while, outside the South, Democrats have a 52–22 seat margin. In the House of Representatives, the Republicans have an 80–62 advantage in southern seats. Outside the South, Democrats hold a 195–98 edge in Representatives. The region that was once an isolated bastion of the Democratic Party was, at least in 2008, the sole bastion of the Republican Party.

The One-Party Democratic South

The end of Reconstruction in 1877 eliminated any prospect of black equality in nineteenth-century America.[3] In the following years, African-American rights were severely undermined as the Fourteenth and Fifteenth Amendments were left largely unenforced and segregation and disfranchisement became wide-spread in the South. The right of states to enforce segregation was upheld in 1896 in the famous Supreme Court decision *Plessy v. Ferguson*, which promulgated the separate but equal doctrine. Segregation in the South extended to public educa-tion from primary school to the university, libraries, cemeteries, public trans-portation vehicles and transit stations, movie theaters, restaurants, and athletic contests.[4] Many southern and border states outlawed interracial marriage until such prohibitions were overturned by the U.S. Supreme Court in the 1967 deci-sion, *Loving v. Virginia*.

In most of the South, blacks were denied access to the ballot box by a vari-ety of mechanisms including literacy tests, poll taxes, grandfather clauses, and extrajudicial intimidation and murder. As the South quickly evolved into a one-party system, the white primary was also developed. Because Democrats won nearly every office in most of the South, a victory in the Democratic primary election was tantamount to winning the general election. Blacks were excluded from the electoral process by measures that permitted only whites to vote in the Democratic primary.[5] By the early years of the twentieth century, few African-Americans voted in the South.

The political instrument of white supremacy in the South was the Democratic Party. Because Abraham Lincoln was a Republican and because the radical wing of the Republican Party had pursued policies promoting black equality during Reconstruction, Democrats were able to marginalize the Republicans in much of the South by labeling them as the party of Yankee domination and black equality. By 1900, the South had largely evolved into a one-party system that was to remain undisturbed for nearly fifty years.[6] The renowned political scientist, V. O. Key, argued that most of the political and institutional arrangements that prevailed in the South during the first half of the twentieth century were centered on ques-tions of race.[7] Candidates sometimes sought political advantage by claiming that they were more committed to preserving white supremacy than were their oppo-nents. The Deep South states of South Carolina, Georgia, Alabama, Mississippi, and Louisiana had the highest black populations and were most committed to the cause of white supremacy and, thus, to the Democratic Party.

From 1880 through 1944, Democrats had a virtual lock on the electoral votes of the southern states. White voters, in the states with the highest black percentages, were most devoted to the segregationist system and therefore most intensely committed to the Democratic Party.[8] Only twice in this period did any southern state cast its electoral votes for a Republican presidential candidate. In 1920, Warren Harding won Tennessee and Oklahoma. More serious defections from the Democrats occurred when they nominated a Catholic, Al Smith of New York, in 1928. With Smith's religion an issue in the campaign, Republican Herbert Hoover carried seven southern states. The five states in Dixie with the highest black populations (Alabama, Georgia, Louisiana, Mississippi, and South Carolina), and the strongest commitment by whites to segregation, remained loyal to the Democratic ticket in 1928, as did Arkansas.[9]

In each of his four successful campaigns for the presidency, Franklin D. Roosevelt (FDR) carried all 13 southern states. In some of the southern states (the outer south) with lower black populations, Republicans received a respectable share of the vote. In some Deep South states, support for the Democrats reached near unanimity. For example, FDR received 98.6 percent of the vote in South Carolina in 1936 and 98.2 percent in 1940. To keep his southern base in line, FDR was reluctant to express overt support for even the most basic civil rights measures. For example, the president refused to take a position on the effort to pass legislation making lynching a federal crime.[10] However, through judicial appointments and the creation of a civil rights section of the Justice Department, FDR did seek to weaken the power of white supremacist politicians in the South.[11]

Southern Democratic sensitivity on the race issue could reach extreme dimensions. In 1936, South Carolina Senator Ellison "Cotton Ed" Smith walked out of the Democratic Convention because a black minister offered the invocation. Smith's colorful account of his departure from the convention hall has become infamous:

> [B]less God, out on that platform walked a slew-footed, blue gummed, kinky headed Senegambian. And he started praying and I started walking. And as I pushed through the great doors, and walked across the vast rotunda it seemed to me that old John Calhoun leaned down from his mansion in the sky and whispered in my ear, "You did right Ed…"[12]

Civil Rights and Strain in the Democratic Coalition

The relationship between the South and the Democratic Party showed severe strains in the 1948 election. In early 1948, President Truman proposed legislation that would make lynching a federal crime, ban racial discrimination in employment, and protect black voting rights.[13] Concerned about winning black votes in contested northern states, the Democratic Party, for the first time in its history, adopted a platform embracing civil rights. Southern segregationists were outraged that, in its effort to reelect President Truman, the Democratic Party had explicitly abandoned its commitment to the white South. Several southern delegates left the convention and later convened in Birmingham, Alabama as the States' Rights Party, to nominate South Carolina's Democratic Governor J. Strom Thurmond as its candidate for president. Thurmond, who later gained fame for serving in the U.S. Senate until he was 100 years old, made the principal priority of the new party clear when he stated that

> ...I am not opposed to the Negro. But I think it in the best interests of law and order, for the integrity of the races, whites and blacks should be kept in separate schools, theaters, and swimming pools....We of the South think it is better not to admit persons of other races into churches, restaurants...and other public places.[14]

The commitment of most white southern Democrats to upholding segregation and white supremacy was as strong in 1950 as it had been a half century earlier. The raw racism behind these convictions was stated by even those regarded as the most dignified and genteel southern politicians, including Richard Russell of Georgia who served his state for 38 years (1933–1971)—after whom one of the three U.S. Senate office buildings is named. Russell was regarded as a scholarly and thoughtful man, yet he objected to interracial marriage on the grounds that it would lead to a "mongrel race" and that all mongrel races were doomed to failure. On the issue of equality between the races, Russell stated, "Any White man who wants to take the position that he is no better than the Negro is entitled to his own opinion of himself. I do not think much of him, but he can think it."[15]

Despite the fact that there was a Democrat running as a segregationist candidate and a left-wing independent candidacy by former Vice President Henry Wallace, Harry Truman was able to defeat Thomas Dewey in the election of 1948. Despite Truman's success, the election of 1948 carried a warning to the Democrats. Thurmond carried four Deep South states: Alabama, Louisiana, Mississippi, and South Carolina. Unlike previous state defections in 1920, and more significantly in 1928, Thurmond won states that had some of the highest black populations in the United States. White voters, who were virtually the entire electorate in these states, put the Democrats on notice that there could be political costs to deviating from the segregationist position that had bonded Democrats and white Southerners for many decades.

Neither political party was particularly eager to take up the cause of civil rights in the 1950s and early 1960s. Other political actors would make political neutrality an increasingly difficult political stance. In 1954, the U.S. Supreme Court declared that segregation was inherently unequal and ruled that racial segregation in public schools was unconstitutional. A year later, led by the young minister Martin Luther King Jr., blacks in Montgomery, Alabama, launched a boycott of the city's bus system to protest the indignities of segregation on the buses. In 1960, black college students in Greensboro, North Carolina, attracted national attention as they "sat in" at lunch counters where they were forbidden to dine because of their race.[16] Republican Dwight Eisenhower, who was elected president in 1952 and 1956, asserted that laws could not change human hearts with regard to racial issues. Eisenhower stated that he would enforce federal law and did so by sending federal troops to implement federal court orders to integrate Central High School in Little Rock, Arkansas, in 1957. Eisenhower, however, refused to publicly state his views on the *Brown v. Board of Education* decision. Adlai Stevenson, the Democrat who lost to Eisenhower in 1952 and 1956, was also reluctant to take a stand in favor of civil rights. Stevenson stated that he believed the Brown case had been correctly decided, but he opposed using federal troops to enforce school integration.[17]

In the election of 1960, Democrat John F. Kennedy and Republican Richard Nixon sought to win black votes by cautiously supporting civil rights. In the three elections of 1952, 1956, and 1960, the South's electoral votes were split between Democrats and Republicans. While race was the defining factor in the region's politics, it is important to note that Republicans were able to win southern electoral votes before the Democrats were identified as the party of civil rights and the party of the overwhelming majority of black voters. At this time, Republicans did well among the growing numbers of middle-class, college-educated voters who voted for the GOP as did similar voters outside the South.[18]

The Republican and Democratic parties were truly differentiated on civil rights most distinctively in 1964. By 1964, President Lyndon Johnson had clearly embraced many of the basic demands of the civil rights movement. Most notably, Johnson had signed the 1964 Civil Rights Act that banned racial discrimination in employment, public facilities, and accommodations. The Republicans nominated Arizona Senator Barry Goldwater, the leader of the party's conservative wing. Goldwater voted against the Civil Rights Act and campaigned hard for votes in southern states. Goldwater's efforts, however, were hampered by his opposition to federal programs that were popular in many parts of the South. Goldwater opposed federal subsidies to farmers, proposed making Social Security contributions voluntary, and favored privatizing the Tennessee Valley Authority—a source of jobs and cheap electricity in several southern states. In losing a national landslide to Lyndon Johnson, Goldwater carried the five Deep South states with the highest proportion of black voters (Alabama, Georgia, Louisiana, Mississippi, and South Carolina). In Mississippi, where few blacks were permitted to vote in 1964, Goldwater won a remarkable 87 percent of the vote. Johnson managed to win, though by relatively small margins, the eight states in the outer South.[19]

By 1968, the white South was in full-scale rebellion against the national Democratic Party that had passed the 1965 Voting Rights Act, the 1968 Fair Housing Act, and a host of social programs that were aimed at helping the poor. The general election in 1968 was a three-way race between Vice President Hubert Humphrey—a strong champion of civil rights—Republican Richard Nixon, and the former Democratic governor of Alabama, George C. Wallace who had attracted national attention by standing in a doorway at the University of Alabama in a futile attempt to block the admission of black students.[20]

Wallace was known for his flamboyant stands on social and racial issues. Wallace taunted hippy college students who shouted obscenities at him, that there were two four letter words he was sure that they did not know; SOAP and WORK. As he campaigned across the country, Wallace delighted his supporters by explaining that Alabama did not have riots because in his state the first person who showed an inclination to riot was shot in the head. Wallace mocked the intellectuals who protested the Vietnam War as impractical people who could not park a bicycle straight.[21] A few months before the election, some polls showed Wallace getting a quarter of the vote.[22]

Wallace was a potential threat to Republican Richard Nixon who sought votes in the South by running as a moderate conservative. Republicans feared that if Wallace won most of the South's electoral votes, the election would be decided in the U.S. House of Representatives where Democrats had a substantial majority. Nixon presented himself as a candidate who would not repeal civil rights laws, but opposed busing and other measures that involved the federal government in enforcing integration upon the South. Earl Black and Merle Black describe Nixon as the candidate of those white southerners who were willing to abandon strict segregation, but did not favor integration.[23] Nixon also appealed to conservative white southerners with his denunciations of the liberal Supreme Court headed by Chief Justice Earl Warren and by promising to restore law and order to a nation that had witnessed a rise in crime and riots in many cities. South Carolina's Strom Thurmond, now a Republican, worked vigorously on Nixon's behalf. Thurmond argued that Nixon was an electable conservative and that a vote for Wallace was a vote to elect the liberal Humphrey to the presidency.

While Nixon narrowly defeated Humphrey in the 1968 election, George Wallace made an impressive showing. Wallace won five southern states (Alabama, Arkansas, Georgia, Louisiana, and Mississippi,) and finished a strong second in North Carolina, South Carolina, and Tennessee. Nixon carried seven southern states. Humphrey, with the help of native son Lyndon Johnson, was able to win only Texas. Humphrey's showing in the South was the worst performance of any Democratic candidate since the end of Reconstruction. The election of 1968 marked a new era in southern and national presidential politics. The white South was in open rebellion against the national Democratic Party.

The Emergence of a Republican Presidential South

In the 1970s and 1980s, the Southern white electorate evolved away from the Democratic Party. While race was a key, it was not the only factor in the trans-formation of southern politics. The majority of southern whites deviated from liberal Democratic norms on a number of key issues. Based on national election surveys, Earl Black and Merle Black found that just over half of all white south-erners in the 1980s were loyal Republicans. These southern white Republicans favored large defense budgets, believed religion should play a significant role in national life, opposed racial quotas, and were ill-disposed toward gays and les-bians. Over a fifth of the southern electorate was made up of white swing voters who were not firmly committed to one political party. These swing voters were culturally conservative. They were opposed to racial quotas, favored the death penalty, and believed that prayer should be permitted in public schools.[24] Whites were a majority of the electorate in every southern state and most of them were conservative on racial and nonracial issues.

After 1968, the Democrats reformed their presidential nominating process to require that delegates be chosen in primaries or caucuses. These reforms weakened the power of party leaders and elected officials who had been able to select or appoint delegates in many states. Because more liberal voters participated in Democratic primaries, between 1972 and 1988 the party often nominated presidential candidates who had difficulties competing in the South.[25] At times, Southern Democrats, however, have been able to parlay strong support in their native region into enough support to win the Democratic presidential nomination.[26]

Table 6.1 compares electoral votes won in the South and the rest of the nation in eight presidential elections from 1972 through 2008. In only one of the elections did the Democratic candidate win a majority of the Southern electoral votes. In fact, in an era when the South was quickly becoming a Republican stronghold, the South was essential in putting Jimmy Carter of Georgia in the White House. The 1976 election deviates from all other elections discussed in this chapter. Since the Civil War, no southerner had been elected president of the United States. Carter appealed to the South to finally elect one of its own to the presidency (Carter was the first southerner elected directly to the presidency since Zachary Taylor in 1848). As a small-town peanut farmer, evangelical Christian, and a politician with an uncanny ability to appeal across racial lines, Carter carried most of the South and narrowly won the presidency in 1976. Although he did not win the Southern white vote, Carter carried about

Table 6.1   Southern and non-Southern electoral votes, 1972–2008

	South		Non-South	
	D	R	D	R
1972 McGovern (D) v. Nixon (R)	0	147	17	374
1976 Carter (D) v. Ford (R)	127	20	170	221
1980 Carter (D) v. Reagan (R)	12	135	37	354
1984 Mondale (D) v. Reagan (R)	0	153	13	385
1988 Dukakis (D) v. Bush (R)	0	153	112	273
1992 Clinton (D) v. Bush (R)	46	117	324	51
1996 Clinton (D) v. Dole (R)	58	105	321	54
2000 Gore (D) v. Bush (R)	0	163	267	108
2004 Kerry (D) v. Bush (R)	0	168	252	118
2008 Obama (D) v. McCain (R)	55	113	310	60

Source: http://www.uselectionatlas.org/accessed May 13, 2009.

47 percent of the whites and, combined with overwhelming black support, won 11 of 13 Southern states. One white man in Mississippi likely spoke for many when he explained his vote in 1976, by saying that he voted for Carter because he was "…a good old southern boy."[27] By 1980, when Carter was beset by economic and foreign policy problems, he did no better among white voters in his native South than in other regions of the country when he was beaten handily by Ronald Reagan.

Reagan played a great role in consolidating Republican dominance of the South in presidential elections. Reagan was the first Republican president to openly embrace an alliance with the conservative Christian movement, now known as the Religious Right, which fought against legal abortion, gay rights, and for public school prayer and a greater role for religion in public life. Over the course of his political career, Reagan consistently opposed civil rights bills. Reagan also won the approval from a large majority of southern whites with his support for large military budgets and assertive foreign policy. When he left office, one poll indicated that Reagan was regarded as a racist by about three-fourths of black Americans, but he was popular among a majority of whites—and especially popular among Southern whites.[28]

In three presidential elections, Democrats nominated northern liberals who did not fare well in the North or the South. George McGovern and Walter Mondale each carried just one state (McGovern won Massachusetts and Mondale carried Minnesota, while both of them carried the District of Columbia). George H. W. Bush decisively defeated Michael Dukakis in 1988. Dukakis did win 10 states and 112 electoral votes, but none of them were in the South.

In 1992 and 1996, the Democratic ticket comprised two southern candidates, Bill Clinton of Arkansas and Al Gore of Tennessee. In each of the elections the Republicans carried a majority of the southern electoral votes, but Democrats were able to win some electoral votes in the South. In both 1992 and 1996, the Clinton-Gore ticket carried Arkansas, Kentucky, Louisiana, and Tennessee. In 1992 the Democrats also carried Georgia, which reverted to the Republicans in 1996. However, in 1996 Clinton won Florida, which as the fourth most populous state, was a very desirable target. By winning southern states and coming close in others, Clinton was able to make the Republicans expend resources that had to be diverted away from crucial battleground states outside the South. (Presidential candidates may wish to force their opponents to spend funds in a state even when they believe they have relatively little chance of carrying it. For example, when John Kerry's campaign announced that it was buying television ads in Virginia in May 2004, many political observers believed the campaign was trying to lure the Bush campaign into spending funds in a state that most believed would vote Republican in November.[29])

The most remarkable regional disparity occurred in the 2000 presidential election. In 2000 Al Gore won the nationwide popular vote on his way to becoming one of the few presidential candidates to win the popular vote, but not attain the presidency. Gore also won 72 percent of the electoral votes outside the South, but failed to carry a single state in the South. Only by winning all 13 southern states was George Bush able to overcome Gore's strength in the Northeast,

West Coast, and the upper Midwest. Gore even failed to carry his own state of Tennessee, which had twice elected him to the U.S. Senate and which had, in 1992 and 1996, voted for the Clinton-Gore ticket. Gore's inability to carry a single state in his home region at a time when he was part of an incumbent administration and in a period of peace and prosperity was largely attributable to a conservative region's rejection of the perceived Democratic permissiveness on issues of sexual morality and other social issues. In 2004, George W. Bush won the national popular vote by a margin of about 2.5 percent. The regional disparities exhibited in 2000 persisted four years later as Bush swept all 168 of the South's electoral votes, while Kerry won 69 percent of the electoral votes outside the South. (In 2008, Obama won 84 percent of the electoral votes outside the South.)

There has been a cottage industry of literature advising the Democrats on how they should win the presidency in view of their southern problem. Thomas Schaller has argued that Democrats should ignore most of the South with the exception of the least "southern of the southern" states such as Virginia and Florida and run against the conservative cultural values of a Republican party rooted in the South to win other regions of the country.[30] Others such as Virginia strategists Steve Jarding and David "Mudcat" Saunders have advocated a strategy aimed at reassuring blue-collar southern voters, sometimes dubbed NASCAR voters, on cultural issues, while emphasizing economic populism.[31] Schaller argues that Democrats lack the credentials on cultural issues such as abortion, gay rights, and guns to compete for most southern white voters. Whatever the Democrats' remedy for their southern white voter problem might ultimately be, table 6.2 indicates that southern whites have consistently been far more favorable to Republicans than whites in other regions of the country.

Unfortunately, the 2008 exit polls did not present a breakdown of racial voting on a region-wide basis. An examination of state polls indicates that the pattern of southern white aversion to Democratic presidential candidates continued in 2008. Barack Obama received 30 percent or less of the popular vote in just 8 of 50 states. All eight of these states were in the South, including three states

Table 6.2 White support for the Republican presidential candidate by region, 1972–2004

	1972	1976	1980	1984	1988	1992	1996	2000	2004
Whites in the Northeast	65	50	52	57	54	36	37	44	50
Whites in the Midwest	65	52	55	64	57	39	43	53	56
Whites in the South	76	52	61	71	67	49	56	66	70
Whites in the West	60	54	55	66	58	47	44	51	54

Source: Data from Donald W. Beachler, "The South," in Kevin J. McMahon, David M. Rankin, Donald W. Beachler, and John Kenneth, eds., *White, Winning the White House, 2004: Region by Region, Vote by Vote* (New York: Palgrave Macmillan, 2005).

where Obama won less than 15 percent of the white vote: Alabama, Louisiana, and Mississippi.

Florida: The Southern Battleground State

Florida has become an ever more important state in presidential politics as rapid population growth has given the state more electoral votes after every census. In 1969, Florida had 10 electoral votes. After the 2000 census figures led to the reapportionment of the U.S. House of Representatives, Florida's electoral votes increased from 25 to 27, the fourth highest in the nation behind only New York (31), Texas (34), and California (55).

Florida gained immense notoriety in 2000 as a result of the disputes over discarded votes, unreadable ballots, and legal wrangling that ended when the U. S. Supreme Court, in a 5–4 decision in the case of *Bush v. Gore*, ended all recounts and in effect made George W. Bush the president-elect.[32] The final official popular vote in Florida was 2,912,790 for Bush and 2,912,253 for Gore, a margin of just 537 votes. Bush officially carried Florida by less than 0.01 percent of the popular vote.[33] Many Democrats believed that the 97,488 votes garnered by leftist independent candidate Ralph Nader cost Gore the presidency. With the capture of Florida's 25 electoral votes, George W. Bush had 271 or one more electoral vote than the majority of 270 needed to become the president of the United States.

Florida was among the earliest Southern states to enter the Republican camp. Dwight Eisenhower won the state in 1952 and 1956, and between 1952 and 1992, Democrats won the state only twice (1964 and 1976). As table 6.3 indicates, from 1972 through 1988, Democratic candidates not only did poorly in Florida, they generally ran well behind their national percentage of the vote.[34] Unlike most other southern states, Florida has been a competitive state for Democrats in the last five presidential elections, however.[35] Aided by demographic changes and the candidacy of independent Ross Perot, Bill Clinton lost the state by only 1 percent of the vote in 1992, and carried Florida by about 5 percent in 1996.[36] In the five most recent presidential elections, Democrats have received about the same percentage of the popular vote in Florida as they have in the nation as a whole. In 2008, Barack Obama ran about 2 percent behind his national percentage of the

Table 6.3 Florida and the nation in presidential elections, 1972–2008

	1972	1976	1980	1984	1988	1992	1996	2000	2004	2008
U.S, Democratic vote	37.5	50.1	41.0	40.6	45.6	43.0	49.2	48.4	48.2	52.9
Florida Democratic vote	27.5	51.9	38.5	34.7	38.15	39.0	48.0	48.9	47.1	50.9
Difference	**−10**	**+1.8**	**−2.5**	**−5.9**	**−7.1**	**−4.0**	**−1.2**	**+0.5**	**−1.1**	**−2.0**

Source: Dave Leip, http://www.uselectionatlas.org/accessed May 13, 2009.

vote. Obama was only the second Democrat to win a majority of the popular vote in Florida since 1964.

Florida is, in many ways, a cross-section of the United States.[37] The northern portion of the state borders rural sections of Alabama and Georgia and many white voters there share the conservative values of whites in more traditional southern states. The Hispanic and black populations in Florida are just a few points above the nation average for each ethnicity. Many relatively affluent Midwesterners have retired to the Gulf Coast of Florida and have made the region south of Tampa predominantly Republican. Retirees and other migrants from the Northeast have made Broward and Palm Beach counties, just north of Miami, very Democratic in presidential elections.

Foreign policy plays a larger role in Florida politics than in most other states. A large Cuban population in Miami-Dade County has traditionally demanded that the U.S. government maintain a harsh policy against the Castro regime. In 2000, Al Gore would almost certainly have been elected president of the United States if the Clinton administration had not returned Elian Gonzalez, a Cuban refugee orphan, to his father in Cuba. Traditionally Republican, Cuban-American voters in Florida turned out in very large numbers for George W. Bush in an effort to penalize the Clinton administration's handling of the Gonzalez matter.

In 2004, the Bush administration enacted tighter restrictions on Cuban-Americans visiting their families in Cuba. Prior to 2004, families were allowed an annual visit to Cuba of unlimited duration. The new policies permitted one visit of two weeks every three years. The amount of money that could be sent to the island was restricted and no funds could be sent to anyone who was not an immediate family member. The Bush administration argued that such measures would hasten Castro's decline, but many observers thought the primary purpose of the restrictions was to court votes among Cubans in a pivotal Electoral College state. Others thought that the policies might backfire as younger Cubans and refugees who had come from Cuba since 1980 might resent the restrictions on travel to the island. In 2004, John Kerry promised that if he were elected he would allow more family visits to Cuba.[38] In 2008, Barack Obama also vowed to ease restrictions on travel to Cuba and the transmission of money to family members.

Due to the large numbers of Jewish voters in south Florida, American Middle East policy is a bigger concern in Florida than all but a few other states. Both the Republican and Democratic presidential nominees inevitably compete in their pledges of fidelity to the state of Israel. In recent elections, Jewish voters in Florida, like Jews elsewhere in the United States, have voted heavily Democratic.

Since it is a retirement haven, Florida also has a disproportionate share of elderly voters. In 2008, 16 percent of the national electorate was age 65 or older. In Florida, however, senior citizens were 22 percent of the electorate. Florida had the highest percentage of elderly voters of any state in the nation. Issues such as the solvency of Social Security and the expansion of Medicare to cover prescription drug benefits have greater resonance in Florida than elsewhere in the United States.

Florida was supposed to be a difficult state for Obama, especially after George W. Bush's five-point win in 2004, and Republican Charlie Crist's 7 percent victory in the 2006 gubernatorial race seemed to demonstrate that Florida was leaning Republican. In 2008, Florida's primary election date violated party rules, and the state was stripped of its delegates to the Democratic National Convention.

Neither Hillary Clinton nor Barack Obama campaigned in the state before the January 29 primary. Still, both candidates' names appeared on the ballot and more than 1.7 million voters participated. Clinton won by a decisive 50–33 percent margin. In subsequent primaries, Obama frequently lost to Clinton among demographic groups such as Latinos, senior citizens, and Jews who are important elements of the Florida electorate.

Despite the apparent demographic disadvantages that Obama faced in Florida, and summer polls showing McCain leading in the contest for the state's 27 electoral votes, the Obama campaign was fully committed to contesting Florida. Obama invested $39 million in the state, and by October his campaign was outspending McCain on television advertisements by a 3–1 margin. The Obama campaign also dispensed Steve Hildebrand, one of the Democratic Party's top field organizers, to Florida in October to concentrate on organizing an immense get-out-the-vote effort.[39]

Obama carried Florida by 237,000 votes or 2.8 percent of the popular vote. McCain received about 70,000 more votes than George W. Bush did in 2004, while Obama won about 700,000 more votes than did John Kerry. Obama carried the state while winning just 16 of 67 counties. His margin of victory was built by winning large margins in the largest metropolitan areas in the southern and central portions of Florida. Obama carried the populous south Florida counties of Miami-Dade, Broward, and Palm Beach by double-digit margins. He won Orange Country (Orlando) by 18 percent (Kerry won Orange County by less than 1 percent) and, unlike Kerry, carried the populous Gulf Coast counties Pinellas (St. Petersburg) and Hillsborough (Tampa). Notably, Obama also won Alachua County (Gainesville), home of the University of Florida and Leon County (Tallahassee), which contains the state capital and home to Florida State University and traditionally African-American, Florida A&M University. Obama won a higher percentage of the vote than Kerry in all of these counties except Leon County where he and Kerry both received about 61.5 percent of the vote.

As it did in other battleground states, the Obama campaign worked to increase its vote totals in Republican areas of Florida. Duval County, which contains the city of Jacksonville, is close to Georgia and contains many conservative white voters, while blacks constitute about 32 percent of the county population. In 2004 George Bush won the county by a 16 percent margin, which provided him with a popular vote margin of over 61,000 votes. In 2008, McCain won the popular vote in Duval County by 2 percent and a popular vote margin of only 8,000.

Exit polling indicates that Florida's three major ethnic groups: whites, African-Americans, and Latinos constituted about the same percentage of the electorate in 2008 as they had in 2004. Obama won about 42 percent of the white vote as did John Kerry. He increased the Democratic margin among black voters substantially; winning 95 of the African-American vote to 4 percent for McCain, as opposed to Kerry's 86–13 margin among black voters. In 2004, George W. Bush won Latino voters in Florida by a 56–44 margin. Obama carried Florida Latinos by 57–42 percent.

Two factors contributed to the change in the Latino vote, including large-scale migration of non-Cuban Latinos into Florida. These new Latino migrants are especially concentrated in the central region of the state. In Orange County, where about 22 percent of the population is black, the Census Bureau estimated that by 2007 a quarter of the population was Latino, an increase from 19 percent in 2000. Kerry prevailed over Bush in Orange County by 800 votes whereas Obama won by 86,000 votes. Osceola County, just south of Orange County, saw very rapid population growth in the 2000s and a dramatic swing in its presidential vote. Bush won the county by 5 percent in 2004, while Obama won it by 20 percent four years later. By 2007, the Census Bureau estimated Osceola County to be 40 percent Latino, up from 29 percent in 2000.[40]

The Cuban-American vote was more Democratic in 2008 than in previous presidential elections. The polling firm Bendixen and Associates polled in Miami-Dade County, the center of the Cuban population in Florida, and found that Obama won 35 percent of the Cuban-American vote. Younger Cuban-Americans were less focused on Cuba as an exclusive issue, while older voters in the community seemed motivated by old foreign policy loyalties. In Miami-Dade County, 84 percent of Cuban-Americans over the age of 65 voted for McCain, while 55 percent of Cuban-Americans 29 or younger voted for Obama.[41]

Unfortunately, exit polling in 2008 did not include figures for Jewish voters in Florida. Based on Obama's very strong performances in Miami-Dade, Palm Beach, and Broward Counties, the centers of Jewish population in Florida, and a national poll finding that Obama won 78 percent of the Jewish vote across the country, it seems that Obama did not fare much worse than Kerry's 80 percent of the Florida Jewish vote in 2008.

Obama did slightly worse than Kerry among Florida voters over 65 winning 45 percent to Kerry's 48 percent. Obama improved by 3 percent over Kerry among 61 percent of Florida voters aged 29 or younger.

Obama carried Florida by improving the Democratic performance among African-American and Latino voters and, despite predictions to the contrary, holding on to the same share of the white vote that John Kerry won in 2004. Obama's victory in the state continues the pattern of Florida being the contested state with the largest number of electoral votes.

The 2008 Presidential Election in the South

In 2008, Democrats faced a far different and more favorable set of circumstances than they had in 2004. As his presidency drew to a close in 2008, George W. Bush, the incumbent Republican president, had better job approval ratings in the South than in other parts of the country, but a majority of voters in each southern state disapproved of his performance as president. In the summer of 2008, gasoline prices were over $4 a gallon across the nation. In the two months preceding the election, the American financial system appeared to be on the verge of collapse as major insurance companies, investment banks, and mortgage guarantors failed, and in many cases required government bailouts. The Congress appropriated $750 billion to assist the nation's banks. Moreover, each of the first nine months of the year saw a net loss of jobs in the U.S. economy. On a variety of domestic policy issues, 2008 was a difficult year to be the candidate of the party that occupied the White House for the past eight years. While John McCain attempted to position himself as a maverick who was different from the unpopular president, his efforts to distance himself from Bush were compromised by the fact that in the Republican primaries McCain had been careful to present himself as a loyal Republican. In general this meant embracing the basic economic philosophy of the Bush administration, which favored substantial tax cuts that Democrats argued favored the wealthy, and supporting a philosophy that advocated very limited government regulation of business. McCain had opposed Bush's tax policy when he ran against Bush for the Republican presidential nomination in 2000 and voted against administration tax policy in 2001 and 2003, but by 2008 McCain was a firm proponent of making nearly all the Bush tax cuts permanent. In the Republican nomination process, McCain had proclaimed that he voted with the president more than 90 percent of the time. In response, residents of battleground states, north and south, were treated to a barrage of Obama commercials (made possible by the Democratic candidate's vast and unprecedented fund-raising capacity), depicting McCain proclaiming his loyalty to the president as he was shown stating that he had supported the now unpopular president more than 90 percent of the time.

As they had in 2004, the Democrats nominated a northern liberal for president in 2008. Obama, unlike Kerry, was from Illinois—a state less stereotypically liberal than Massachusetts—but in his brief career in the Senate, Obama had complied a liberal record very similar to that of Kerry who had been defeated in every southern state in 2004. For example, the liberal interest group Americans for Democratic Action had given both Kerry and Obama a 95 in 2005 and a grade of 100 in 2006. Kerry and Obama had each received a 0 from the conservative Club for Growth in 2006.[42] (Interest groups award a "grade" to members of Congress based on the percentage of roll call votes the senator or representative voted in agreement with the group's position on selected pieces of legislation.)

As the first African-American to receive his party's presidential nomination, Obama faced special challenges and opportunities across the nation and in the South. In the protracted primary battle for the Democratic nomination between Senators Obama and Clinton, the primary electorate was divided along racial lines in 12 of 13 southern states. Only in Virginia was Obama able to win a majority of both white and black voters. Georgia was the only southern state in which Obama was able to remain within 10 points of Clinton among white voters. In most states, Clinton won landslide victories among white voters, as well as overwhelming victories among Latinos in Texas and Florida (see table 6.4). Obama won huge majorities among African-Americans in all 12 states where exit polls captured enough black voters for there to be a significant sample. Given the fact that whites cast a majority of the vote in all southern states in the general

Table 6.4   The 2008 Democratic primaries in the South

	Obama state vote	Clinton state vote	Clinton white vote	Obama white vote	Clinton black vote	Obama black vote	Clinton Latino vote	Obama Latino vote
Alabama	56	42	72	25	15	84	—	—
Arkansas	26	70	79	16	25	74	—	—
Florida	33	50	53	23	23	75	59	30
Georgia	67	31	53	43	11	88	—	—
Kentucky	30	65	72	23	7	90	—	—
Louisiana	56	37	59	30	13	86	—	—
Mississippi	61	37	70	26	8	92	—	—
North Carolina	56	42	61	37	7	91	—	—
Oklahoma	31	55	56	29	N/A	N/A	—	—
South Carolina	55	27	36	24	19	78	—	—
Tennessee	41	54	67	26	22	77	—	—
Texas	48	51	55	44	16	84	66	32
Virginia	64	36	47	52	10	90	—	—

Source: http://www.cnn.com/ELECTION/2008/primaries/ accessed May 13, 2009.

Note: All figures are percentages of the vote statewide or by ethnic group.

election, the racial polarization evident in the primaries did not augur well for the Democratic nominee in the South in the fall contest.

The Obama campaign was obliged to compete in a region hostile to Democratic presidential candidates as well as one with a long pattern of racially polarized voting. Given the winner-takes-all method that all states but Maine and Nebraska use to allocate electoral votes, the Obama campaign, like all others, was forced to make decisions about where to allocate its resources. Initially four states were selected for extensive television advertising and an extensive network of field offices that were devoted to registering and turning out voters deemed likely to vote for Obama. The Obama campaign decided to make a serious attempt to win Virginia, Georgia, Florida, and North Carolina.

The Obama campaign aired more than $2,000,000 in television ads in Georgia during the spring and summer before deciding that it was unlikely to win Georgia and dropping its media buys in August and redeploying some of its paid staff to North Carolina.[43] On the Friday before the election, the Obama campaign announced that it was spending a modest amount ($100,000) of money on television advertising in Georgia in response to polls that indicated that the race in Georgia was close and that there was a massive African-American turn-out in the state's early voting. Black voters, who were about a quarter of the total electorate in the general election in Georgia in 2004, constituted 35 percent of those casting ballots before Election Day in 2008.[44] Republican consultant and pollster Matt Towery explained of Georgia, "[Y]ou cannot be the fastest grow-ing state in the nation for African-American population and be drifting toward becoming a massively Republican state."[45] In November, John McCain defeated Barack Obama by a 52–47 percent margin in Georgia. (The decision to concede Georgia for two months may have cost Obama another 15 electoral votes.) For

Democrats, Obama's showing represented a significant improvement over 2004 when George W. Bush defeated John Kerry by 58–41 percent.[46]

At the end of the campaign Obama was contending for the other three southern states that he had decided were potentially attainable. The day before the election he campaigned in Jacksonville, Florida, Charlotte, North Carolina, and Manassas, Virginia.[47] The last day was well spent as Obama won all three states capturing 55 southern electoral votes.

Table 6.5 indicates that Obama's four target states were different from most other southern states in some important demographic factors. The four southern battleground states had the highest percentage of adults over age 24 with a college degree.[48] Only Virginia had a rate of college graduates well above the national average of 24.2 percent. The importance of higher education levels for the voting preferences of white voters varied considerably even in the battleground states. In Virginia, Obama did 12 percent better among white college graduates than among other whites (44–32). In North Carolina, Obama performed 5 percent better among white college graduates than among nongraduates. In Florida (+2 percent) and Georgia (+3 percent), Obama performed only marginally better among white college graduates than among other white voters.

While all four southern battleground states had substantial black populations, they also have increasingly diverse populations in general. The four battleground states have larger Asian populations than any southern state other than Texas. They also possess growing Latino populations. Texas has long had a large and growing Latino population and it still has by far the largest Latino population in the South. As younger Cuban-Americans enter the electorate and as non-Cuban Latinos vote in greater numbers in Florida, Democratic strength has grown as a breakdown of racial voting in 2008 indicates. Barack Obama was the first Democrat to win the Latino vote in Florida in a presidential election since at least 1988 when exit polling was first conducted in Florida.[49] While just 5 percent of Virginia voters were Latino, Obama's 31 percent margin (65–34) provided him with a quarter of his six-point margin in the state.[50] Asians were included in the "all other" category in the exit poll in Virginia. This All Others group was about three-fifths Asian and constituted 5 percent of the electorate. Obama carried the All Others category by 37 percent of the vote, which provided him with a net gain 1.85 percent of the total electorate in Virginia.[51] In Virginia, the southern state where Obama had his best showing, half of his margin of victory was provided by Latinos, Asians, and those grouped under All Others.

Obama achieved his 55 southern electoral votes and his impressive showing in Georgia in a variety of ways. In Virginia, he improved on the 2004 Democratic performance among whites and blacks, as he did in North Carolina. In Florida, his much stronger showing among an increasingly diverse Latino population and a very strong performance among blacks contributed mightily to his victory. In Georgia, the source of the Obama surge was rooted in the increasing black population of the electorate, from 25 to 30 percent, and winning 98 percent of those voters—a 10 percent improvement on John Kerry's 2004 vote among Georgia's African-Americans. While the 4 percent of the Georgia electorate that was Latino or Asian was too small for reliable estimates of its vote, if these groups

Table 6.5 Selected Southern demographics by state

	College graduates 2000	Asian population 2000	Asian population 2007	Latino population 2000	Latino population 2007	Black population 2000	Black population 2008	Democratic presidential vote change, 2004–2008
Alabama	19.0	0.7	1.1	1.7	2.7	25.9	25.9	2
Arkansas	16.7	0.7	1.6	3.2	5.3	15.6	16.2	–6
Florida	22.3	1.6	2.7	16.8	20.6	14.2	15.9	4
Georgia	24.3	2.1	3.4	5.3	7.8	28.5	30.0	6
Kentucky	17.1	0.7	1.2	1.5	2.2	7.3	7.6	1
Louisiana	18.7	1.2	1.4	2.4	3.2	32.3	31.9	–2
Mississippi	16.9	0.6	1.0	1.4	2.0	36.2	37.2	3
North Carolina	22.5	1.4	2.2	4.7	7.0	21.4	22.3	6
Oklahoma	20.3	1.3	1.7	5.2	7.2	7.5	7.8	0
South Carolina	20.4	0.9	1.2	2.4	3.8	29.4	28.7	3
Tennessee	19.6	1.0	1.3	2.2	3.5	16.3	16.8	–2
Texas	23.3	2.7	3.5	32.0	35.6	11.3	12.0	6
Virginia	29.5	3.7	4.9	4.7	6.6	19.4	19.9	7

Source: http://factfinder.census.gov/home/en/official_estimates_2007.html/ accessed May 12, 2009.

Note: College graduates are the percentage of the population over 25 holding at least a bachelors degree.
All numbers are percentages of the total state population.

Table 6.6 Ethnic voting in the South, 2004–2008

	McCain white vote	Change in GOP white vote 2004–2008	Obama black vote	Change in Democratic black vote 2004–2008	Obama Latino vote	Change in Democratic Latino vote 2004–2008	Obama all others	McCain all others
Alabama	80	8	98	7	—	—	—	—
Arkansas	63	5	95	1	—	—	—	—
Florida	56	0	96	9	57	13	—	—
Georgia	77	–1	98	10	—	—	—	—
Kentucky	64	–1	90	3	—	—	—	—
Louisiana	75	9	94	4	—	—	—	—
Mississippi	85	3	98	8	—	—	—	—
North Carolina	68	–4	95	10	—	—	—	—
Oklahoma	71	0	N/A	N/A	—	—	—	—
South Carolina	78	–2	96	11	—	—	—	—
Tennessee	65	–2	94	7	—	—	—	—
Texas	74	–1	98	11	63	13	—	—
Virginia	68	–8	92	5	65	NA	68	31

Source: http://www.cnn.com/ELECTION/2008/ accessed May 12, 2009.

voted like Latinos and Asians elsewhere in the nation, they likely favored Obama (see table 6.6).

Looking to the Future: The Converging South and the Neo-Confederate South

Every presidential election is, of course, a unique event and the problem with studying these elections is that there are very few cases to examine. Still, demographic and voting patterns indicate that there may be two Souths. The four states examined to this point in the chapter have diverse populations and the most educated populations. They are unlikely to become Democratic strongholds (and in the absence of a black Democratic nominee they will not likely produce quite as high a Democratic percentage of the vote). Still, as more Asians and Latinos who reside in these states obtain citizenship, they may provide for a modest, but important, uptick in the Democratic percentage of the vote. With a burgeoning Latino population, Texas might become the fifth converging southern state.

Other states in the South saw their overall Democratic presidential vote or their white vote for president decline from 2008 to 2004. These states generally have lower Latino and Asian populations than the converging southern states. They also have lower rates of college graduates than the four states where Obama won or lost narrowly in 2008. Some of these states also have long histories of strong support for white supremacy. Alabama and Mississippi were the two states that gained notoriety for racial violence against black civil rights workers in the 1960s. In Louisiana, Ku Klux Klan leader David Duke was a serious, but unsuccessful contender, in the 1990 Senate race and the 1991 gubernatorial election.[52] In 2008, the Republican share of the white vote in Louisiana was 84 percent compared to 75 percent in 2004. (Louisiana did elect Bobby Jindal, a Republican whose parents were immigrants from the Indian state of Punjab, governor in 2007.) In the five Deep South states of Arkansas, Georgia, Louisiana, Alabama, and Mississippi, Obama won a smaller percentage of the vote than did John Kerry in all 49 counties where whites constitute at least 90 percent of the population.[53] Some of these states saw their already low percentages for Democratic candidates drop from 2004 to 2008 as the Democratic nominee switched from a white northern liberal to a black northern liberal. Socially conservative Oklahoma was the only state in the nation in which Barack Obama did not carry a single county.[54] In five Little Dixie counties in southeastern Oklahoma populated by conservative white Democrats, McCain ran 14 percent ahead of Bush's 2004 performance.

Adam Nossiter of *The New York Times* summed up the trend in the bifurcated South by arguing that states along the Atlantic coast had been influenced by an influx of more prosperous and more educated voters. Southern counties that were more supportive of John McCain than of George W. Bush in 2004 were "less educated, poorer, and whiter."[55] Speaking of the fact that 90 percent of Alabama whites voted for McCain, University of Alabama at Birmingham historian Glenn Feldman stated, "Race continues to play a major role in his state....Alabama unfortunately continues to be shackled to the bonds of yesterday."[56]

Going forward some states may continue to resemble the traditional South with partisan voting patterns highly polarized along racial lines. These states will be Republican base states. Other states, most notably Virginia, North Carolina, Florida, and Georgia, are more likely to be battlegrounds states in all but land-slide presidential elections.

In 2008, a great deal of attention was paid to the youth vote. In the prima-ries and in the general election, Barack Obama drew big crowds on many col-lege campuses and young people formed an important contingent in his large corps of get-out-the-vote volunteers. In the electorate overall, Obama won about two-thirds of the vote among those voters 18–29 years of age. Among white vot-ers, Obama won 43 percent of the national vote. Whites aged 18–29 provided Obama with 54 percent of their votes. The youngest voters were the only group of whites that supported Obama over McCain. Table 6.7 examines the white vote in the South to see whether there was similar movement to Obama among young whites in the South. In all but two southern states, young white voters gave a higher percentage of support to Obama than did older whites. The age difference in southern white voting for Obama varied greatly, but certain states have results that merit comment. In North Carolina, a state with a large college population, Obama carried 56 percent of young white votes as he narrowly carried the state. In four other southern states, Obama won more than 40 percent among young white voters. The greater support for the Democrat among the youngest gener-ation of southern whites in a number of states may be an indicator that future presidential elections in the South will be more competitive. On the other hand, it should be noted that in some Deep South states such as Mississippi, Alabama, and Louisiana, young white voters, while slightly more supportive of Obama than older whites, gave him a very low level of their support. There will likely be no youth movement aiding the Democrats in the Deep South.

Table 6.7   Age and the white vote for Obama in the South

	18–29	30–44	45–64	65+
National	54	41	42	40
Alabama	13	10	9	N/A
Arkansas	34	29	32	24
Florida	44	38	43	43
Georgia	20	32	19	22
Kentucky	42	33	34	36
Louisiana	17	16	12	13
Mississippi	18	12	10	N/A
North Carolina	56	32	33	30
Oklahoma	31	30	25	N/A
South Carolina	24	31	22	29
Tennessee	45	28	34	33
Texas	30	27	25	30
Virginia	42	38	38	38

Source: http://www.cnn.com/ELECTION/2008/ accessed May 12, 2009.

Note: The number in each cell is the percentage of the white vote for Obama.

A continuing source of Republican strength in the South will be the far higher number of conservative Protestant voters than in the rest of the nation. The 2008 exit poll asked voters whether they were white evangelical or born-again Christians (WEBACs). As table 6.8 illustrates, 26 percent of the American electorate were WEBACs and 35 percent of white voters nationwide identified themselves as evangelical or born-again Christians. Only 24 percent of all WEBACs voted for Barack Obama, while 62 percent of all other voters cast a Democratic ballot in the presidential race. In the South, only one state, Florida, a state only geographically southern, had a WEBAC electorate below that of the nation as a whole. The only other southern state close to the national percentage in WEBACs was Virginia. It is almost certainly no accident that Florida and Virginia were two of the three southern states won by Obama. Most other southern states are well above the national average in their WEBAC percent of the electorate and the percentage of white voters who consider themselves evangelical or born-again Christians. While issues such as abortion and gay rights were not as prominent in the 2008 election as in 2004, the strong WEBAC support for John McCain indicates that conservative religious belief among white protestants is a strong predictor of Republican voting behavior and a factor that bodes well for Republican prospects in future southern elections.

In future presidential elections, the South will likely continue to be the Republican's strongest region of the country. The very large number of WEBACs, racially polarized electorates in some states, and low educational levels should benefit the Republicans in many parts of the South. Democrats should be competitive, as they were in 2008, in states with higher educational levels and growing Latino populations. In-migration may make some southern states decidedly less southern. Florida is a southern state in geography only and, as the Washington

Table 6.8 White evangelical or born-again voters

	WEBAC %	WEBAC % of white voters	WEBAC % for Obama	% of all non-WEBACS for Obama
National	26	35	24	62
Alabama	47	72	8	64
Arkansas	56	67	20	64
Florida	24	34	21	61
Georgia	37	57	10	67
Kentucky	45	53	25	57
Louisiana	32	49	6	54
Mississippi	46	74	6	75
North Carolina	44	61	25	68
Oklahoma	53	63	21	52
South Carolina	40	56	15	64
Tennessee	52	62	22	62
Texas	33	52	16	57
Virginia	28	40	20	64

Source: http://www.cnn.com/ELECTION/2008/ accessed May 12, 2009.

Note: WEBACs is an acronym for White Evangelical or Born Again Christians.

suburbs south of the Potomac River grow and become more Democratic, Virginia is the southern state beside Florida that is likely to be increasingly southern in name only. A population influx is also altering politics in North Carolina. (In addition to their success in the 2008 presidential election, Democrats gained three Senate seats and five House Seats in Virginia and North Carolina in 2006 and 2008.) Republicans may still have a considerable advantage but, in close elections, several dozen southern electoral votes will be fiercely contested.

Notes

1. Earl Black and Merle Black, *The Vital South: How Presidents Are Elected* (Cambridge, MA: Harvard University Press, 1992).
2. Texas was the only southern state that Humphrey won in the 1968 election.
3. The major historical work on Reconstruction is Eric Foner, *Reconstruction: America's Unfinished Revolution, 1863–1877* (New York: Harper and Row Publishers, 1988).
4. Jack Bloom, *Class, Race, and the Civil Rights Movement* (Bloomington, IN: Indiana University Press, 1987). Also see, Neil R. McMillen, *Dark Journey: Black Mississippians in the Age of Jim Crow* (Champaign-Urbana, IL: University of Illinois Press, 1990).
5. The legal and political mechanisms of black disfranchisement are discussed in a classic work by V. O. Key first published in 1949, *Southern Politics in State and Nation* (New York: Random House, 2000).
6. Dewey Grantham, *The Life and Death of the Solid South: A Political History* (Lexington, KY: University of Kentucky Press, 1992).
7. Key, *Southern Politics in State and Nation.*
8. Grantham, *The Life and Death of the Solid South*. Also, Earl Black and Merle Black, *Politics and Society in the South* (Cambridge, MA: Harvard University Press, 1987).
9. Ibid.
10. Harvard Sitkoff, *A New Deal for Blacks; The Emergence of Civil Rights as a Political Issue in the Depression Decade* (New York: Oxford University Press, 1981).
11. Kevin J. McMahon, *Reconsidering Roosevelt on Race: How the Presidency Paved the Road to Brown* (Chicago, IL: The University of Chicago Press, 2004).
12. Alan Brinkley, "The New Deal and Southern Politics," in James C. Cobb and Michael Namorato, eds., *The New Deal and the South* (Jackson, MS: University of Mississippi Press, 1984).
13. Black and Black, *The Vital South.*
14. Ibid., p. 144.
15. Robert A. Caro, *The Years of Lyndon Johnson: Master of the Senate* (New York: Vintage Books, 2002), p. 194.
16. Taylor Branch, *Parting the Waters: America in the King Years* (New York: Simon and Schuster, 1988).
17. Black and Black, *The Vital South.*
18. Black and Black, *Politics and Society in the South.*
19. Theodore White, *Making of the President, 1964* (New York: New American Library, 1964).
20. Dan T. Carter, *The Politics of Rage: George Wallace, the Origins of the New Conservatism, and the Transformation of American Politics* (Baton Rouge: Louisiana State University Press, 2000).
21. Ibid.

22. Theodore White, *The Making of the President, 1968* (New York: Atheneum, 1969).

23. Black and Black, *The Vital South*.

24. Ibid.

25. Nelson W. Polsby, *The Consequences of Party Reform* (New York: Oxford University Press, 1983). Nicol C. Rae, "The Democrats' Southern Problem in Presidential Politics," *Presidential Studies Quarterly* 22 (1992): 135–152.

26. Donald W. Beachler, "The South and the Democratic Presidential Nomination, 1972–1992," *Presidential Studies Quarterly* 26 (1996): 402–414.

27. Earl Black and Merle Black, *The Rise of the Southern Republicans* (Cambridge, MA: Harvard University Press, 2002), p. 213.

28. Ibid., and Dan T. Carter, *From George Wallace to Newt Gingrich: Race in the Conservative Counterrevolution, 1963–1994* (Baton Rouge: Louisiana State University Press, 1999).

29. Jim Rutenberg, "Kerry, in Show of Confidence Plans $18 Million Ad Push," *The New York Times*, May 29, 2004, p. A11.

30. Thomas F. Schaller, *Whistling Past Dixie: How Democrats Can Win without Dixie* (New York: Simon and Schuster, 2008).

31. Steve Jarding and David "Mudcat" Saunders, *Foxes in the Henhouse: How the Republicans Stole the South and the Heartland and What Democrats Must Do to Run 'em Out* (New York: Touchstone, 2006).

32. The 2000 presidential election in Florida is analyzed in Steven C. Stauber and William C. Hulbarry, "Florida: Too Close to Call," in Robert P. Steed and Laurence Moreland, eds., *The 2000 Presidential Election in the South: Partisanship and Southern Party Systems in the 21st Century* (Westport, CT: Praeger, 2002).

33. Jeffrey Toobin, *Too Close to Call: The 36 Day Battle that Decided the 2000 Election* (New York: Random House, 2002).

34. Mark Stern, "Florida," in Laurence W. Moreland, Robert P. Steed, and Tod A. Baker, eds., *The 1984 Presidential Election in the South: Patterns of Southern Party Politics* (New York: Praeger, 1986). Also, William Hulbarry, Anne Kelly, Lewis Bowman, "Florida: The Republican Surge Continues," in Robert P. Steed, Laurence W. Moreland, and Tod A. Baker, eds., *The 1988 Presidential Elections in the South: Continuity amidst Party Change* (New York: Praeger, 1991).

35. The 1996 Election in Florida is analyzed in Kathryn Dunn Tenpas, William E. Hulbarry, and Lewis Bowman, "Florida: An Election with Something for Everyone," in Laurence W. Moreland and Robert P. Steed, eds., *The 1996 Presidential Election in the South Southern Party Politics in the 1990s* (Westport, CT: Praeger, 1997).

36. The evolution of presidential politics in Florida from the 1970s through the 1990s is discussed in Donald W. Beachler, "The Clinton Breakthrough? Presidential Politics in Florida," *Political Chronicle* 11 (Spring 1999): 1–12.

37. Michael Barone and Grant Ujifusa, *The Almanac of American Politics, 2004* (Washington, DC: The National Journal, 2004).

38. Susan Milligan, "New U.S. Travel Restrictions Irk Some Anti-Castro Cubans," *Boston Globe*, July 4, 2004.

39. Beth Reinhard, "For Obama, Florida Still Counts," *Miami Herald*, October 18, 2008; miamiherald.com.

40. Much of Osceola County is part of the greater Orlando area.

41. Casey Woods, "Obama First Democrat to Win Florida's Hispanic Vote," *Miami Herald*, November 6, 2008; miamiherald.com.

42. Michael Barone and Grant Ujifusa, *The Almanac of American Politics, 2008* (Washington, DC: The National Journal, 2007).

43. Jim Galloway and Aaron Goula Sheinin, "Obama to Trim Staff in Georgia," *Atlanta Journal-Constitution*, September 10, 2008.
44. Early Voting Statistics are available at http://elections.gmu.edu/early_vote_2008.html.
45. Shaila Dewan and Robbie Brown, "Black Turnout May Hold the Key," *The New York Times*, November 2, 2008.
46. Chuck Todd and Sheldon Gawiser argue that because black turnout was 30% of the electorate, the Democrats' potential in Georgia might have reached its peak of 30% in 2008. Chuck Todd and Sheldon Gawiser, *How Barack Obama Won: A State by State Guide to the Historic 2008 Presidential Election* (New York: Vintage, 2009).
47. Jeff Zeleny, "Obama Plans a Four Day Hunt for More Democratic Votes," *The New York Times*, October 31, 2008.
48. The education figures are from the 2000 census; see Barone and Ujifusa, *The Almanac of American Politics,* 2008.
49. Julia Preston, "In Big Shift Latino Vote Was Heavily for Obama," *The New York Times*, November 7, 2008.
50. A 31% win among five% of the electorate nets a candidate 1.65% advantage in the statewide popular vote.
51. A 37% win among five% of the electorate provides a candidate a net advantage of 1.85% of the statewide popular vote.
52. Duke won 44% of the vote for the U.S. Senate in 1990 and 39% of the vote when he ran for governor in 2007.
53. Stephen Ohlemacher, "Obama's Victory May Show the Way to Win in the Future," *Associated Press*, November 9, 2008.
54. Ron Jenkins, "As Nation Went Blue, Oklahoma Applied an Extra Coat of Red," *The Washington Post*, November 9, 2008, p. A18.
55. Adam Nossiter, "For South, a Waning Hold on Politics," *The New York Times*, November 11, 2008, p. A1.
56. Ibid.

7

The Midwest

Middle America's Margins

David M. Rankin

As the 2004 presidential election drew to a close, electoral pundits and strategists were transfixed on the state of Ohio. Early exit polls had indicated that John Kerry might actually come out ahead in the Buckeye state and with it the 20 electoral votes that would determine the Electoral College margin. In the end, Ohio would eventually swing by three points to George W. Bush at the center of the most competitive region in the country in which Ohio and the Midwest mirrored the three-point national popular vote margin that gave President Bush a second term.

Election night 2008 would be far from the suspenseful election night of 2004 and light years from 2000, but Ohio would still serve as a critical barometer for the evening's count. After all, no Republican has ever won the presidency without Ohio and only two Democrats since 1892. Thus when early results indicated Ohio was going to Obama, Bob Schieffer of CBS News summed up what most analysts already knew, that without Ohio he could not see McCain winning. Even Republican operative Karl Rove now working as an electoral analyst for Fox News admitted that without Ohio there was no chance for a McCain-Palin victory.

With Ohio as the center, the Obama and McCain campaigns focused a great deal of time and resources on upper Midwest states.[1] The region provided for not only the margin of victory in 2004 but also had six of the most competitive states nationwide in that election. Among such states recently had been Minnesota, once a Democratic stronghold in the region, but a very close race in 2000 and 2004. With electoral designs on the region, Republicans held the national nominating convention in Minneapolis-St. Paul. However, before John McCain could even accept his party's nomination the Obama-Biden ticket had already kicked off the general election with a barnstorming bus tour in the Midwest the day after the Democratic Convention, with multiple stops over two days in Ohio and Michigan.

Recent history demonstrated that the road to the White House winds through upper Midwest battleground states and both parties looked to launch and end their campaigns close to the Great Lakes. Beyond campaign strategy, the story of Barack Obama and this transformative moment evoked thoughts of the nation's first Republican president, Abraham Lincoln. A century and a half later, the "land of Lincoln" stretched more favorably into Democratic terrain with Obama handily winning Illinois and substantially increasing margins across what had been competitive Midwest states in recent elections. Obama topped it off with one of the biggest Election Night surprises, an Electoral College win for Democrats in Indiana for the first time since 1964.

A Grand Old Entrance Out of the Midwest

The rocketing electoral fortune of Illinois' Barack Obama from what has become one of the most solid Democratic states is a cruel irony in the historical development of the Grand Old Party (GOP). After all, the national Republican Party emerged out of Illinois and the Midwest region with Abraham Lincoln's surprising *and* monumental victory in the critical election of 1860.[2] But the election of Lincoln, a candidate sympathetic to the abolition of slavery, was the final breaking point between Northern and Southern states leading to Civil War, 1861–1865. For the ensuing 100 years, the Republican Party would be associated with more urban industrial interests of the rapidly developing upper Midwest and Northeast while Democrats were the party of the South and more agrarian-based states.

After the impeachment and near removal of Lincoln's successor, the Unionist Andrew Johnson of Tennessee, the United States elected three straight Republican presidents from Ohio: Ulysses S. Grant for two terms (1869–1877), Rutherford B. Hayes (1877–1881), and James Garfield elected in 1881 and assassinated shortly thereafter. Republican Benjamin Harrison of the neighboring Great Lake state of Indiana was elected in 1888, and three more Republican candidates from Ohio, William McKinley (1897–1901), William Taft (1909–1913), and Warren Harding (1921–1923) were also elected. With the exception of Chester Arthur, who took over for Garfield and served out the term until 1885, Theodore Roosevelt of New York (1901–1909) was the only Republican from outside the upper Midwest elected president until Calvin Coolidge from Massachusetts (1923–1929).

The only successful Democratic candidates elected president during the period, 1860–1928, were Grover Cleveland of New York (1884 and 1892) and Woodrow Wilson from New Jersey (1912 and 1916). Still, it was the upper Midwest that would become a significant piece of New York native Franklin Delano Roosevelt's Democratic New Deal Coalition that in the critical election of 1932 shattered the long-running Republican advantage in the Electoral College.[3] Under Roosevelt's leadership, the Democrats became strongly associated with the labor union movement increasing in conjunction with the rapidly growing industrial base of the Great Lakes and Midwestern river-ways.[4] After

FDR's death following four straight electoral victories (1932–1944) a Democrat won from the central region of the Midwest for the first time, when FDR's successor Harry Truman of Missouri secured a narrow electoral victory. However, President Truman's 1948 decision to integrate the armed forces set off permanent fissures in the southern base of the Democratic Party, leading to the Dixiecrat challenge of former South Carolina Democrat Strom Thurmond in the 1948 election.

The Democratic Party still relied on Midwest working-class whites, Catholics, urban liberals, and African-Americans moving from the South to work in industrial cities from Detroit to Cleveland.[5] And the local party machine under Democratic Chicago Mayor Richard Daley peaked during the presidential elections of the 1960s. In the close 1960 election between Richard Nixon and John Kennedy, many Republican loyalists believed that Daley had somehow improperly helped deliver the critical votes in Illinois in favor of Kennedy, not unlike accusations later leveled by embittered Democratic activists in Florida in 2000 and Ohio in 2004.

Civil Rights, Conflict, and Chicago

After taking the oath as president after Kennedy's assassination in November 1963, Texan Lyndon B. Johnson (LBJ) garnered 61 percent of the popular vote over Arizona Republican Senator Barry Goldwater in the 1964 election. An immediate objective of President Johnson was to press for congressional passage of the 1964 Civil Rights Act and the 1965 Voting Rights Act initiated in the final stages of the Kennedy administration and an outgrowth of the civil rights movement. These actions succeeded in putting the black vote firmly into the Democratic column as the African-American population became an increasingly larger component of the urban population throughout the Great Lake states and Missouri. On the other hand, these Democratic administration federal directives not only alienated the formerly Democratic and states-rights oriented southern white base, it fractured the once solidly Democratic blue-collar white vote in the Midwest.

In 1964, LBJ swept the Midwest, including all of the states that helped Nixon run such a close race in 1960. Johnson won in the industrial upper Midwest and across the Central Plains. But he would be the last Democratic presidential candidate to win Kansas, Nebraska, and the Dakotas, and, until Obama's narrow win, Indiana. The Johnson administration's handling of the Vietnam War and his personal decision to not seek the presidency in 1968 fractured his own gains in Great Lake states. The Democratic Party had split over policy in Vietnam and primary challengers New York Senator Robert Kennedy, before his assassination upon winning the 1968 California primary, and Minnesota Senator Eugene McCarthy, were roundly criticizing the Johnson administration and gaining significant support among the antiwar movement. When former Minnesota Senator and LBJ's Vice President Hubert Humphrey accepted the nomination at the 1968 Democratic Convention in Chicago, the tense standoff between police and antiwar protesters exploded on national television.

The 1968 Republican candidate, Richard Nixon, capitalized on broadcast images of Mayor Daley's Chicago police scuffling with protesters. Nixon seized the moment to call upon America's "silent majority" fed up with the nation's violent division, presumably a failing of the incumbent Democratic administration, to elect him for a return to traditional Midwestern-style values, law, and order. Nixon's electoral strategy relied extensively on winning in the Midwest region.[6]

Humphrey lost narrowly, largely because of voter backlash to the Chicago convention riots. In 1972, Senator George McGovern, who was a vocal critic of the Vietnam War, lost in a landslide to Nixon. Nixon swept the entire Midwest region in 1972, including McGovern's home state of South Dakota. Despite the fact that Humphrey was the vice president during the military escalation of the war in Vietnam, and McGovern was a decorated World War II veteran, Democrats were increasingly labeled as the weaker party on defense. This began to resonate among white working-class men in the Midwest who increasingly perceived Republicans as the "tougher" party on military matters and national security. Many of these white working-class voters increasingly viewed the Democrats as less a party of their Midwest values and interests and a party more concerned with civil rights, minorities, and liberal elite.[7]

Ironically, it was the overzealous actions of the Committee to Re-Elect the President (CREEP) that led to Nixon's resignation in 1974 as a result of the 1972 Watergate break-in at the offices of the Democratic National Committee, ensuing cover-up and crisis, which reopened an opportunity for Democrats in the Midwest. For a region that birthed the Republican Party and was home to so many of its presidents, it took nearly fifty years and the resignation of a president until the next and only other Republican president was to come from the upper Midwest, Gerald Ford of Michigan.

Former House Leader Ford presided over a Republican congressional delegation consisting heavily of Midwesterners before he replaced Nixon's Vice President Spiro Agnew in 1973. And Ford might have won the White House in 1976 had he not pardoned Nixon for the Watergate crimes, thereby losing narrowly to Georgia upstart Jimmy Carter. Ford lost the presidency but won many states that Nixon charted out as part of a Midwest strategy. Carter captured Wisconsin, Missouri, and Ohio, states won by Nixon in 1968 and 1972, as well as Minnesota, which Nixon won in 1972 but not in 1968. Ford held Illinois, Iowa, and his home state of Michigan, and also won the plains states that Nixon won every time he ran for president in 1960, 1968, and 1972.

Carter conveyed a populist image on the 1976 campaign trail, with born-again Christian faith and his peanut farm, despite the fact that he was trained as a nuclear engineer at Annapolis. A "down home" campaigning style and persona appeared to resonate with Midwestern voters, particularly the increasingly volatile voting bloc of white working-class voters, once firmly in the New Deal coalition, now up for grabs.[8] These voters were faced with multiple challenges and concerns as once secure jobs of the industrial base were dwindling based on domestic economic transition and foreign competition. Whole towns and cities were threatened throughout a Midwest region that relied extensively on industries that simply could no longer compete and exist, or had to dramatically scale back local production and workforce.

Collaring the Reagan Democrat in the Industrial Midwest

A feeling of helplessness in the once proud industrial base of America was amplified by the energy shortage, Iranian hostage crisis, and the Soviet invasion of Afghanistan all occurring on President Carter's watch. Thus, when one-time New Deal Democrat, former movie actor and California Republican Governor Ronald Reagan rode in from the mythical Wild West, his symbolic message to "restore American pride" and take down the Soviet "Evil Empire" resonated with this new bloc of swing voters.

The Democratic New Deal coalition had been successful because of the significant inroads among the working-class population in the upper Midwest into the 1960s, but Nixon had a strategy to bring the industrial Midwest back into the Republican fold.[9] This strategy would be mastered in 1980 and 1984 with the emergence of swing voters who came to be known as "Reagan Democrats," including white working-class Midwesterners who had since abandoned the dwindling New Deal Coalition to help Reagan secure the White House for two terms.[10]

Whether intentional or not, race was a defining feature that split critical elements of the white vote from the New Deal coalition leading Midwestern white voters to align themselves increasingly with the Republican ticket and Midwestern black voters to almost uniformly vote Democratic.[11] Class, long the mainstay of division between voting Republican or Democratic in the Midwest, became less relevant for voters than did race.[12] Working-class whites in the Midwest became increasingly likely to support Republican presidential candidates, with white males emerging as the most dependable Republican bloc.[13]

The emerging gender gap, on the other hand, opened up a new opportunity for Democrats to win back upper Midwest states. While Democrats were only able to win Vice President Walter Mondale's home state of Minnesota during Reagan's sweep of the Midwest in 1980 and 1984, the 1988 Democratic candidate Michael Dukakis won Iowa and Wisconsin. It marked the first time that a Democratic candidate had won Iowa since 1964 and only the second time a Democrat won Wisconsin since the LBJ landslide, and Iowa and Wisconsin supported Nixon in 1960. The 1988 victory in Iowa and Wisconsin would mark a turning point in favor of Democratic success within the two formerly solid Republican states, by relying increasingly on women, the college-educated, unmarried, and urban residents.[14]

Many college-educated, single, and urban women, in particular, were increasingly drawn to the Democratic presidential candidacies in part because of a more vocal Republican Party stance on the pro-life side of the divisive abortion issue. Conversely, noncollege graduates, lower-income, and rural residents focused less on economic issues while considering more of the social implications of their vote for president and party. Values of morality to patriotism competed with economic platforms, and at times "values trumped issues" in Midwest minds.[15]

The values debate became intertwined with religious belief and practice in electoral politics.[16] With Reagan's strategic embrace of Jerry Falwell's "Moral Majority" the Republican Party was becoming a party for the religious conservative, and many such newly engaged voters resided in the rural Midwest. In 1988, the Bush-Quayle campaign continued Republican domination of the Great Plains states while holding Illinois, Michigan, Missouri, and Ohio, despite the fact that these states had been hit hard over the 1980s with job loss and economic downturn.[17]

In 1980, Reagan focused on what he considered the failings of the Democratic incumbent administration asking voters, "Are you better off now than you were four years ago?" In 1992, Democratic candidate Bill Clinton would use similar tactics when he sought to win back the very voters Reagan had successfully moved from the traditional Midwestern Democratic base, reminding "Reagan Democrats" of the job loss and economic hardship of the region during the Reagan/Bush years. While 1992 Clinton campaign lore focuses on the "war room" in Little Rock, Arkansas, a centerpiece of Clinton's electoral strategy hinged on Stanley Greenberg's polling and focus groups in Macomb County, Michigan.[18]

Macomb County resembled many counties across the industrial Midwest and helped the Clinton campaign to win back many blue-collar "Reagan Democrats" through campaign appeals to the economic and health care needs of the working- and middle class. According to Greenberg, these voters were feeling squeezed by the conservative economic policies of the Republican Party and neglected by the liberal social policies of Democrats. Clinton turned electoral attention to the domestic and economic concerns of the white working class while also relying on groups that were a firm new part of the Democratic base, including college-educated women, minorities, singles, and urban residents.

Clinton's Midwest strategy was successful, winning back Missouri and Ohio for the first time since 1976, Michigan for the first time since 1968, Iowa and Illinois for the first time since 1964. Clinton effectively swept the Great Lakes states with the exception of Indiana, an electoral feat he would duplicate in 1996 over Kansas Senator Bob Dole. Thus, it was perfectly symbolic for the 1996 Democratic Convention to return to Chicago for the first time since the 1968 party implosion in order to celebrate Clinton's impending reelection, the first Democrat reelected since FDR. Illinois, the launching pad of the Republican Party by Abraham Lincoln, was solidly Republican from the 1968 through the 1988 presidential elections. However, starting with the 1992 presidential election, Illinois would become the most dependable Democratic state in the Midwest.

Shifting Suburbs across Urban and Rural Terrain

The presumed 2008 Democratic presidential nominee, Senator Hillary Clinton, had been raised in a Republican household in the Chicago suburbs before moving on to Wellesley and Washington but would eventually lose the nomination to Barack Obama, who got his start in Chicago politics as a community organizer before serving Illinois as a State and U.S. senator. Both candidates claimed

Midwestern ties as to why they were best suited to win swing states in a region with unique urban and rural balance. But there was little balancing act as Obama spoke to the enthusiastic throngs gathered in Grant Park in downtown Chicago on the occasion of his victory speech on election night. It was a scene that symbolized how far America and Chicago had come since 1968 when divisive riots nationwide followed Martin Luther King's assassination and young protesters battled police during the Democratic Convention in the very same park. The chant developed in 1968s Grant Park that "the whole world is watching" echoed 40 years later when Chicago welcomed the first African-American president elected in the nation's history.

Illinois took longer to shift from Republican to Democrat than did a young Hillary Rodham, but by 2008 when Illinois voted by 25 points and Chicago by a 72-point margin (86–14) for Obama, the state had moved firmly Democratic. While Chicago may have been excited by the prospect of one of its residents occupying the White House, Obama's margin in the Windy City was about the same as that for John Kerry in 2004. Illinois has become a Democratic foothold in the Midwest not so much because of changes across the region or even as part of the 2008 election but as an electoral outgrowth of an expanding, diverse metropolitan area along Lake Michigan increasingly spilling into surrounding suburbs.

It has largely been an electoral game of rural versus urban population math when it comes to winning in the upper Midwest. For example, Bush lost the state of Illinois to Gore by 10 points in 2000 and Kerry by 12 points in 2004 despite winning by solid margins in central and southern Illinois. Gary, Indiana, a predominantly industrial city with a sizable African-American population, voted solidly for the 2000 and 2004 Democratic candidates despite the fact that Democrats lost the state of Indiana by double-digit margins to George W. Bush. Political geography is critical to understanding this electoral dynamic. As the Indiana *and* Illinois state maps shift south and decidedly more rural toward the Kentucky border, the terrain becomes decidedly more Republican.

Across the Mississippi River from southwestern Illinois is the city of St. Louis from which rises the Gateway Arch. The arch, at one time the symbolic division of the American East and West, could today serve to signify the arching divide between urban and rural America, between the industrial heartland and the Great Plains. Missouri was a state that Clinton won twice, but Gore lost by three points and Kerry by seven. Neither Gore nor Kerry lost based on the urban area surrounding the arch but on the vote outside of St. Louis as well as Kansas City. As the map extends to western borders of Missouri, it is approaching the geographic midpoint of the United States and epicenter of Republican strength in the Electoral College (see table 7.1).

Certain Great Lake states remain competitive for Republicans and Democrats because they consist of significant metropolitan areas and rural communities, college towns and farming towns, industry and agriculture, highly paid professionals and blue-collar, career women and stay-at-home moms, churchgoers and non-churchgoers, substantial white and black populations, all of which fuel a division over government policies, social and economic viewpoints.[19] However, there are Midwest rural states in which few of these distinctions are prominent,

Table 7.1 Electoral College partisan trends in the Midwest Region, 1968–2008

	68	72	76	80	84	88	92	96	00	04	08	00+	04+	08+
Rural Red												+26	+28	+12
Kansas	R	R	R	R	R	R	R	R	R	R	R	21	26	15
Nebraska	R	R	R	R	R	R	R	R	R	R	R	29	35	15
North Dakota	R	R	R	R	R	R	R	R	R	R	R	28	27	8
South Dakota	R	R	R	R	R	R	R	R	R	R	R	23	22	8
Rust Purple														
Indiana	R	R	R	R	R	R	R	R	R	R	D	15	21	1
Lake Blue														
Illinois	R	R	R	R	R	R	D	D	D	D	D	12	10	25
Shading Blue												+2	+2	+13
Michigan	D	R	R	R	R	R	D	D	D	D	D	5	3	16
Minnesota	D	R	D	D	D	D	D	D	D	D	D	2	4	10
Wisconsin	R	R	R	R	R	D	D	D	D	D	D	0.2	0.4	14
Battleground												+2	+3	+5
Iowa	R	R	R	R	R	D	D	D	D	R	D	0.3	1	9
Missouri	R	R	D	R	R	R	D	R	R	R	R	3	7	0.1
Ohio	R	R	D	R	R	R	D	D	R	R	D	4	2	4

Source: Table compiled by author.

Note: The 00+, 04+, and 08+ columns calculate the popular vote margin for each state and the average popular vote margin for solid red, solid blue, and the closer battleground states. For example, George W. Bush won Indiana by a 21-point popular vote margin in 2004 and Barack Obama with a 1-point margin in 2008. The average red state popular vote margin was 28 points in 2004 and 12 points in the 2008 election. Additional percentage points < 0.5 are rounded down (e.g., 2.4% = 2%) and additional percentage points > 0.5 are rounded up (e.g., 15.6% = 16%) unless the overall percentage of the state popular vote is less than 1 (e.g., 0.1%, 0.9%).

populations are predominantly rural, religious, older, married, and white, and these states have voted Republican for president without exception since 1968.

Despite Clinton's success in winning back the industrial Midwest, Kansas, Nebraska, and the Dakotas have voted Republican in every presidential election since 1968. Gore and Kerry lost by 27 points on average across the states. There is an entrenched Republican culture in these states not unlike the one-time southern embrace of the Democrats. In Kansas, the state's identity was forged in the Lincoln Republican tradition as free soil Jayhawks battled across the border with slave-holding Missourians.[20]

Kansan Dwight "Ike" Eisenhower was the only Great Plains native elected to the White House, in 1952 and 1956. While Ike made his military career and political residence outside Kansas, his election success signified fortunes ahead for Republicans in the breadbasket of America. When the longtime U.S. Senate leader from Kansas, Bob Dole, received the 1996 Republican nomination Kansas remained solidly "red" as did its neighboring Plains states. Heading into the twenty-first century, Kansas became an even more solid lock for Republicans in presidential elections. Kansans like Eisenhower and Dole have since disappeared from political life and a new breed of Midwesterners were jockeying for partisan control even in solidly Republican states. Electoral divisions extended beyond rural and urban to splintering suburban areas, increasingly divided into an inner and outer suburban ring from Plains states into the upper Midwest.

Suburban Impact

With the red-blue divide of recent elections much Republican success was placed on mobilizing rural voters and hoping for lower urban turnout (and vice versa for Democrats), which certainly has been important, but the electoral balance has increasingly relied on shifting suburbs sprawling across the upper Midwest. In the 2000 exit poll, Bush narrowly won the Midwest 49–48 percent in which Midwest suburbs voted 49–47 percent for Bush. Bush won the 2004 Midwest suburban vote 55–45 percent, significantly increasing his national popular vote. As Democrats were building (and relying) on large urban numbers, Democratic margins were increasingly tied to suburban gains and losses. Despite difficult losses overall, 2004 provided indications of Democrats' competitiveness in upper Midwest suburbs. And in 2006 and 2008, Democrats rode some of these Midwest suburban gains to control of Congress and the presidency.

Eisenhower's 1952 win was the GOP's first national-suburban victory, the same year in which Republican Senator Robert Taft of Ohio declared, "The Democratic Party will never win another national election until it solves the problem of the suburbs." While the Democrats have won the White House since 1952, they had only won 50 percent or more of the suburban vote once (1964) until the 2008 election. Responding to such patterns, Charles Mahtesian wrote that "from the building of the first tract houses of Levittown to the rise of McMansion subdivisions, the Democratic Party has had a suburban blind spot," arguing that Democrats failed to "grasp the potency of issues" important to suburbia, "such as law and order, tax relief, personal responsibility, and the role of religion in public life."[21]

Yet by Democratic design or by demographic change the tendency for suburbanites to vote Republican declined, if not turned. Inner suburbs, those most closely adjoining central cities became more racially, culturally, and economically diverse and also more competitive.[22] Clinton made inroads in the older, close-in suburbs in part by reframing Democratic positions on race, class, and personal responsibility resonating in places such as suburban Detroit's Macomb County.[23]

Still, Republicans continued to find strength in newer, outer suburbs, or exurbs. Stanley Greenberg describes "Exurbia," composed in large part of displaced voters from the older cities, older inner suburbs, and rural areas within the Midwest, as "Republican loyalist territory."[24] One such example is Scott County, Minnesota, which increased rapidly in population by more than 50 percent during the 1990s. In 1996, Dole lost Scott County by six points, but Bush won the county in 2000 by 15 points.[25]

Mahtesian describes burgeoning exurbs with a "large number of young, white married couples with children…with McMansions, mega-churches, and big-box/big consumption lifestyle." In 2004, President Bush won 62 percent of the exurban and 57 percent of the emerging suburban vote, a total cast of 17.5 million votes in an election Bush won by 3 million. Some of the most important votes came in rapidly expanding suburbs around Cincinnati and Columbus, Ohio.[26] Kerry kept Ohio close by breaking even in the surrounding area of Cleveland, but lost the Ohio suburban vote by two points. And Bush had a significant rural advantage of at least 20 points in Ohio in 2000 and 2004.

The strategy, or necessity, of winning big in urban areas to offset rural *and* suburban losses provided little room for error for Democratic candidates. In 2004, Kerry won Michigan with an overwhelming urban advantage but Bush kept it close by winning rural and suburban Michigan, similar to what happened with Gore in 2000. Without huge margins in metropolitan areas, Democrats scraped by or lost Midwestern states. In Missouri, Kerry could not find enough urban votes to offset Bush's commanding lead among rural voters.[27] Although Kerry narrowly carried St. Louis suburbs, Bush won the overall Missouri suburbs in 2004 just as he had in 2000—increasing his edge in suburban Kansas City.

When Bush lost in the upper Midwest, he *actually* did poorer in the growing suburbs. In Minnesota, Bush won the rural and suburban vote but could not replicate 2002 Republican Senate candidate Norm Coleman's success in the fast-growing suburban-collar counties around the Twin Cities. Without running up totals there, Bush could not overcome Kerry's advantage in Minneapolis and St. Paul. Norman Ornstein of the American Enterprise Institute, speaking of Minnesota and the Twin Cities suburbs, noted, "[T]he old stereotypes about the suburbs, where middle-class whites have fled and become more conservative and Republican just isn't true anymore."[28]

In 1972, Nixon won Chicago and Cook County. But between 1970 and 1997, Chicago lost 60 percent of its manufacturing jobs, and in the 1990s Chicago became one of the leading areas for information technology. The metropolitan area now has twice as many professionals and technicians as production work-ers. In *The Emerging Democratic Majority*, John Judis and Ruy Teixeira argue that Democrats are countering Republicans through the emergence of the "ideo-polis," described as metropolitan, postindustrial regions growing at more than twice the rate as the rest of the country. Ideopolises develop around information technology, entertainment and media, major universities or research centers, concentrations of professionals and technicians, immigrant and ethnic diversity, artistic and gay communities, which includes Chicago's Cook County.[29]

Dane County, home to the University of Wisconsin, Madison, and the fastest-growing county in the state, relies heavily on biomedical research and went for Gore in 2000 by nearly 30 points. Upscale suburban Oakland County, recording the largest Michigan county growth in the 1990s and home to the high-tech sec-tor of the auto industry, voted overwhelmingly Republican in the 1980s, but has turned Democratic.[30] Judis and Teixeira claim, "The New Deal coalition of the Upper Midwest, once dominated by blue-collar workers and small farmers, now includes a large contingent of professionals, and Democratic success in these coun-ties signaled the diminution of race as a divisive factor and the re-identification of the Democrats as the party of prosperity among these voters."[31]

The Republican Party has countered with a persistent program of tax cuts, strong defense, and social conservatism that reaches rural and suburban, upper- and lower-income whites. In 2004, *Washington Post* writer Mike Allen noted, "Minnesota and Wisconsin have been trending Republican and strategists believe that they can turn them by targeting suburbs, along with rural areas that used to be solidly Democratic, with promises of a muscular foreign policy, preservation of traditional values and lower taxes." But in the upper Midwest suburbs, Bob von Sternberg of the *Minneapolis Star Tribune* pointed out that "Republicans' low tax message and social conservatism doesn't necessarily play well with all parts of that changing population. Many suburbs are struggling with the effects of sprawl and aging public infrastructure that Democrats are more likely to address with calls for increased government spending." Mark Kirk, a Republican representa-tive from the North Shore suburbs of Chicago and a member of the Suburban Agenda Caucus warned, "[S]uburban voters are less focused on culture war issues like same-sex marriage and abortion than on safety, education and environmen-tal protection."[32] And Kirk's district had changed dramatically, from 62 percent for George H. W. Bush in 1988 to 53 percent for Kerry in 2004.

Illinois, which voted consistently Republican for president until 1992 has not voted Republican since and suburban shifts look to make that even less likely into the near future. In 2004, a *Chicago Daily Herald* analysis of presi-dential voting patterns throughout the suburbs found that over five presiden-tial elections once-solidly Republican suburbs had swung their support to the Democratic candidate by 15 points while not one suburban township has grown more Republican.[33] George H. W. Bush won with healthy margins in suburban Cook, Kane, Lake, and DuPage counties and, though George W. Bush won every suburban county except Cook, the margin had shrunk considerably.

Population and attitude shifts made traditionally Republican suburban dis-tricts such as DuPage competitive, with younger voters more liberal on social issues from gay rights to stem cell transplants. With the city and downstate more locked up for either party, Dick Simpson argues in the *Chicago Sun Times* that "the balance of power in the state and the nation depends on the suburban vote" and "one might speculate, as DuPage goes, so goes the country."[34] *In 2008 Obama won DuPage 55–44 percent, reversing a 54–45 margin for President Bush.*

Bellwether Region?

The 2004 Midwest exit poll mirrored the 51–48 national popular vote margin for President Bush with close contests in six states. In 2008 the Midwest exit poll showed a 54–44 margin for Obama, still the closest to the national popular vote difference of seven points but a greater discrepancy than in 2004. Ohio lived up to its billing as a bellwether but Missouri narrowly missed the presidential pick for the first time since 1956. Obama's Midwest margin grew higher with a significant surge in Democratic leaning states and smaller margins, if not losses in typically dependable Republican states. Obama also made inroads into the New South and New West, but solidified a significant national margin by sweeping the upper Midwest.

For 40 years "rural red" Midwestern Plains states have voted by large margins for Republican presidential candidates, and until 2008 Indiana voted with them. As for the seven other Midwest states won by both parties since 1968, they have played a key part in close elections when they are not swept up in a national landslide (see table 7.2). For 20 years following the fractious 1968 Democratic Convention Illinois and Iowa voted Republican and, except for Minnesota, the other upper Midwest states voted overwhelmingly Republican. In 1976 Carter battled to win Ohio, Missouri, and Wisconsin, otherwise Republicans were running up substantial Midwest margins in these states and in the overall electoral count. With little success in the Great Plains and Deep South, a sweep of these seven Midwest states provided Clinton with nearly half of what turned out to be a substantial electoral margin in 1992 and 1996. With the Northeast increasingly locked up for Democrats and the South for Republicans, a close battle for six of these states in 2000 and 2004 made for election night nail-biters. Yet with southern and Great Plains locked up George W. Bush could lose the majority of competitive Midwestern states, so long as he held the bellwether states of Ohio and Missouri. Obama, on the other hand, became the *first* Democrat to win the election without Missouri by sweeping the upper Midwest, adding Indiana for good measure.

When Indiana fell to Obama, it confounded tidier red-blue depictions that painted the electoral map in 2000 and 2004, or for 40 Hoosier-red years in the case of Indiana. But in other ways, it made for a more geographically consistent regional victory based on trends and dynamics in neighboring Great Lakes states. Although margins were noticeably lower across the Central Plains in 2008, these rural red states still voted as they had for 40 years for the Republican ticket.

The composition of voters in rural red Midwestern states stack the odds heavily in a Republican candidate's favor, even when the national context cries

Table 7.2 Midwest margins in "competitive" states, 1968–2008

	68	72	76	80	84	88	92	96	00	04	08
National vote popular margin	0.7	23	2.1	10	18	8.5	5.5	8.5	-0.5	2.4	7
Illinois	3	19	-2	8	13	2	14	18	-12	-10	25
Ohio	2	21	0.3	11	19	11	2	6	4	2	5
Michigan	-7	14	-5	6	19	8	7	13	-5	-3	16
Missouri	1	24	4	7	21	4	10	6	3	7	-0.1
Wisconsin	4	10	2	5	9	-4	4	10	-0.2	-0.4	14
Minnesota	-13	5	13	-4	-0.2	-7	12	16	-2	-4	10
Iowa	12	17	-1	12	8	-10	6	10	-0.3	1	9
*Midwest margin electoral total**	*73*	*113*	*58*	*103*	*97*	*78*	*100*	*100*	*32*	*38*	*85*
National vote electoral margin	**110**	**503**	**57**	**440**	**512**	**315**	**202**	**220**	**5**	**35**	**192**
Electoral total	*301*	*520*	*297*	*489*	*525*	*426*	*370*	*379*	*271*	*286*	*365*
Party winner	**R**	**R**	**D**	**R**	**R**	**R**	**D**	**D**	**R**	**R**	**D**

Source: Table compiled by author.

Note: The table includes Midwest states won by both Republican and Democratic presidential candidates, 1968–2008. Popular vote margins are in bold for states won by the Electoral College winner. Popular voter margins are assigned a negative value for states lost by the Electoral College winner. * The total of electoral votes gathered across the seven Midwestern states for the Electoral College winner.

out for change and a "throw the bums out" kind of mood prevails. In *What's the Matter with Kansas?*, Thomas Frank explained that "one thing unites all different groups of Kansans, millionaires and trailer-park dwellers, farmers and thrift-store managers and slaughterhouse workers and utility executives, they are almost all Republicans."[35] While this may be a bit of a heartland exaggeration, the 2008 Kansas exit poll had a 49–26 percent advantage in Republican versus Democratic identifiers and as Frank points out such hyper-partisan allegiance may impede economic considerations when weighing which party to blame. In the same exit poll, 64 percent of Kansans thought the economy was the most important issue and voted for McCain in a state where disapproval of President Bush was at 63 percent. It may be that such Republicans are voting their interest for economic solutions they prefer enacted, which might explain why 57 percent of neighboring Nebraskans agreeing the economy was the most important issue voted by 15 points for McCain despite 61 percent disapproval for Bush.

As Frank notes, there are also noneconomic factors that drive support for Republicans in heartland states, including social issues and religion. In the 2008 exit poll, 41 percent of Kansas voters were white evangelicals and 92 percent of this group voted for McCain. Furthermore, while McCain managed a narrow one-point margin with the Kansas urban vote, he had a 36-point margin among rural voters, which made up 44 percent of voters compared with 36 percent considered urban.

Rural voters account for nearly half of the electorate in Midwest red states compared with about one-third of Midwest blue states. Red Midwest states have higher percentages of whites, married, religious, evangelicals, and Republican identifiers, all groups that voted in large numbers for President Bush and continued to support McCain. These social groups also supported the president's reelection in states that Kerry carried, albeit not by the same margins, but more importantly were offset by higher relative numbers of groups that favored the Democratic candidate—including blacks, unmarried, less religious, younger voters and Democratic identifiers.

Economic differences have had a limited impact in rural red-state voting, with Bush winning by substantial margins among lower- and higher-income groups. In the traditionally staunch Republican state of Indiana, President Bush had a 4-point margin with voters making less than $50,000 a year, winning those making $30,000–$50,000 by 12 points and by 4 points for the $15,000–$30,000 bracket. In 2008, a tipping point for Indiana might have been the differing impact of economic-class voting. Obama won the $15,000–$30,000 range of voters by 26 points, and had a 14-point advantage with Indiana voters earning less than $50,000 a year.[36] Negative economic perceptions arguably had as much to do with shifting the upper Midwest Democratic as any other issue in 2008; yet other social forces still emerged.

Plumbing for Votes in the Buckeye State

Republicans long appealed to more affluent voters in the Midwest and nationwide based on what was perceived as economic and tax policies more beneficial to this income bracket. In *Red State, Blue State, Rich State, Poor State*, the authors conducted a comprehensive statistical analysis to essentially reiterate the point that higher-income groups were still more likely to vote Republican regardless of region or state, red or blue.[37] And in states such as Ohio, Missouri, and Indiana 2008 exit polls show that higher-income groups did skew Republican, yet in the deepest blue state of Illinois this was not the case. In fact, a three-point margin for Kerry grew to nine for Obama among this affluent group. States such as Illinois may simply find Democratic solutions to the economy more appealing or other issues may override perceived higher-economic class benefits from Republican tax positions.

This is a real concern for Republicans, losing ground with a traditionally supportive bloc of higher-income voters, particularly in an upper Midwest region that has been among the most competitive in recent elections. And this extends to the type of college-educated professionals inhabiting metropolitan areas from Chicago to Columbus. While Democrats counted on noncollege-educated voters as part of a more traditional coalition (winning these Illinois voters by a 32-vote margin in 2008), the cultivation of college-educated voters (by 13 points in Illinois for Obama) makes for a challenging electoral coalition.

Turning higher-income, college-educated voters was a key part of Obama's success in upper Midwest battleground states. While losing Indiana college grads by nine points in 2008, it was a leap from the 42-point deficit for Kerry. And Obama won college graduates in Missouri by one point, 15 points higher than Kerry, narrowly losing the Show Me state. While Missouri just missed showing us the presidential winner, Ohio maintained its status as the nation's bellwether. Obama won Ohio by four points, where noncollege- and college graduates shifted Democratic.

Voter preferences and concerns in Ohio representing critical changes from the 2004 election demonstrate why Ohio remains an electoral barometer for the nation.[38] Ohio is a confluence of region, whether Pennsylvania on the eastern side, Kentucky on the southern side, and the Indiana heartland on its western border. The north of Ohio resembles the more urban centers of Detroit and Chicago while the southern reaches are more similar to the states it borders.

McCain and Obama poured time and money into the Buckeye state, but unlike 2004 when Republicans had a slight edge in ground mobilization Democrats were better funded to turn out the vote in 2008. African-American turnout helped Obama in Ohio and other Great Lakes states, but white voters were also less likely to support McCain than Bush. Swinging support among white voters helped Obama's surge in states such as Michigan and Wisconsin, with a 13-point increase among white men, and winning white women in these states by double digits. Despite losing the white female vote in Indiana by three points, Obama narrowed the margin from a 31-point deficit in 2004.

Obama increased Democratic margins in the urban vote by more than 20 points in states such as Michigan to a 67-point margin and Ohio to 41 points, but it was the suburban vote that helped turn states such as Ohio—winning back a group that Bush carried twice. The suburbs also swung from Bush to Obama in Michigan, Wisconsin, and Illinois. Obama narrowly lost the overall suburban vote in Missouri, but kept the state close by increasing Democratic margins in the St. Louis suburbs with a 55–44 percent win.[39] In the Twin City suburbs, surrounding the site of the 2008 Republican Convention, Obama prevailed by 30 points.

As Stan Greenberg had charted out for Clinton in 1992, success in suburban Oakland/Macomb County, Michigan, equaled victory in the nation. Bush won the county 51–47 in 2004 but it turned 55–43 for Obama. And Obama made inroads in what had been very strong Republican suburban areas in Central Ohio, reducing the deficit there from 18 in 2004 to 5 points and taking the lead in what had been an evenly divided Northeastern Ohio—a region with university towns, small cities, and rural areas. He was the first Democrat to win Hamilton County in 44 years, using a big turnout in Cincinnati, and also cut into the fast-growing and usually Republican-collar counties around Cincinnati.[40] Obama won big in the six urban counties, boosting a 30-point margin for Kerry in Cuyahoga County (with the city of Cleveland) to 47 points with 86 percent of the vote, matching his numbers in Chicago.

While Obama's historic candidacy helped mobilize and turnout critical voters the national climate also contributed to voter desire to hit the polls, particularly in Midwest states where the economy had taken a large toll. Even before the pleas of the big three Detroit automakers for a Washington bailout, economic concern was high in these manufacturing states.[41] For example, in 2004 59 percent of Michigan voters felt the state economy was not so good or poor, compared with 30 percent of South Dakota voters, and Michigan ended up swinging their vote against Bush. But by 2008 86 percent of even South Dakotans were very or somewhat worried about economic conditions, in a climate in which the economy would be far and away the number one issue for voters, and not in a positive way.

The economy was listed as the most important issue in 2008 by at least 60 percent of voters in all upper Midwest states, surging on average by 40 points from 2004 exit poll rankings. And whether voters directed more blame at McCain for stating the "fundamentals of the economy are still strong" in the face of such concern or whether what he really meant by fundamentals was the American worker, the issue clearly hurt the Republican more than it did Obama. In 2008, Ohio had one of the country's highest unemployment rates at 7.2 percent with tremendous foreclosure rates in many of its metro areas including Cleveland, Akron, Toledo, and Dayton, and Obama delivered what his campaign called his closing argument speech in Canton, an industrial city in northeastern Ohio. His focus remained on the economy, job creation, and the middle class, stating, "After 21 months and three debates, Senator McCain still has not been able to tell the American people a single major thing he'd do differently from George Bush when it comes to the economy."

Ohio was also home to Samuel Joseph Wurzelbacher, a Toledo resident who had questioned Obama at a campaign stop and was thrust into the national spotlight and *Saturday Night Live* parody after McCain referenced him as "Joe the Plumber" multiple times throughout the final presidential debate as a means to criticize Obama's tax plan. Like Joe Six-Pack, both parties were once again aiming for white blue-collar voters unsettled by hard economic times as well as foreign threats and challenges.

McCain's references to Joe the Plumber and his assurances that he was not another George W. Bush might have worked in states such as Missouri. Kerry had a 39-point advantage with those who felt the state economy was not so good, but McCain held a 21-point margin among Missouri voters who viewed the national economy as not so good. Despite importance attached to the economy alongside high levels of disapproval for President Bush, Obama only had a five-point advantage for those listing the economy as most important in states such as Missouri and Indiana. And of those who saw the national economy as "not so good" in these states, including Ohio, they sided heavily with McCain.

But it was the voters who saw the national economy as poor where Obama pulled huge margins over McCain. And in places such as Michigan, where 60 percent of respondents thought the economy was poor or in Ohio where it was 53 percent, it had more of an impact. Indiana was an important example of how the Republican presidential candidate had been punished for such negative economic perceptions. In 2004, 20 percent of Indianans viewed the state economy as poor and voted for Kerry by 20 points, but four years later 43 percent viewed the national economy as poor and supported Obama by 34 points (see table 7.3).

In 2004 negative economic perceptions were connected more directly to votes against President Bush and while the sheer level of economic angst hurt McCain, he kept it closer than might otherwise be expected based on other issue considerations.[42] Clinton won Ohio in 1992 and 1996 largely on an economic platform, yet Gore lost the state in part because of Clinton's success in making the economy a less concerning issue and his own personal conduct making values and personal character a more important concern. In 2004, the war on terrorism, the moral values issue, and anti-gay marriage amendments helped push Bush over the top in Missouri *and* Ohio.

While Obama had a five-point margin in Missouri for the 61 percent who thought the economy was most important, McCain had a 44-point advantage among the 34 percent who thought the "candidate shares my values." Whether the "candidate shares my values" question captured the same feelings that propelled moral values to the top issue of 2004 in many of these states, it was an issue that also helped the Republican candidacy, particularly in Missouri. Attempts had been made throughout the campaign to raise doubts about Barack Hussein Obama in that he had associated with "questionable" figures that may not share Middle America values. There was the brief uproar that followed Reverend Wright's post–9/11 sermon blasted across You Tube that suggested America had brought such attacks on itself, punctuated with inflammatory rants about America and its policies. There were the McCain and Palin questions concerning Obama's association with Weather Underground founder, Bill Ayers, who had been labeled a domestic terrorist by the FBI for his radical anti-Vietnam group, despite the fact Obama only intersected with Ayers as a middle-aged University of Illinois-Chicago Professor involved in local education projects.[43]

Although the issue importance attached to terrorism was lower in all states compared with 2004, Missouri was the only competitive Midwest state in which

Table 7.3   Demographic and issue impact in the Midwest

Democratic candidate margins in states	OH 04	OH 08	MO 04	MO 08	IN 04	IN 08	IL 04	IL 08
Demographics								
White men	−13	−8	−11	−16	−31	−16	−3	−7
White women	−10	−5	−19	−15	−31	−3	−2	11
18–29 year olds	14	25	3	20	−5	27	29	44
30–44 year olds	−5	4	−13	−1	−33	−5	5	33
45–64 year olds	−4	7	−7	−5	−13	−1	14	9
65+ year olds	−16	−11	4	13	−26	−26	−4	10
First-time voters	8	27	17	23	NA	35	NA	NA
$50,000 income	16	21	5	16	−4	14	21	49
> $50,000 income	−16	−3	−17	−11	−33	−8	4	11
> $100,000 income	−22	−16	−19	−8	−42	−9	3	9
No college degree	0	6	−3	−1	NA	2	NA	32
College graduate	−7	6	−14	1	NA	−3	NA	13
White evangelicals	−52	−44	−51	−41	−55	−39	NA	−26
Independents	19	8	−5	−6	−5	11	16	12
Moderates	18	23	9	23	2	21	17	35
Urban	17	41	39	34	−7	22	41	49
Suburban	−2	1	−4	−3	−30	−9	−1	5
Rural	−20	−11	−33	−19	−14	−11	−7	3
Evaluation and impact								
Disapprove of President	46	71	46	71	35	67	51	77
Vote impact	89	39	89	32	89	38	87	41
Disapprove of war in Iraq	40	64	43	NA	36	54	50	71
Vote impact	80	50	75	NA	61	58	77	59
Iraq War most important	13	11	17	11	15	11	21	9
Vote impact	44	22	49	22	37	22	51	NA
Terrorism most important	17	8	18	10	19	8	18	6
Vote impact	−80	−76	−74	−83	−82	−75	−68	NA
Health care important	5	10	4	9	4	9	5	8
Vote impact	50	31	66	32	NA	37	60	NA
Economy most important	24	61	23	61	17	60	20	68
Vote impact	66	9	67	5	33	5	72	31
Economy not good*	38	40	37	47	42	48	37	42
Vote impact	27	−25	39	−21	−12	−19	29	5
Economy poor*	19	53	8	44	11	43	10	50
Vote impact	80	38	72	38	20	34	49	49

Source: The table is compiled from 2004 and 2008 state exit polls for Ohio, Missouri, Indiana, and Illinois.

Note: For demographics, positive numbers in the columns reflect the percentage point margin of victory on the variable for Kerry and Obama. Negative numbers reflect the point margin for Bush and McCain. On evaluation, the numbers represent the percentage pertaining to the question and the vote impact is the percentage point margin for candidates based on the variable in the row above it. *In 2004 the exit poll question referred to the state economy and in 2008 to the national economy.

the vote impact on the terrorism issue was more favorable to the Republican candidate than as part of President Bush's reelection. However, by 2008 disapproval of Bush and the war in Iraq overwhelmed most ground McCain had on the issue of terrorism, as domestic issues favoring the Democratic candidate such as health care now challenged national security questions as pressing voter concerns.

Fertile Ground on Midwestern Soil

Scammon and Wattenberg described a "forty-seven year old housewife from the outskirts of Dayton, Ohio, whose husband is a machinist" as the proto-typical Democratic defector of the 1970s.[44] With crosscutting target voters that ranged from NASCAR Dads to Security Moms in 2004, Democrats and Republicans sought to close the gender gap in Ohio. Democrats sought to appeal to working-class male interests, including jobs and health care.[45] Republicans aimed for protective suburban mothers in the post–9/11 environment on issues of national security and the war on terrorism.[46] In 2008 the Midwestern white male vote, whether Joe Six Pack or Joe the Plumber, a key to Democratic and then Republican success in upper Midwest states, moved heavily to Obama-Biden with white women breaking in even higher numbers for the Democratic ticket.[47] Missouri was the only competitive Midwest state in which Obama lost ground among white men, a state in which he did not do much better among white women.[48]

Obama had crossed historic terrain in the Midwest and America since announcing his candidacy in Springfield, Illinois, and then propelling his bid for the nomination with a win in the Iowa caucus on January 3, 2008. The Iowa win not only dealt frontrunner Hillary Clinton a devastating early defeat, it also announced to white and black America that a biracial son of a white woman from Kansas and an African father named Barack Hussein Obama could win over white Midwestern voters.[49] And Obama followed up with a nine-point general election victory in Iowa, a state Kerry lost narrowly and Gore had barely won. Obama gained ground across all Midwest states, cutting into all 2000 and 2004 rural red state margins and increasing margins in the bluest states by double digits.

In the end there was just too much desire for change in most of these states, a dynamic that Obama tapped at the start of his campaign. From the Iowa cau-cuses where youth participation had surged from 2004 and largely for Obama, to Election Day in Iowa where Obama won 18–29-year-olds by 20 points (up from three points in 2004), the youth vote made it clear that they embraced Obama as the "Change We Need." College-age voters or recent college graduates had been a particular boon for the Kerry campaign in the upper Midwest with 18–29-year-olds giving Kerry a substantial margin despite the fact that Bush won all age groups by a large margin across the red states. Kerry can credit the youth vote with helping him win tight races in states with substantial college towns such as Minnesota, Michigan, and Wisconsin. But Obama's support among 18–29-year-olds dwarfed that for Kerry and also stretched into typically safe Republican states. Obama won the 18–29-year-old vote in Indiana by 27 points, a group that President Bush had won by 5 points. While losing all other age groups in South Dakota by at least 10 points, Obama won 18–29-year-olds by 2 points—a group Bush won by 12 points in 2004. And in three Midwest states that Kerry barely carried Obama won the 18–29-year-old vote by 32 points on average compared with a 15-point average margin in 2004, boosting the average margin of victory across these states by over 10 points.

Midwestern Mirrors

Despite Missouri's failure to deliver the presidential winner in 2008 Ohio and the Midwest region served notice that GOP losses would be widespread, a barometer of the national mood stretching back to the 2006 elections. Following the 2004 elections, the Midwest delegation to the U.S. House of Representatives consisted of 60 Republicans and 40 Democrats. Even in states that Gore and Kerry both carried, Republicans held a 26–24 House member advantage. At the heart of Republican advantage in the Midwest was a rural, conservative constituency, evident in House delegations from Indiana, Iowa, Nebraska, and Kansas. But holding it together were suburbs in red and blue states. In 2002 Charlie Cook focused particularly on "collar counties" ringing urban areas in the upper Midwest, such as Wayne (Detroit), Cuyahoga (Cleveland), and Cook (Chicago), as holding the balance of power in Congress, noting that collar counties tend to have a greater than average share of "persuadable" or swing voters.[50]

Increasing disfavor with President Bush, war in Iraq, the economy, scandal, and corruption, would unravel the Republican Midwestern advantage. In 2006, a sour mood cost Republicans in heartland states such as Iowa, Indiana, and Kansas. Voter discontent at the state and national levels in Indiana knocked out Republican incumbents in three districts that had all voted for Bush by an average 2004 margin of 17 points. In Indiana's eighth district, 2006 Democratic challenger Ellsworth beat Republican Hostettler 61–39 percent. Defeated Kansas House incumbent Jim Ryun's district had voted by 18 points for Bush.

The late 1990s had a Republican surge in Minnesota and neighboring states Wisconsin and Iowa. Yet in 2006, Democrats knocked off a six-term House Republican representing Minnesota who had won his previous 2 races by more than 20 points, and beat another House incumbent in Iowa. Democrats also took the open seats of failed Republican gubernatorial candidacies of Iowa's Jim Nussle and Wisconsin's Mark Green. The Wisconsin district had gone by nine for Bush, Gutknecht's Minnesota district by two points. The only Democratic pickups that voted against Bush in 2004 were in Iowa. With ties to disgraced lobbyist Jack Abramoff, one scandal-scorched district was the typically reliable Republican district of Ohio's Bob Ney. With an open seat left by Ney's resignation, Democrat Zachary Space beat Joy Padgett, 62–38 percent in a district that voted by 12 points for Bush in 2004.

Demographic shifts also brought formerly safe Republican seats into sight for Democrats.[51] Incumbent Deborah Pryce, the number 4 GOP House leader, narrowly hung on by a little more than 1,000 votes near Columbus in what she called "hands down the toughest reelection fight of her 14 year career, after winning 62 percent of the vote in 2004."[52] GOP consultant Alex Gage noted such suburban districts are new bellwethers for voting shifts in which "voters most likely to defect from the Republican Party tend to be moderate, independent, or GOP-leaning women, older men, and people who are well educated . . . a demographic found in Northern and Midwestern suburban rings."[53]

In 2008, Democrats knocked out another incumbent Ohio Republican and picked up Pryce's open seat from which she had retired since her close call.

Democrats also picked up the wealthy suburban ninth district in Michigan, represented by Joe Knollenberg since 1993, and in Republican hands for 65 years. In Illinois Democrats picked up the seat retiring Republican Weller held for seven terms, stretching from the southwestern Chicago suburbs. After knocking out two Republican incumbents in Michigan and picking up an open seat in Illinois, Democrats strengthened their regional advantage to eight seats among states that voted Democratic in 2004 and 2008.[54]

Kansas Republicans regained a seat in 2008 to bring red states back to the four-seat advantage they had following Bush's reelection. In the delicate red-and-blue balance in the Midwest, Democrats not only picked up Ohio, Iowa, and Indiana as part of the 2008 presidential election, Democrats now had a 2-member advantage across states they trailed by 14 members in 2005. Overall in the Midwest, Democrats had a 53–47 House member advantage mirroring the national popular vote margin for Obama (see table 7.4).

Table 7.4 Congressional elections and party delegation in the Midwest region

State	House #GOP 2007	House #DEM 2007	House #GOP 2009	House #DEM 2009	Senate 2007		Senate 2009	
					R	D	R	D
Red states 04/08								
Kansas	2	2 (+1)	3 (+1)	1	2	0	2	0
Missouri	5	4	5	4	1	1	1	1
Nebraska	3	0	3	0	2	0	2	0
North Dakota	0	1	0	1	0	2	0	2
South Dakota	0	1	0	1	1	1	1	1
Red states total	**10**	**8**	**11**	**7**	**5**	**5**	**5**	**5**
Red state pickups		*+1*	*+1*			*+1*		
04 Red to 08 Blue								
Indiana	4	5 (+3)	4	5	1	1	1	1
Iowa	2	3 (+2)	2	3	1	1	1	1
Ohio	11	7 (+1)	9	9 (+2)	1	1	1	1
Flip states total	**17**	**15**	**15**	**17**	**3**	**3**	**3**	**3**
Flip state pickups		*+6*		*+2*		*+1*		
Blue states 04/08								
Illinois	9	10	8	11(+1)	0	2	0	2
Michigan	9	6	7	8 (+2)	0	2	0	2
Minnesota	3	5 (+1)	3	5	1	1	0	2
Wisconsin	3	5 (+1)	3	5	0	2	0	2
Blue states total	**24**	**26**	**21**	**29**	**1**	**7**	**0**	**8**
Blue state pickups		*+2*		*+3*				*+1*
Midwest total	**51**	**49**	**47**	**53**	**9**	**15**	**8**	**16**
Midwest pickups		*+9*	*+1*	*+5*		*+2*		*+1*

Source: Table compiled by author.

Note: House and Senate # refers to Democratic and Republican seats in each state, with gains and losses as a result of the 2006 and 2008 elections in parentheses and italics. Red states 04/08 represent states that voted for both Bush and McCain, blue states 04/08 for both Kerry and Obama, and flip states for Bush and Obama.

As Al Franken would say as his *Saturday Night Live* character Stuart Smalley stared into a mirror as part of his Daily Affirmations, "I'm gonna help people. Because I'm good enough, I'm smart enough, and doggonit, people like me!" Holding no previous elected office but a sharp wit, the author of comedic yet dead serious books such as *Lies and the Lying Liars Who Tell Them* as well as pointed criticism of the president on the liberal Air America satellite radio were increasingly in sync with public disfavor with the Bush administration, particularly in Minnesota where disapproval of the president was at 73 percent in 2008 exit polls. And when Franken won a combative recount over incumbent Republican U.S. Senator Norm Coleman Democrats controlled all eight Senate seats in Midwest states that voted for Democratic presidential candidates in 2004 and 2008. In 2006 Democrats had picked up U.S. Senate seats in Missouri and Ohio to draw even in five red states and three states that had flipped to Obama, and with Franken's win doubled up Midwest delegation to the U.S. Senate, 16–8.

In 2002, President Bush helped Republicans with narrow victories in Senate races in Minnesota and Missouri and in 2004 a national party effort to knock out Senate Majority Leader Tom Daschle in South Dakota was successful. But by 2006 and 2008, President Bush was more of a drag on his party's fortunes. In 2006, Sherrod Brown, a relatively liberal House member who voted against the war resolution and the Patriot Act, won the Senate seat from Ohio with a substantial margin of the urban vote while carrying the suburban vote by two points. In Missouri, political scientist Dave Robertson also predicted that an anti-GOP suburban shift could hurt U.S. Senate Republican incumbent Jim Talent.[55] The St. Louis suburbs were critical to Talent's narrow win in the 2002 special election, prevailing by the narrowest margin of any GOP candidate that year. Yet in 2006, Claire McCaskill, the Democratic winner, won the St. Louis suburbs, constituting 35 percent of the state vote by 50–48 percent.

In Minnesota, Amy Klobuchar won an open seat vacated by the retiring U.S. Senator Mark Dayton with a huge margin of 20 points in 2006. Her opponent, Republican House member Mark Kennedy, represented suburban and exurban counties around the Twin Cities. Klobuchar, however, won the Twin Cities suburbs by 10 points and Minnesota's suburbs by 13 points.

As he led the 2006 effort to retake the House, Rahm Emanuel of Illinois, now President Obama's Chief of Staff, quite pointedly stated that "the future of both parties is in the suburbs."[56] And some of the most competitive suburbs are in the upper Midwest surrounding Chicago, Detroit, and Cleveland, but not necessarily in places such as suburban Atlanta and Houston, where Republicans have had a more dominant regional advantage.[57] Thus Democratic gains in Midwest states have Republican leaders worried.[58] As a foreshadowing of what was to come in 2008, 2006 Democratic gubernatorial candidate Ted Strickland won by the most lopsided margin since Republicans took total control of Ohio government in 1994. Strickland won 72 of 88 counties, the most by a Democratic gubernatorial candidate in Ohio since the early twentieth century. Michigan Governor Jennifer Granholm and Kansas Governor Kathleen Sebelius also won reelection by comfortable margins and are considered rising female stars in the Democratic Party.

Republicans can take some comfort that former Bush administration official, Mitch Daniels, was reelected as governor of Indiana by a solid margin despite the fact the state moved from Hoosier red to rust purple.[59] And the GOP has the schadenfreude that comes with the arrest of Democratic Illinois Governor Rod Blagojevich over his illegal demands for Obama's open Senate seat. In 2002 Blagojevich broke a seven-election-long Democratic Party losing streak, and in 2006 he had doubled his victory margin in suburban Cook County.

Illinois, where Republicans began their national ascent under Lincoln, and Obama began his historic rise to the White House, looks to be safely in Democratic control for the near future. However, scandal and context can shake up suburban votes in competitive Midwestern states as we have witnessed over the course of this new century. From Springfield, Illinois, through the Iowa caucus to Canton, Ohio, Obama rode the message of change and hope out of the Midwest and into the White House as congressional Democrats have gained a representative advantage in the region. But with electoral success comes greater accountability and as both parties have learned over time, Ohio and the upper Midwest region will likely foreshadow electoral forces rippling across the nation.

Notes

1. Robert Barnes and Michael Shear, "Obama and McCain Take Post-Debate Sparring to Crucial Midwest," *Washington Post*, October 9, 2008, p. A10; Peter Slevinn and Juliet Eilperin, "Final Weekend Push Starts in Midwest," *Washington Post*, November 1, 2008, p. A2.
2. V. O. Key, Jr., "A Theory of Critical Elections," in Jerome Chubb and Howard Allen, eds., *Electoral Change and Stability in American Political History* (New York: Free Press, 1971).
3. Kristi Anderson, *The Creation of a Democratic Majority, 1928–1936* (Chicago, IL: University of Chicago Press, 1979).
4. Taylor Dark, *The Unions and the Democrats* (Ithaca, NY: Cornell University Press, 1999).
5. Everett Carll Ladd, Jr. with Charles D. Hadley, *Transformations of the American Party System: Party Coalitions from the New Deal to the 1970s* (New York: Norton, 1975).
6. Kevin Phillips, *The Emerging Republican Majority* (Garden City, NY: Anchor Books, 1970).
7. Edward G. Carmines and James A. Stimson, *Issue Evolution: Race and the Transformation of American Politics* (Princeton, NJ: Princeton University Press, 1989).
8. John Petrocik, *Party Coalitions: Realignment and the Decline of the New Deal Party System* (Chicago, IL: University of Chicago Press, 1981).
9. Theodore White, *America in Search of Itself: The Making of the President, 1956–1980* (New York: Harper and Row, 1982).
10. Ruy Teixeira and Joel Rogers, *America's Forgotten Majority: Why the White Working Class Matters* (New York: Basic Books, 2000).
11. Katherine Tate, *From Politics to Protest: The New Black Voter in American Elections* (Cambridge, MA: Harvard University Press, 1994).
12. Jeffrey Stonecash, *Class and Party in American Politics* (Boulder, CO: Westview Press, 2000).

13. Robert Huckfeldt and Carol Weitzel Kohfeld, *Race and the Decline of Class in American Politics* (Urbana, IL: University of Illinois Press, 1989).

14. Francis E. Rourke and John T. Tierney, "The Setting: Changing Patterns of Presidential Politics, 1960 and 1988," in Michael Nelson, ed., *Elections of 1988* (Washington, DC: CQ Press, 1989), pp. 1–24.

15. John Kenneth White, *The New Politics of Old Values*, Second Edition (Hanover, NH: University Press of New England, 1990).

16. David Keege and Lyman Kellstedt, *Rediscovering the Religious Factor in American Politics* (Armonk, NY: Sharpe, 1993).

17. Peter Goldman and Tom Mathews, *The Quest for the Presidency: The 1988 Campaign* (New York: Simon and Schuster, 1989).

18. Stanley Greenberg, *Middle Class Dreams: The Politics and Power of the New American Majority* (New Haven: Yale University Press, 1995).

19. John Sperling, *The Great Divide: Retro vs. Metro America* (Sausalito, CA: Polipoint Press, 2004).

20. Thomas Frank, *What's the Matter with Kansas?: How Conservatives Won the Heart of America* (New York: Metropolitan Books, 2004).

21. Charles Mahtesian, "Suburban Blind Spot," *National Journal*, April 29, 2006.

22. William Frey, *Melting Pot Suburbs: A Census Study of Suburban Diversity* (Washington, DC: Brookings Institution, 2001).

23. Greenberg, *Middle Class Dreams*.

24. Stanley Greenberg, *The Two Americas: Our Current Political Deadlock and How to Break It* (New York: St. Martin's Press, 2004), p. 108.

25. Ibid.

26. James Barnes, "It's the Suburbs Stupid," *National Journal* 36 (2004): 1.

27. Philip O'Connor and Greg Jonsson, "Rural Vote Again Provides Bush's Margin of Victory in Missouri," *St. Louis Post-Dispatch*, November 3, 2004, p. A11.

28. Bob von Sternberg, "Suburbs Paint '08 Election a New Hue," *Minneapolis Star Tribune*, September 24, 2007, p. 1A.

29. John Judis and Ruy Texeira, *The Emerging Democratic Majority* (New York: Scribner, 2002), pp. 72–76.

30. Ibid., p. 105.

31. Ibid., p. 108.

32. Timothy Egan, "Battle for Control of the House Focuses on the Suburbs, Inner and Outer," *New York Times*, June 16, 2006, p. A24.

33. Sara Burnett, Eric Krol, and John Patterson, "GOP's Weakening Grip on Suburbs," *Chicago Daily Herald*, November 14, 2004, p. 1.

34. Dick Simpson, "Dems Gaining in Battle for DuPage," *Chicago Sun Times*, August 3, 2007, p. 37.

35. Frank, *What's the Matter with Kansas?*, p. 28.

36. Abdon Pallasch, "Obama Fights for Hoosier Vote," *Chicago Sun Times*, October 24, 2008.

37. Andrew Gelman and others, *Red State, Blue State, Rich State, Poor State* (Princeton, NJ: Princeton University Press, 2008).

38. John C. Green, "Ohio: The Heart of It All," *The Forum* 2:3 (2004): 1–5; *The Economist*, "The Big, Bellwether Battlefield; Swing States: Ohio," August 2, 2008.

39. Jo Mannies, "Obama Invaded Some GOP Territory," *St. Louis Post-Dispatch*, November 12, 2008, p. B1.

40. Joe Hallett, Jonathan Riskind, and Mark Niquette, "Total State Approach Aided Obama," *The Columbus Dispatch*, November 6, 2008, p. 1A.

41. Paul Kane, "GOP Slide in Michigan Hews to Economy," *Washington Post*, November 1, 2008, p. A4.

42. Adam Nossiter, "In Missouri, Slow Economy Helps Obama," *New York Times*, October 18, 2008, p. A12.

43. Scott Shane, "Obama and 60's Bomber: A Look into Crossed Paths," *New York Times*, October 3, 2008.

44. Richard Scammon and Ben Wattenberg, *The Real Majority* (New York: Coward-McCann, 1970), p. 30.

45. Nicholas Kristof, "Kerry's Blue-Collar Bet," *New York Times*, July 7, 2004, p. A21.

46. Mike Allen, "Bush Makes Pitch to 'Security Moms': President Hopes to Narrow Gender Gap at Expense of Democratic Issues," *Washington Post*, September 18, 2004, p. A14.

47. Joe Hallett, "Republicans Lost Ground More than Democrats Gained It," *The Columbus Dispatch*, November 9, 2008, p. 5H.

48. Jo Mannies and Tom O'Neil, "Missouri's Bellwether Status Likely Is Over," *St. Louis Post-Dispatch*, November 5, 2008, p. 4.

49. Alexander Marks, "Obama Gaining among Rural Voters," *Christian Science Monitor*, October 14, 2008.

50. Daron Shaw and Seth McGee, "Suburban Voting in Presidential Elections," *Presidential Studies Quarterly* 33:1 (2003): 125.

51. Rhodes Cook, "Cities and Suburbs a Winning Combination for Democrats," *The Wall Street Journal*, November 27, 2008.

52. Jim VandeHei, "Republicans Losing Security Moms," *Washington Post*, August 18, 2006, p. A1.

53. James Barnes, "It's the Geography, Stupid," *National Journal*, April 29, 2006.

54. Jessica Brady, "Midwest: Democrats Gain in Michigan and Ohio," *Roll Call*, November 6, 2008.

55. Jo Mannies, "Democrats Won't Pass Kirkwood by Anymore," *St. Louis Post-Dispatch*, November 10, 2005, p. B3.

56. Egan, "Battle for Control of the House Focuses on the Suburbs, Inner and Outer."

57. Shaw and McGee, "Suburban Voting in Presidential Elections."

58. Joe Hallett, "Ohio GOP to Focus on Fixing Identity Crisis," *The Columbus Dispatch*, November 7, 2008, p. 1B.

59. Peter Schnitzler, "Can State Remain in the Swing?" *Indianapolis Business Journal*, November 10, 2008.

8

The West

On the Electoral Frontier

David M. Rankin

In an historic spectacle before about 80,000 people crowded into Denver's Invesco Field, 45 years to the day of Martin Luther King's "I have a dream" speech, Barack Obama accepted the Democratic nomination for president of the United States. Emotions were a mile high at the football home to the Denver Broncos, with a stadium of delegates and audience members who had made the trek hollering along to campaign slogans such as "Yes We Can." It was the first time that a major party candidate had accepted the presidential nomination in an outdoor stadium since 1960 when Senator John F. Kennedy unveiled his New Frontier speech at the Los Angeles Memorial Coliseum.

It is not likely that the Democratic Party imagined historic racial barriers would be lifted in the mile-high city when the site was selected for the 2008 Democratic national convention, 100 years after the Democrats last convened in Denver. Yet Democratic strategists were fully aware that Colorado is an emerging centerpiece for success in the West region and a prime location to launch efforts to take back control of the electoral map.[1] Adjoining western states stretching through Colorado, New Mexico, Arizona, Nevada, Oregon, and Washington had been increasingly competitive because of demographic transformation and resulting policy confrontations.[2]

The transformative spirit of the West has often charted a new direction in American elections, politics, and governance. Indeed, a western conservative movement that would guide Republican success for decades was born in the earlier efforts of Arizona Senator and presidential candidate, Barry Goldwater, and carried forward in resounding presidential reelection victories by California's Richard Nixon and Ronald Reagan. But by the time Goldwater's one-time disciple, Arizona Senator John McCain, also made history by selecting Alaska's Sarah Palin as a running mate, a Republican brand of social conservatism was having far less success outside of the reddest rural western states despite a GOP ticket with a distinctly rugged western flair.[3]

Into the Wild West

This would not be the first time that the Western region unveiled new frontiers, historically or electorally. The American West of the nineteenth century was a place to explore and develop new terrain, yet the region meant little for about the first 100 years of the Electoral College. As western territories became states they developed partisan ties and at times a unique brand of presidential voting. The first western states, California and Oregon, voted with the north for Republican candidate Abraham Lincoln in the critical election of 1860, even though California supported the Democrat Buchanan in 1856.[4] By 1864, Nevada had joined the Union and voted with the west for Lincoln's reelection.

The western states continued to support victorious Republican presidents, with the exception of 1880, and in 1884 all three states went Republican even as Democrat Grover Cleveland won the presidency. By 1892, the addition of four new states altered the electoral balance in the expanding west. While Oregon, Washington, Montana, and Wyoming all voted Republican, California supported Cleveland in his second successful presidential bid, while Idaho and Nevada voted for the People's Populist Party candidate, James Weaver. The "Wild West" embrace of a reform candidacy was a harbinger for the next two elections. Ohio's William McKinley won the critical election of 1896 with the support of the upper Midwest, Northeast, California, and Oregon,[5] but Nebraskan William Jennings Bryan on the Democratic and Populist Party ticket won the other western states, which now included Colorado. The west split 5–4 in the 1900 McKinley and Bryan rematch.

Assuming the presidency after the 1901 assassination of President McKinley, Theodore Roosevelt swept the west in 1904. Bryan was again the 1908 nominee when Democrats held the first national convention out west, in Denver. Bryan won Colorado and Nevada gaining west voters who viewed Washington, DC, as a corrupt, distant influence on their lives. In 1912 California and Oregon supported Teddy Roosevelt's Progressive candidacy. Roosevelt, known by then as a reformer, had as a Republican president and conservationist established federal protection of western natural sites, parks and monuments, which would at times continue to be a source of local and national debate. Roosevelt lost his Progressive candidacy in which Utah voted for the Republican Taft, and the rest of the western states for the Democrat Woodrow Wilson. In 1916, Wilson recaptured the entire west except Oregon. Beside Wilson, Republican domination included the west from 1908 to 1928, and from 1920 to 1928 the entire west supported three straight Republican presidential candidacies.

Between 1908 and 1960, the Democratic Convention did not again convene west of St. Louis with the exception of 1928 in Houston to nominate Alfred E. Smith to face the Republican Herbert Hoover. The Stanford-educated Hoover was president from 1929 to 1933. From 1933 to 1968 there was only one Republican president, the Kansan Dwight "Ike" Eisenhower, 1953–1961, until Ike's Vice President and California native Richard Nixon regained Republican control of the White House.

Franklin Delano Roosevelt had tremendous western success winning all states in 1932 and 1936, losing only Colorado in 1940, and Colorado and Wyoming in 1944. The far west states, particularly California, grew in part because of economic displacement from the Great Depression, also affecting the central Plains from which many had left. In a saga of American migration featured in California resident John Steinbeck's *The Grapes of Wrath*, families from the Depression-era Dust Bowl packed everything onto jalopies to find work in a largely agrarian California. The FDR administration simultaneously fueled the west's economy with governmental assistance with World War II demanding military equipment and aircraft. Aerospace companies grew propelled by military contracts, including Lockheed Martin in southern California and Boeing in Seattle. These industry giants also employed a large unionized workforce with solid wages, a critical western piece of the Democratic New Deal coalition.[6] However, early western cracks in the Democratic juggernaut were exposed as Colorado joined neighboring Plains states voting Republican.

The government also utilized states such as Nevada and New Mexico for extensive military testing, including the first detonation of an atomic bomb. Strategic placement and space made San Diego a major naval base and the military a focus in many western states. Economic and social transition also transformed partisan affiliation. After FDR's successor Harry Truman narrowly won the presidency in 1948 relying heavily on support out west, Eisenhower swept the west for Republicans in the next two elections. Like the Midwest, the unionized workforce supported Democrats, while the military culture and industry was increasingly Republican. As the former World War II Allied Commander Eisenhower himself warned of a military-industrial complex; yet his administration presided over its escalation. Individualism and government dependence were developing as strange bedfellows in the west as Republicans became the party of opposition to federal government authority associated with Democrats, while fueling the west's growth through government contracts and spending.

Until 1956, no Republican national convention was held west of Kansas City. But California was increasing in importance. When Hoover was elected president in 1928, California had 13 electoral votes. California was up to 32 votes by 1956. Thus, Eisenhower became the first presidential candidate to accept his party's nomination west of the Rockies by accepting his bid for reelection in San Francisco.

With California's increasing importance the Democrats followed the Republicans by holding their 1960 convention in Los Angeles, where John Kennedy introduced the New Frontier. Kennedy faced Vice President Richard Nixon, a hard-nosed, cunning campaigner, and with relatively humble southern Californian roots that contrasted sharply with Kennedy's privileged east coast pedigree. Nixon's personal story and a fighter instinct alienated many voters and east coast elite, but he resonated with the individualistic "pull yourself up by your own bootstraps" mentality of many western voters. In 1960, Nixon won every mainland western state except Nevada and New Mexico, winning the new state of Alaska while losing the other new state of Hawaii. Still, Nixon lost the Electoral College narrowly to Kennedy, following up that tough defeat by losing

to Democratic candidate Edmund "Pat" Brown in California's 1962 guberna-
torial election. After losing in two straight attempts for political office a dour
Nixon pined before reporters, "You won't have Nixon to kick around anymore."
But Nixon would be back, having laid the groundwork in the west for a successful
Republican run.

Electoral focus was moving west for Republicans with the 1964 convention in
San Francisco for the second time in three elections. With the prospect of facing a president who took office following Kennedy's 1963 assassination, Nixon
avoided another futile electoral attempt. Arizona Senator Barry Goldwater
secured the Republican Party nomination and lost to Lyndon Johnson in an historic landslide.

In Goldwater's acceptance speech he uttered the defining statement,
"[E]xtremism in the defense of liberty is no vice and...moderation in the pur-
suit of justice is no virtue," and the Johnson campaign portrayed the senator as
too conservative, if not radical, for the average American voter. Goldwater was
swept in the west with the exception of Arizona. However, Goldwater appealed
to states-rights white voters alienated by what they felt were intrusive policies of
the Democratic Kennedy and Johnson administrations. In his critique of government largess and the Democratic Party that he argued promoted such policy,
Goldwater laid the ideological foundation for Republican electoral success for
decades in the west.[7]

In 1968, California was again a focus of the race for the presidency. Democratic
primary challenger, Robert Kennedy, had just finished his acceptance speech in
Los Angeles after winning the California primary when he was assassinated. Yet
Kennedy's earlier assault on the Vietnam War policies of the Johnson administration, exacerbated by fractious Chicago Democratic convention riots, opened
up the door for two-time electoral loser, Richard Nixon.

Nixon was a strategic politician and his campaign built upon much of
Goldwater's strategy to win not only in the South but also the West.[8] He advocated
that more power and decision-making should return to the states and played to
the small-town values of a rustic west alienated by urban-centered protest and
conflict. In 1968, Nixon carried the west except Hawaii and Washington, adding Nevada and New Mexico, two states he lost in 1960. In 1972, Nixon won the
entire west in a landslide reelection while locking the region in as a Republican
stronghold in presidential elections.[9] In 1976, President Gerald Ford swept the
mainland west despite losing the election to Jimmy Carter after pardoning Nixon
following his 1974 resignation over the Watergate crisis.

In 1980 Republican candidate Ronald Reagan carried the west *and* Reagan
won the presidency. On his path to the White House, Reagan accomplished what
Nixon could not. In 1966, Reagan defeated Pat Brown to become California governor, winning reelection in 1970. Reagan had graduated from Eureka College in
Illinois and started his career in broadcasting in his native Midwest. But Reagan
made his name in Hollywood as a movie actor predominantly in the 1940s and
1950s. However, Reagan's last role before elected office was perhaps most fitting.
From 1965 to 1966, Reagan hosted the popular television series entitled *Death
Valley Days* also known as *Call of the West*.

From the Democrat Reagan to Reagan Democrats

By 1960, the Democrat Reagan was increasingly enamored with Republican presidential candidates out west. Unlike much of Hollywood supporting Kennedy for president, Reagan gave more than 200 speeches as a "Democrat for Nixon," and in 1962 he officially changed his party affiliation to Republican. In 1964, Reagan became the cochair of California Republicans for Goldwater, and in one of his many speeches on behalf of Goldwater, Reagan delivered an attack on big government and Johnson's "Great Society" programs. Reagan soon succeeded to the leadership of the conservative movement within the Republican Party.

Whether it was his movies, his personality, or his policies, Reagan struck a nerve in California and throughout the west with Nixon- and Goldwater-inspired attacks on government and in defense of states rights and lower taxes, which resonated from the suburbs to rustic western terrain. Reagan also promoted defense spending and American military superiority, which helped him in military-reliant communities across the west and with white blue-collar workers who once staunchly supported the Democrats.[10] Reagan, a former FDR Democrat himself, successfully converted many former members of a crumbling New Deal Coalition.[11] Reagan reinforced the growing perception of the Republican Party as an advocate of smaller government symbolized by his famous statement, "Government is not the solution to the problem, government is the problem."

Reagan utilized and solidified electoral forces that Nixon set in motion, sweeping the west in his bid for reelection in 1984 mirroring Nixon's own landslide reelection.[12] The Reagan persona symbolized the "rugged individualism" of the Wild West, which lent itself to the philosophy of the free market and slashing government programs.[13] President Reagan reinforced the western myth as the cowboy riding his horses, chopping wood, and entertaining dignitaries on his rustic California ranch.

Electoral success had a future electoral price in the west as the Reagan coalition attracted western working-class whites through social conservatism.[14] This strategy included allying with conservative religious organizations necessitating, among other social debates, an increasingly partisan pro-life position on the fractious abortion issue.[15] The 1988 Bush-Quayle ticket swept the Mountain West and Southwest but the Democratic Dukakis-Bentsen campaign made inroads on the West coast, winning Washington and Oregon, aided by expanding metropolitan areas and more socially moderate viewpoints.[16]

Furthermore, President Bush's decision to raise taxes to contend with the federal deficit despite asking voters to read his lips to the contrary did not play well in many western states. Western voters again threw support behind a reform-minded third-party candidacy, the independent Ross Perot, and the 1992 Clinton-Gore ticket could build upon the urban-based Pacific Coast success of the Dukakis 1988 campaign to gather western states rebelling over economic policies of the incumbent administration.[17] In 1992 Democrats regained California, the largest electoral prize with 54 electoral votes, and with Perot stealing off a chunk of the vote, Clinton also won longtime Republican states Nevada, New Mexico, Colorado, and Montana.

The Clinton administration, in turn, alienated voters in states such as Montana with support for gays in the military, gun control, and environmental laws that butted heads with many local views and interests. In his 1996 reelection over Kansas Senator Bob Dole, Clinton lost Montana and Colorado back into the Republican column.[18] Clinton did hold Nevada and picked up Arizona for Democrats for the first time since 1948, but both returned to Republicans in 2000 (see table 8.1).

Electoral lines had been carved into the western landscape. In 2000 and 2004, Republican candidate George W. Bush won rustic Mountain West states by an average margin of at least 34 points. Democratic strength had moved to the coast where California's 55 electoral votes had been trending as blue as the Pacific surrounding Democratic Hawaii. Thus, competition revolved around six remaining competitive western states. Democrats won by single digits in each of the past two elections in Oregon and Washington. New Mexico went narrowly to Gore in 2000 and narrowly to Bush in 2004. Nevada, Arizona, and Colorado went Republican in 2000 and 2004 but by single-digit margins and with demographic trends that made Democrats hopeful.

Table 8.1   Electoral College partisan trends in the West Region, 1968–2008

	68	72	76	80	84	88	92	96	00	04	08	00+	04+	08+
Rustic red												+36	+34	+22
Alaska	R	R	R	R	R	R	R	R	R	R	R	31	26	22
Idaho	R	R	R	R	R	R	R	R	R	R	R	40	38	25
Montana	R	R	R	R	R	R	D	R	R	R	R	25	20	2
Utah	R	R	R	R	R	R	R	R	R	R	R	41	45	28
Wyoming	R	R	R	R	R	R	R	R	R	R	R	41	40	32
Pacific blue														
California	R	R	R	R	R	R	D	D	D	D	D	12	10	24
Hawaii	D	R	D	D	R	D	D	D	D	D	D	18	9	45
Shading blue														
Oregon	R	R	R	R	R	D	D	D	D	D	D	5	4	16
Washington	D	R	R	R	R	D	D	D	D	D	D	6	7	17
Blue surge														
Nevada	R	R	R	R	R	R	D	D	R	R	D	4	3	12
New Mexico	R	R	R	R	R	R	D	D	D	R	D	1	1	15
Battleground														
Arizona	R	R	R	R	R	R	R	D	R	R	R	6	10	9
Colorado	R	R	R	R	R	R	D	R	R	R	D	8	5	9

Source: Table compiled by author.

Note: The 00+, 04+, and 08+ columns calculate the popular vote margin for each state and the average popular vote margin for solid red, solid blue, and the closer battleground states. For example, George W. Bush won Alaska by a 26-point popular vote margin in 2004 and John McCain by a 22-point margin in 2008. The average red state popular vote margin was 34 points in 2004 and 22 points in the 2008 election. Additional percentage points <0.5 are rounded down (e.g., 2.4%=2%) and additional percentage points >0.5 are rounded up (e.g., 15.6%=16%) unless the overall percentage of the state popular vote is less than 1 (e.g., 0.1% 0.9%).

Obama's Pacific Wave Crashes into the McCain-Palin West

When Barack Obama interrupted the final days of his campaign to visit his dying grandmother in Hawaii, he had dramatically traversed the American experience since his older childhood days known as Barry "O-Bomber" for his jump shot on the basketball court at Punahou High School. In an autobiographical *Dreams from My Father*, Obama recounted coming of age on the islands as a biracial child raised during this formative period by his white grandparents from Kansas. But by 2008 when a cresting Hawaiian voting wave grew from a 9-point margin for Kerry to a 45-point advantage for Obama, the Democratic candidate's multiracial heritage and experience would seem more familiar to Pacific Coast residents as votes surged by double digits for Obama.

States lining the Pacific have always attracted new residents and migrants, and California was already a relatively diverse state when Republicans were racking up victory after victory on the west coast. Besides Hawaii, these states were solidly Republican from 1972 to 1984, yet Reagan was the last Republican to sweep the Pacific Coast. More recently, Democratic presidential candidates have gained the electoral advantage within the coastal states as the population changed dramatically from even the 1970s and 1980s, with even more diversity in race and lifestyle alongside rapid population growth and concentration in metropolitan areas. Republican presidential candidates, on the other hand, have continued to rule throughout the Mountain West states where the population has not changed nearly as much and remains predominantly white, rural, and older. The biggest challenge for both parties has thus been states exhibiting both trends, rural throughout large swaths of the state but rapidly expanding in metropolitan areas with the sort of younger, diverse residents flooding into coastal cities.

In 2004, urban rich areas helped tilt the west region exit poll to Kerry 50–49, but the rural-dominated mountain, desert, and plains helped Bush run up incredible electoral margins of victory across multiple less-populated states. An urban-rustic divide was starkly apparent in a region in which Bush won 9 out of 13 states but Kerry received 77 of the 124 electoral votes. Bush won the white vote by 33 points in red states while narrowly losing white voters in states that went to Kerry.

In 2008 rustic red states again voted by substantial numbers for the Republican ticket, with 4 of these states by at least a 22-point margin. While the youth vote was the story for Obama across most states, in Utah McCain won the 18–29-year-old vote, 62–33 percent, and in Idaho, 56–41 percent. In Alaska, 18–29-year-olds increased their support for the Republican ticket from a 22-point advantage in 2004 to a 24-point margin.

Whether 44-year-old Alaska Governor Sarah Palin on the ticket appealed to these younger voters[19] McCain-Palin actually did worse among Alaskan voters 45 and older than did Bush-Cheney in 2004, albeit still winning all Alaskan age groups with comfortable margins. Much was made of the first female Republican vice presidential candidate, yet McCain-Palin won Alaskan men by double the margin of Alaskan women. Nevertheless, McCain-Palin carried both men and women by at least double-digit margins in the rustic red states, with the exception of Montana where white men supported the Republican ticket by nine points and white women by six points.

Hunting for Votes with a Hockey Mom

Red western states consist of fewer professional and college-educated women, and more women who are married and living in rural areas. In these states, Bush won convincingly among white men and women. Democrats have had an advantage in more urban-dominated blue western states more populated by women who are nonwhite, unmarried, college-educated, and professionals, and who vote increasingly for Democrats on economic and social policy.[20] In 2004 white women gave Kerry a 12-point advantage and white men gave Bush a 7-point margin in blue states.

Palin's placement on the Republican ticket and Hillary Clinton's absence from it did little to stem the gender gap across Democratic-leaning western states. Support for the Democratic ticket increased among white women from 2004 in all western states carried by Obama. In Nevada and Colorado, white female voters flipped their vote from Bush to Obama. In California, Oregon, and Washington, an advantage with white female voters moved into double digits for the Democratic ticket. Although Palin referred to herself as a "hockey mom" with 5 children including a newborn in tow, California mothers with children under 18 voted 64–36 percent for Obama, while unmarried women in the state with no kids voted for Obama, 75–25 percent.[21]

Stanley Greenberg interviewed what he called "Super-Educated Women" in Seattle's King County, describing such voters as "the most committed to the regulatory state" in which "they reject aggressive individualism, whether in personal behavior or for the country."[22] And in 2008, working women supported Obama by a 49-point margin in California. Such women, residing in urban and suburban areas, contrast with what Greenberg calls the "F-U Boys" who he finds are "anti-government, pro-NRA, military values, blue collar, without college degrees, under fifty, mainly with young families, like the Republican view on taxes, that American security depends on its own strength, not alliances."[23] Such factors split critical states such as Colorado in 2004 where Democrats ended up winning college graduates by two points while losing noncollege graduates by 17 points and white men by a 19-point margin. In Arizona, Bush had a 27-point advantage among white men and a 19-point advantage among those without college degrees while college graduates were evenly divided in their support for Kerry. Arizona Senator John McCain maintained a 21-point advantage in his home state among white men and still carried noncollege voters by 6 points even though such groups were swinging more significantly to Obama in blue-collar Midwestern states.

Forty years earlier, Arizona Senator Barry Goldwater's presidential campaign was based on his statement to "go hunting where the ducks are,"[24] and in less populated rustic western states there are a lot more people who hunt period and they tend to vote Republican. Kerry lost gun owners' votes by a solid margin among a group that apparently did not view the Democrat's heavily publicized hunting experience in the same light as that of Wyoming native and hunting enthusiast Dick Cheney. Cheney had his own hunting mishaps when he accidentally shot a hunting companion in the face, but western gun owners remained among the most loyal voters for the Republican ticket. Gun owners in Alaska supported McCain-Palin by a 38-point margin and in Montana by 17 points, a state McCain won by 3 points overall. This support is particularly impactful in rustic states in which 75 percent of 2008 voters claimed to be gun owners compared with 30 percent of Californians.

Photos and stories of Alaska Governor Palin gazing down the barrel of a shotgun or skinning a moose may have endeared her to hunting enthusiasts in western states, and her small-town Wasilla roots and family concerns may have seemed more real to many struggling families. Nevertheless, lower-income voters outside of the reddest rustic states did not appear particularly receptive to the Republican message in 2008. Despite Palin's "You Betcha!" folksiness that was both appealing and satirized, Democrats did better among lower-income, working-class voters, particularly in blue states. Obama won with higher margins than 2004 among voters making less than $50,000 a year in states such as California, Washington, and Nevada.

However many houses John and Cindy McCain actually own, an ongoing joke on late night comedy, higher-income voters were not necessarily amused with the Republican ticket. And trends in the most populated, rapidly growing western states are really no laughing matter for Republicans as college-educated higher-income voters have been moving Democratic. Even before the recent economic crisis, Democrats had been gaining among higher-income, skilled professionals in rapidly growing and high-tech areas such as Bellevue and Redmond Washington.[25] Judis and Teixeira refer to the "ideopolis" of Seattle's King County and Portland's Mutnomah County in terms similar to California's Silicon Valley, areas with highly skilled professional voters who "back regulatory capitalism, but are wary of social engineering," which in their minds includes the electoral rejection of the Republican brand of social conservatism.[26] While Kerry won Mutnomah and King County by 22 points each, Obama extended the margin to 56 points in Mutnomah and 44 points in King County.

Overall, Washington college graduates went from a 17-point margin for Kerry to 24 points for Obama. Nevada college graduates moved from six points in favor of Bush to six points in favor of Obama. In California, those making $100,000 or more a year increased a 4-point margin in favor of the Democratic ticket to 15 points in 2008. In Nevada, this wealthier group swung 22 points from Bush to Obama. And in Colorado, an 11-point margin with this high-income group for Bush became a 13-point advantage for Obama.

Abramson, Aldrich, and Rohde note, "Democrats may be appealing to disadvantaged Americans because of the party's economic policies and better educated Americans—especially better-educated women—may reject the interpretation of traditional values emphasized by Republicans in recent elections."[27] Recognizing rapid population and demographic shifts in line with conservative success in other areas, Republicans attempted to make inroads with the burgeoning Latino population in western states.

Si Se Puede!

Ronald Brownstein and Kathleen Hennessey of the *Los Angeles Times* point out that

> more than any single factor, it has been the Latino community's steady growth that has moved these states from reliably Republican toward the tossup category. From 1990 through 2002, the Latino population soared by 272% in Nevada, 115% in Arizona, 93% in Colorado and 38% from a large base in New Mexico, according to census figures. By 2004, Latinos constituted about a fifth of the population in Nevada and Colorado, more than a fourth in Arizona and more than two-fifths in New Mexico.[28]

Democratic candidates increased success in states such as California because of the increasing Latino population and Latino backlash to conservative proposals such as California's Proposition 187.[29] Passed in 1994 but later ruled unconstitutional, Proposition 187 denied public services to illegal immigrants including their children and had the visible backing of Republican Governor Pete Wilson. In 1996 Clinton won over nearly three-quarters of California's Latino vote over Bob Dole, who visibly supported an English-only requirement.

As a candidate who regularly addressed Latino audiences in Spanish, George W. Bush won 35 percent of Latinos nationwide in 2000. Still, Gore beat Bush by 27 points among Latinos and by similar margins in critical western states. In New Mexico, Gore won by 366 votes where 43 percent of the population is Latino. In 2004 Bush won a record 44 percent of the Latino vote for a Republican candidate, surpassing Reagan's 37 percent in 1984. Bush claimed more secure victories in Arizona and Colorado with the relatively strong showing among Latinos, which also helped him over the top in Nevada and New Mexico. Republicans viewed courting Latino voters as a necessity but also sensed an opportunity.[30] Many Latinos have conservative social values and serve in the military, both advantages for Republican candidates.[31] Roberto de Posada, president of the business-oriented Latino Coalition, claims that much Latino opposition to "the gay marriage issue is a concept that worked very, very well for Bush."[32]

Traditional values voting among Latinos did not work as well for McCain in 2008.[33] Proposition 8, which would overturn gay marriage rights in California, narrowly passed; yet California Latinos supported Obama by a 51-point margin over McCain, 20 points higher than Kerry. New Mexico's Latino voters, accounting for 41 percent of the state exit poll, voted 69–30 percent for Obama, turning a 1-point victory for Bush in 2004 to a 15-point win for the Democrat. In Colorado and Nevada, states that swung to Obama after supporting Bush in 2000 and 2004, Latinos made up a much larger percentage of voters in 2008. Nevada Latinos comprised 10 percent of the exit poll in 2004 and 15 percent in

2008, providing Obama a 54-point margin over McCain—33 points more than for Kerry.

Whether Latinos were also motivated to vote for the first nonwhite presidential candidate, the perceived handling of the immigration issue by congressional Republicans probably did not help.[34] For example, of the 35 percent of voters who disagreed with a suggested policy to deport illegal immigrants, there was a 40-point margin for Obama in Colorado, and a 38-point margin on the issue for Obama in Arizona where Latino support moved to a 15-point advantage for Obama in McCain's own state.

Religion had been another component Republican candidates had used to some success with Latinos in western states, but faith played less of a factor when it came to voting for McCain-Palin than it did for Bush. Despite McCain's attempts to cozy up with Religious Right leaders after earlier rifts and the selection of an openly devout Christian running mate, the 2008 Republican ticket even lost some ground with white evangelicals in western states. Although McCain still had a 53-point margin among white evangelicals in Arizona and a 33-point margin among white evangelicals in Oregon, it was still a 20-point drop in both states compared with support for Bush in 2004.

Moral Outrage in a Purpose-Driven Election

Republicans had been making great strides with the evangelical community and churchgoers in rural areas and suburbs populated by megachurches from southern California to northern Colorado. It continued a western path to the White House that Reagan set out. Reagan had done what Goldwater would not. He made conservative religious groups a critical component of the Republican strategy to win the west, and the synergy of Christian faith and the philosophy of limited government translated into Republican domination in the Mountain west.[35] With the solid support of churchgoers, George W. Bush built upon the advantage Reagan established between the Religious Right and the Republican Party. Bush's outspoken Christian faith, support of extensive tax cuts, and faith-based programs solidified nearly universal support of white conservative Protestants and gained overwhelming support from white evangelical voters throughout the west.

The Republican domination of churchgoers had reached a point that former altar boy and Catholic John Kerry lost the Catholic vote by 20 points in western states that went to Bush, including the vote of pro-life Catholic Latinos. And the loss of religious groups and the relative influence of the moral values question were of particular concern for Democrats attempting to reach voters in otherwise competitive western states. Perhaps taking a page from Jim Wallis's *God's Politics: Why the Right Gets It Wrong and the Left Doesn't Get It*,[36] Obama sought to broach how Democratic concerns and policies bridged those of Christian faith, and cut significantly into Republican support among 18–44-year-old white evangelicals.[37]

Obama himself had been under fire for his associations with the bombastic Reverend Jeremiah Wright and had to endure a difficult public split from his early spiritual mentor in Chicago. But Obama would reach out to the Christian community on the largest stage, sitting down alongside John McCain to discuss faith, politics, and policy with Rick Warren, founding pastor of Saddleback Church. With weekly attendance of over 15,000 congregants at the southern California megachurch and having sold 20 million copies worldwide of the *Purpose Driven Life*, Warren provided a very public forum for the Democrat to confront the perspective that only Republicans would directly speak to religious concerns and solutions.

President-elect Obama opened up a bit of the culture war debate by inviting Warren to deliver the invocation at his presidential inauguration even as the presiding concern over the economy and foreign affairs dominated the presidential transition. As Sean Penn's portrayal of the first openly gay elected official in the late 1970s, the assassinated San Francisco supervisor Harvey Milk, was generating Oscar buzz, Warren's selection upset many in the gay community because of his support of Proposition 8. While similar measures previously passed in 27 states, thousands of gay couples had already married in California in the aftermath of a State Supreme Court ruling.

Many credit or blame the anti-gay marriage amendment on the 2004 ballot in many states for turning out religious conservative voters and swinging the election. The gay marriage issue had particular salience and divisiveness in a region with the 1998 Wyoming murder of Matthew Shepard because of his homosexuality as well as the high-profile decision by San Francisco Mayor Gavin Newsom to recognize gay marriage. Whatever the effect on turnout, the nearly one-third of voters who felt there should be no legal recognition of gay couples voted by a 46-point margin in the west for President Bush. With the amendment on the Oregon ballot in 2004, the race was significantly closer than anticipated with 32 percent of voters classified as white evangelicals. The gay marriage debate made moral values a more important issue for certain west voters, providing Bush with a significant advantage.

Although gay activists expressed outrage that the 2008 election could advance the historic standing of a previously discriminated group while at the same time denying the rights of another,[38] the issue itself did not turn critical states as it had in 2004.[39] Although McCain won California supporters of Proposition 8, 61–38 percent, Obama won those opposed by an even higher margin, 85–13 percent. In Arizona there was more of an impact in which supporters of Proposition 102, which passed 56–44 percent defining marriage as only a union of one man and one woman, voted for McCain by 76–22 percent and those opposing the proposition for Obama, 72–27 percent. Yet other than Palin's Alaska, Arizona was the only western state to basically hold its 2004 vote margin for the Republican ticket.

In the 2004 west region exit poll 22 percent of respondents felt that moral values was the most important issue, ranking it ahead of Iraq (19 percent), terrorism (19 percent) and the economy/jobs (17 percent). Most importantly, moral values ranked at the top in western states that Bush carried, such as Arizona and Colorado, as opposed to those he did not, such as California where the importance of moral values trailed Iraq and terrorism and was on par with concern about the economy. In 2008 McCain and Palin again sought to court voters on the values question by suggesting that Obama was more in tune with Hollywood players in Tinseltown than the values of a small town. One McCain ad compared Obama's widespread allure with the paparazzi-style celebrity of a Paris Hilton or Britney Spears.

There were also echoes of Obama's April 2008 You Tube moment when he uttered at a fund-raiser in San Francisco that for many rural Americans, "[i]t's not surprising then they get bitter, they cling to guns or religion or antipathy to people who aren't like them or anti-immigrant sentiment or anti-trade sentiment as a way to explain their frustrations." But whatever attempts McCain and Palin would make to seize on such moments to raise doubts about Obama, they could not override the reality that most Americans *were* frustrated with the state of affairs. Even in Arizona where 29 percent of respondents who agreed that a candidate that shares my values was the most important candidate quality and voted by a 35-point margin for McCain, they were overshadowed by the 31 percent who thought a candidate who brings change to be more important—providing a 73-point margin for Obama.

At the top of the desire for change was disapproval of President Bush, the war in Iraq, and significant concern and negative views over the economy. In Arizona, Bush's disapproval jumped from 42 percent in 2004 to 62 percent in 2008, and disapproval of the war in Iraq moved from a clear minority to a clear majority; so perhaps McCain's "maverick" style and reform rhetoric appealed enough to hold his own Republican-leaning state. But outside of the reddest rustic states, the desire for change was too much in a climate in which concern with the economy swallowed other issue concerns.

All Bets Are Off

More evenly divided views on the economy, the war in Iraq, and thus the president helped Bush win reelection. Moreover, in critical western states there was a relatively favorable economic evaluation, which made it harder for Kerry to gain certain voters out west based on an economic criticism of the Bush administration.[40] In 2004 nearly twice as many voters in Nevada (74 percent) as in Ohio (38 percent) rated the state economy as excellent or good and those voters solidly backed the incumbent. Furthermore, more western voters believed Bush's tax cuts helped rather than hurt the economy and more voters trusted Bush than Kerry to handle the economy. Bush's economic approach, for the most part, resonated in a region that had embraced similar policies under Reagan.

But even in a state known for high-stakes gambling, reckless financial risks leading to the 2008 economic meltdown had Nevada voters in a foul mood.[41] Nevada's foreclosure rate was the worst in the country and its unemployment rate was at a 23-year high.[42] Whereas 5 percent of Nevadans viewed the state economy as poor in 2004, 53 percent saw the national economy as poor in 2008 and voted by a 40-point margin for Obama. The economy was now the number one issue for 63 percent of Nevadans compared with 16 percent four years earlier.

In California, a state at the epicenter of the mortgage crisis due to exploding housing prices and subsequent collapse, 55 percent saw the national economy as poor compared with 13 percent viewing the state economy as poor in 2004. Expanding metropolitan areas on the Pacific Coast from Los Angeles to Seattle had been moving to the Democrats on social issues but the 2008 meltdown also pushed these states away from Republican solutions for economic reasons.[43] Like California, the economy surged in importance in Oregon and Washington from 19 percent of voters to 54 and 60 percent, respectively, and these voters heavily supported Obama.

The backlash to President Bush was particularly high in Pacific Coast states, up from 52 to 77 percent disapproval in California and at 72 percent disapproval in both Oregon and Washington. In Nevada, a state Bush carried twice, disapproval for the president surged from 46 to 73 percent. With negative numbers such as these for the Republican incumbent president, relatively competitive states in 2004 became double-digit victories for Obama.

Even in Utah, a state Bush won by 45 points in 2004, disapproval of the president reached 52 percent. In Alaska, disapproval jumped from 37 to 61 percent. Still, in such Republican heavy states, McCain sold himself as enough of a change from Bush and a better alternative than Obama, particularly on national security. While Tina Fey spoofed Sarah Palin's answer to questions about the Alaska governor's foreign policy qualifications in that she could see Russia from her house, McCain still won substantially on the terrorism issue with western voters. The problem for McCain was that terrorism was far less of an issue for voters than in 2004, and disfavor with the war in Iraq had increased.

In 2004, approval for the war in Iraq and President Bush was at least 65 percent in every rustic red western state. Four years later, even in McCain's Arizona 55 percent approval for the war in Iraq had turned to 62 percent disapproval. And in states such as Nevada, where approval for the war turned to strong disapproval, Nevadans also turned Democratic.

Drilling for Votes in Hazardous Waters

The mythology of the American west is a land of endless opportunities and wild, where gambles and risks go with the territory. But as open spaces and waters confront growth and development, electoral divisions have arisen over how to meet community and environmental needs.[44] As metropolitan life extends into once sparsely populated lands there is greater concern by many new residents for solid public schools, clean air and water, public access to environmentally friendly recreational activities—valued in university communities such as Eugene, Oregon. With high percentages of undergraduates and postgraduates, Colorado and Washington are top "New Economy" states in which, John Kenneth White explains, "the environment is an important issue to well-educated New Economy voters who desire its preservation and see it as a values issue."[45] New West Democrats such as Montana Governor Brian Schweitzer, reelected in 2008, describe new jobs in line with environmental restoration.

There is also rural conservative backlash to 1980s-style economic wealth and 1960s-influenced social values embodied by what David Brooks calls "bourgeois bohemians."[46] Their expansion encroaches upon local interests of the agrarian and rustic west, long accustomed to unhindered access to logging, mining, fishing, hunting, and land. When the federal government imposes environmental protections and gun restrictions, it infringes upon traditional ways of life in rural communities. At least that is how voters in states such as Alaska and Idaho tend to view federal directives they associate with Democratic presidents, and thus vote Republican.

A rhetorical attack on distant federal directives and largess was at the center of the reform discourse of the self-described maverick McCain. And his selection of Alaska's "reformer in chief" to be his running mate was aimed at voters suspicious of federal intervention in lieu of locally determined economic and environmental decisions. With high gas prices and energy concerns, McCain and Palin led supporters in the chant of "Drill, baby, drill" in terms of opening up further oil exploration and drilling including areas under federal environmental protection. To many Democratic supporters of former vice president and presidential candidate Al Gore and his academy award documentary *An Inconvenient Truth* equating our petroleum-fueled world with a catastrophic rise in global warming, the prospect of expanding U.S. oil industry over environmental protection was unthinkable.

There are very real differences on these issues based upon where one resides in the west region. Despite the wide damage of oil spills associated with the Exxon Valdez in 1989 off the Alaskan coast, 75 percent of Alaskan voters support drilling for oil in the Arctic National Wildlife Refuge, and voted for McCain-Palin by a 77–21 percent margin. Off the California coast, the 1969 Santa Barbara oil spill inserted environmental politics more firmly into political discourse for coastal communities and it only increased in tenor over the next few decades. In the face of soaring gas prices in 2008, 52 percent of California voters did support expanding offshore oil drilling and voted for McCain by a 17-point difference. Yet of the 42 percent who opposed expanding offshore drilling, Obama had an 84-point margin. On emerging issues such as the environment Democrats are increasingly appealing to certain committed western voters at a level similar to Republicans devoted to a pro-life position and gun rights, setting off a western electoral showdown based on demographic trends and divides.[47]

Ain't No Mountain High Enough

An historic candidacy, record funds, demographic shifts, issue concerns, voter mobilization, even inroads among religious voters, helped Obama increase urban and suburban margins while narrowing rural numbers in growing western states. In California, Obama increased a 23-point urban margin in 2004 to a 36-point advantage while increasing the suburban margin from 2004 by 9 additional points. In Washington, suburban voters swung from a 2-point advantage for Bush to a 13-point margin for Obama, while rural voters moved from a 15-point margin for Bush to a 2-point advantage for Obama. In Nevada, a state Bush narrowly won by splitting the suburbs and winning rural voters by a 43-point margin, Obama won by 15 points overall—with a 24-point margin among suburban voters.[48]

Nevada, once known for remote nuclear testing and brief visits to "Sin City," has become the fastest-growing state because people are not just visiting Las Vegas but moving into its surrounding community to set up permanent residence. Clark County, in which Las Vegas is centered, accounts for nearly three-quarters of the state voters, and expanding margins there for the Democratic candidate are moving this state from Republican to Democratic territory. Where Kerry carried Clark County by 3 points, Obama moved it to a 20-point margin.

Democrats have increased their odds in states growing rapidly around metropolitan areas with diverse inner suburbs. Republicans' best bet has included states with predominantly rural areas with fast-growing smaller communities and outer suburbs. Nevada is an accelerated version of trends across the region in which urban areas are solidly Democratic, rural areas Republican, with suburban sprawl becoming battlegrounds. New communities extending beyond Phoenix and Portland are electoral targets as metropolitan sprawl extends into once remote rural communities.

At the center of this emerging electoral balance is Colorado, where the suburban vote swung from eight points for Bush to two points in favor of Obama. Obama increased a Democratic advantage from 7 to 17 points among urban residents and overcame a 27-point deficit for Kerry among rural residents to win the group by 1 point. Central to Kerry and Obama's success in Colorado was the Denver area, an example of an increasingly Democratic, higher-educated, highly skilled, younger, mobile "ideopolis" or what a recent *Brookings* report calls a "Mountain Megalopolis."[49] The Denver/Boulder area is increasingly more likely to resemble Los Angeles voters than other Coloradoans. Kerry won Denver/ Boulder and Los Angeles County, 61–38 percent and 63–35 percent, respectively. And Obama increased the victory margin in Denver/Boulder to 70–28 percent and Los Angeles County to 67–31 percent in his favor.

The similarities developing between higher-income and college-educated voters in Colorado and California likely have to do with the similar preferences and communities in which these groups are increasingly concentrated. Higher-educated and diverse residents are moving into metropolitan areas and university communities, where the highest-paying jobs demand the highest levels of education. Less educated, less skilled, and lower-income residents remain in rural communities with some brushing up against the outer suburbs. Since California has had more densely populated urban areas than Colorado, lower-income and less educated groups are more concentrated among higher-educated professionals in sprawling metropolitan areas. Like voting coalitions of the past, these metropolitan groups tend to share common concerns related to the economic vitality of the broader area while demonstrating more socially tolerant viewpoints due to living with so many diverse residents.[50] In areas such as Denver that increasingly resemble larger California metropolitan growth, there are similar voting patterns taking shape.[51] Obama won the double-digit support for Coloradoans and Californians earning less than $50,000 a year as well as those earning more than $100,000 a year. He had a double-digit advantage among college graduates in both states. This pattern is also evident in increasingly high-tech, high-growth states such as Washington and Oregon, home to Microsoft and Nike.

Success in suburban rings spreading out beyond urban centers was a big part of Obama's western victories. Colorado's Arapahoe and Jefferson counties narrowly went for Bush, 50–49 percent but swung heavily to Obama, 55–44 percent. Adding Adams County, Obama was the first Democrat since 1964 to win the three suburban counties around Denver. Central Colorado, home to suburban communities such as Littleton, Colorado, swung from a 6-point advantage for Bush to a 12-point margin for Obama. Obama made great inroads in suburban areas that have been an important battleground astride more Democratic urban space and Republican domination of the rustic west. Although Obama won the overall rural vote by cutting into the advantage where expanding suburbs buck up against rural communities, he still lost the regions of Eastern and Western Colorado farther removed from suburban sprawl.

The Democratic decision to hold the nominating convention in Denver was driven by a calculation that the state was a missing piece of a westward strategy to winning the Electoral College. As Pacific Coast states have all voted Democratic for president since 1992, Colorado had not voted Democratic since 1992, and like Arizona had only voted once for a Democratic presidential candidate since 1964. Still, Colorado has been in play for both parties as it has resembled Arizona but increasingly looks like California.

Colorado tilted, as did Arizona, to Bush's reelection on key issues and concerns. Fifty-four percent of Coloradoans and 55 percent of Arizonans approved of the war in Iraq, compared with 42 percent of California voters. A majority of voters in Colorado and Arizona approved of President Bush, while in California a majority disapproved. Colorado, like Arizona, had been experiencing a boom in recent years with residents streaming into the state for economic and lifestyle opportunities. And in 2004, 53 percent of Colorado voters saw the state economy as good, similar to Arizona's 55 percent, but quite different from the 37 percent of Californians, who had recalled a sitting governor over the state of affairs.

By 2008, Colorado views were more in line with those of California voters when it came to strong disapproval of President Bush, the war in Iraq, and negativity about the economy. In 2004 moral values was a top issue in Colorado and Arizona but down the list in California, but by 2008 the economy was by far the top concern in all three states. In California and Colorado, voters took out their economic angst on the Republican candidate, whereas McCain managed to win a one-point victory on the issue in his home state. How much McCain's in-state appeal contributed to his victory there may be evident in his support among white women, a group that shifted to Obama in Colorado. McCain also barely held onto white males, usually reliable Republican voters in Colorado and a group narrowly lost to Obama in California despite comfortable margins with this group in states such as Arizona and Nevada.

With the U.S. Air Force Academy in Colorado and the Top Gun jet fighter academy in southern California and a heavy defense industry presence in both

Table 8.2   Demographic and issue impact in the West

Democratic candidate margins in states	CO 04	CO 08	AZ 04	AZ 08	NV 04	NV 08	CA 04	CA 08
Demographics								
White men	−19	−2	−27	−21	−20	−17	−14	2
White women	−11	6	−9	−17	−6	1	5	11
Latinos	38	23	13	15	21	54	31	51
18–29 year olds	4	NA	−2	4	14	36	19	53
30–44 year olds	−3	7	−23	−5	−4	24	6	20
45–64 year olds	−6	14	−6	−14	−5	5	9	22
65+ year olds	−13	−9	−10	−13	−7	−13	6	−2
First-time voters	6	NA	−8	NA	16	54	29	67
< $50,000 income	−1	15	3	3	14	30	18	35
> $50,000 income	−7	7	−16	−15	−12	6	3	19
> $100,000 income	−11	13	−14	−8	−23	−1	4	15
No college degree	−17	−3	−19	−6	1	18	−3	24
College graduate	2	14	0	−12	−6	6	22	22
White evangelicals	73	−53	NA	−60	NA	−45	NA	−43
Independents	7	10	6	5	12	13	23	NA
Moderates	9	28	5	6	12	31	15	36
Urban	7	17	0	7	7	16	23	36
Suburban	−8	2	−20	−42	0	24	5	14
Rural	−27	1	−32	−7	−43	−29	−19	NA
Evaluation and impact								
Disapprove of President	46	69	42	62	46	73	52	77
Vote impact	90	48	89	38	89	49	85	44
Disapprove of war in Iraq	44	60	42	55	44	59	50	67
Vote impact	81	66	77	52	81	71	79	64
Iraq War most important	23	13	21	9	21	9	23	11
Vote impact	46	29	50	41	58	35	62	37
Terrorism most important	19	10	22	11	25	8	20	NA
Vote impact	−78	−77	−76	−85	−76	−81	−69	NA
Health care important	5	10	7	8	6	9	5	NA
Vote impact	55	58	56	NA	78	50	53	NA
Economy most important	18	54	13	61	16	63	16	60
Vote impact	62	14	45	−1	60	22	59	18
Economy not good*	35	39	28	NA	20	39	45	38
Vote impact	40	−19	37	NA	37	−11	25	−9
Economy poor*	9	53	7	NA	5	53	13	55
Vote impact	64	36	70	NA	57	40	50	44

Source: The table is compiled from 2004 and 2008 state exit polls for Colorado, Arizona, Nevada, and California.

Note: For demographics, positive numbers in the columns reflect the percentage point margin of victory on the variable for Kerry and Obama. Negative numbers reflect the point margin for Bush and McCain. On evaluation, the numbers represent the percentage pertaining to the question and the vote impact is the percentage point margin for candidates based on the variable in the row above it. *In 2004, the exit poll question referred to the state economy and in 2008 to the national economy.

states, McCain sought to appeal to his naval aviator past and current concerns with national security. And like other states he did well on the terrorism question as had Bush, but lost ground on the war in Iraq, and most importantly to the relative concern attached to the economy. After Democrats, Independents were an important group to first abandon support of President Bush and the war in Iraq. In Colorado, Independents voted narrowly for Bush in 2000 but against the president in 2004 (see table 8.2).

With an independent streak, 2008 Colorado voters consisted of 39 percent Independents compared with 31 percent Republicans and 30 percent Democrats. Although McCain portrayed himself as an independent-minded maverick, Colorado's Independents had a relatively important voice in support of Obama. Comparably, Arizona's 2008 exit poll consisted of 39 percent Republicans, 32 percent Democrats, and 30 percent Independents. California had 42 percent Democrats, 30 percent Republicans, and 28 percent Independents, giving the two states decisive partisan advantages for presidential aspirants.

Despite its independent impact, Colorado was a microcosm of 2008,[52] and a potentially long-term sign of Republican obstacles in the growing west. Demographic voting trends pushing Pacific Coast states to the Democrats have been emerging in Colorado.[53] Bush's huge margin among white Colorado female voters in 2000 was halved in 2004 and McCain lost this group in 2008. Republican presidential candidates lost Colorado college graduates in 2004 and 2008 after carrying them comfortably in 2000. The Latino population has also expanded dramatically as it has in other western states and for the 58 percent of Colorado voters who felt illegal immigrants should be offered legal status there was a 39-point margin for Obama.

When William Jennings Bryan accepted the 1908 Democratic nomination at the national convention in Denver, the Democrats were at an electoral disadvantage that had translated into an era of Republican domination. It had been the only time either party selected a Western locale north of Texas and east of California to nominate their candidate before Obama's historic acceptance. One hundred years later, the state of Colorado is the centerpiece of a westward electoral strategy. Colorado shares two of the "four corners" border points with New Mexico and Arizona. Arizona's neighbor Nevada borders Oregon, which shares its northern boundary with Washington. These six states were the most closely contested in the west region in 2000 and 2004,[54] but in 2008 Obama won all of them except Arizona. Taking the stage at Invesco Field to accept the Democratic nomination, sports enthusiast Obama referenced the setting by its familiar name of Mile High stadium drawing up imagery of the Denver Bronco's Orange Crush defense that once held opponents' offense in check. But it was McCain-Palin who had much to defend in the west as once competitive territory was lost to the Obama wave.

How the West Was Won

The 2008 West region exit poll had a 57–40 percent victory for Obama, close to the Northeast margin of 59–40 percent and dwarfing McCain's southern margin of nine points. In 2004, Kerry won the Northeast by 13 points but the West only by a single point. More importantly, Obama won 7 western states with 96 electoral votes. Obama picked up three western states that voted for Bush and came close in Montana. McCain came no closer than 16 points (Oregon) in any western state carried by Kerry. McCain won 6 western states, but the largest was Arizona with 10 electoral votes. Half of McCain's states had the Electoral College minimum of 3 votes for a total of 28 electoral votes in the west. California alone has 55 votes yet Republicans have not won the Golden State since the 1988 presidential election.

Democrats are piling up electoral votes in the most populated western states and have made similar headway in the U.S. Congress. In 2009 Democrats hold a 46–23 House seat advantage in western states that voted for both Kerry and Obama. But Democrats picked up the most ground across the three western states that flipped from Bush to Obama. With Bush's reelection, Republican House members outnumbered Democrats across Colorado, Nevada, and New Mexico by an 8–5 margin. However, following the 2008 election, Democrats have the majority of members in each of the states and a 10–3 margin overall.

Demographic trends and growth accelerating in Colorado and Nevada have less in common with more dependably Republican rustic western states and are more familiar to California, and in New Mexico there are also increasingly significant Hispanic populations and voters. New Mexico's Democratic Hispanic Governor Bill Richardson did not win the 2008 presidential nomination, but following the election all of New Mexico's congressional members were now Democrats. Similar dynamics have extended to states such as Arizona, where a combination of Republican scandal, disfavor with Republican leadership, and demographic trends flipped the Arizona delegation from a 6–2 Republican advantage in 2005 to a 5–3 Democratic advantage in 2009. With the one representative minimum in each of four less populated rustic states, a 13–3 advantage in 2005 narrowed to 9–7 for Republicans even in the reddest western states (see table 8.3).

Republicans held their ground in U.S. Senate representation in less populated western states by virtue of the Constitutional provision of two senators per state. Nevertheless, the tide really turned against Republicans nationwide from 2006–2008 and had a particular impact out west. Scandal and corruption have long alienated western voters suspicious of distant Washington dealings. Thus when a wave of scandal implicated numerous Republicans including Montana Senator Conrad Burns, it opened the door for the populist appeal of Democrat Jon Tester. With Tester's 2006 victory the once reliably Republican state now had two Democratic senators, a Democratic governor and Democratic control of the state legislature. Tester's win would provide an ingredient for Democratic success in other western states and in the presidential election, driven by dissatisfaction with the Bush administration and Republican leadership, demographic shifts even in mountain west states, and voter mobilization for change. In a razor-close election, Harvard Professor David King concluded that Tester topped Burns by a surge in youth registration and turnout around the University of Montana campus in Missoula.

Despite Senator Larry Craig's "wide-stance" bathroom arrest and decision to not run for reelection in 2008, Republicans maintained both of Idaho's seats. However, Alaska's Ted Stevens could not overcome the charges against him in

Table 8.3   Congressional elections and party delegation in the West region

State	House #GOP 2007	House #DEM 2007	House #GOP 2009	House #DEM 2009	Senate 2007 R	Senate 2007 D	Senate 2009 R	Senate 2009 D
Red states 04/08								
Alaska	1	0	1	0	2	0	1	1
Arizona	4	4 (+2)	3	5 (+1)	2	0	2	0
Idaho	2	0	1	1 (+1)	2	0	2	0
Montana	1	0	1	0	0	2	0	2
Utah	2	1	2	1	2	0	2	0
Wyoming	1	0	1	0	2	0	2	0
Red states total	**11**	**5**	**9**	**7**	**10**	**2**	**9**	**3**
Red state pickups		*+2*		*+2*		*+1*		*+1*
04 Red to 08 Blue								
Colorado	3	4 (+1)	2	5 (+1)	1	1	0	2
Nevada	2	1	1	2 (+1)	1	1	1	1
New Mexico	2	1	0	3 (+2)	1	1	0	2
Flip states total	**7**	**6**	**3**	**10**	**3**	**3**	**1**	**5**
Flip state pickups		*+1*		*+4*				*+2*
Blue states 04/08								
California	19	34(+1)	19	34	0	2	0	2
Hawaii	0	2	0	2	0	2	0	2
Oregon	1	4	1	4	1	1	0	2
Washington	3	6	3	6	0	2	0	2
Blue states total	**23**	**46**	**23**	**46**	**1**	**7**	**0**	**8**
Blue state pickups		*+1*						*+1*
West total	**41**	**57**	**35**	**63**	**14**	**12**	**10**	**16**
West pickups		*+4*		*+6*		*+1*		*+4*

Source: Table compiled by author.

Note: House and Senate # refers to Democratic and Republican seats in each state, with gains and losses as a result of the 2006 and 2008 elections in parentheses and italics. Red states 04/08 represent states that voted for both Bush and McCain, blue states 04/08 for both Kerry and Obama, and flip states for Bush and Obama.

losing a tightly fought election. In Oregon, once popular incumbent Senator Gordon Smith likely lost his seat for the crime of being a Republican in a state already trending Democratic in an electoral climate very unforgiving of any perceived partisan ties to the Bush administration and policies. And four years after the Hispanic Salazar brothers won a Senate and House seat in Colorado, the state elected Democrat Mark Udall by an 11-point margin to turn both Senate seats Democratic. Mark joined his first cousin, Tom Udall, who won a U.S. Senate Seat in New Mexico, 61–39 percent. Out of six U.S. Senate seats in these crucial battleground states, Republicans are down to a single U.S. senator in Nevada.

There was speculation should Alaska's Ted Stevens survive the election to instead be expelled by the U.S. Senate, Sarah Palin could be a potential candidate to fill his position. While that did not come to pass, it remains to be seen whether the Alaska governor will parlay her sudden exposure to help rebuild the Republican Party out of the west. Whatever Palin's future, Republicans will need to do better with female voters, particularly higher-educated women populating metropolitan and suburban areas in this growing region. Democratic Governor Christine Gregoire won reelection in 2008, joining Democratic Senators Patty Murray and former Microsoft executive Maria Cantwell in Washington State. Democratic Senators Barbara Boxer and Diane Feinstein have represented California since 1992.

California's Republican Governor Arnold Schwarzenegger faces Democratic opposition from the women in his own life. Similar to her daughter, the governor's wife Maria Shriver joined other members of the Kennedy clan in her vocal support for Barack Obama. After gaining office in a 2003 recall election of the Democratic California governor that featured the likes of former child actor Gary Coleman of *Different Strokes* and an adult film star, Schwarzenegger won reelection in 2006. With success in an increasingly Democratic state, Stanford political scientist Morris Fiorina contends, "Arnold Schwarzenegger is the kind of socially moderate Republican who can win elections in California" in which "the unusual nature of the recall election saved the Republican Party from itself."[55]

Nevertheless, recent trends have not been kind to Republicans in the west region. With San Francisco Representative Nancy Pelosi Speaker of the House and Nevada's Harry Reid the Senate Majority Leader, there is a distinctive western air to Democratic congressional leadership. Ironically, California was once the launching ground for a Reagan coalition that dominated not just the West but also the Electoral College. Central to that coalition's longevity was the support of emerging voters that would also stretch into congressional gains. In 1984, as part of an electoral landslide Reagan won 59 percent support among 18–29-year-olds nationwide, the largest percentage for a presidential candidate from the youth vote until Obama crushed it with 66 percent. While Reagan won with a 19-point margin among this age group, Obama won by 34 points. In California, the margin for Obama was 53 points, in Nevada it was 36 points, and in Montana at 24 points. Like the symbolic imagery of change in Obama's campaign material, where the letter O captures a rising sun stretching into a hopeful horizon, the western frontier holds the promise of electoral opportunity and success.

On the Electoral Horizon

Beyond Barack Obama's candidacy and convincing victory, numerous aspects of the 2008 election inspire historical reflection as our democratic nation traversed groundbreaking terrain. Responding to the present, presidential elections evoke the past while shaping the future. The 2008 election evoked seminal moments in history from Lincoln's transformative rise from Illinois in 1860 to JFK's youthful appeal of 1960. With an optimistic message of change in troubled times we are reminded of the sweeping implications of FDR's 1932 victory and Ronald

Reagan's election in 1980. In 2008 immediate concerns and emerging trends also confronted electoral realities shaped from the past where unflinching voting patterns since the 1960s gave way in Indiana and Virginia.

For the first time a Democrat won the presidential election without Missouri, yet Ohio remains a bellwether as no Republican has ever won the presidency without the Buckeye state. With its unique balance of urban, rural, and urban populations, Ohio and the Midwest remain vital to control of the presidency and Congress. Despite the enduring support of Plains states, Republicans will need to battle for suburban voters in Great Lakes states in order to make the electoral count.

The necessity of competing in the upper Midwest reflects the Democratic domination of the Northeast. In 2004 and 2008, the Republican presidential candidates could only win the state of West Virginia, with its 5 electoral votes. And with the 2008 defeat of longtime House incumbent Christopher Shays of Massachusetts, there is not a single New England Republican representative.

Democrats must also continue to contend for the upper Midwest due to persistent Republican advantage in the South. The recent success in New South states such as Virginia and North Carolina and the swing state of Florida notwithstanding, John McCain still won the South by a margin of 113–55 electoral votes. And with the exception of Georgia, southern margins for McCain were all at least double-digits. That said, Democratic success in rapidly developing metropolitan, high-growth, higher-educated, younger, and increasingly diverse New South states is a concern for Republicans not just in the region but across the nation, namely out west.[56]

As the eastern half of the United States has flipped upside down in party strengths since the 1960s, the west has increasingly provided for the balance of power. While original Republican strength emerged out of the upper Midwest and Northeast, Republican candidates Nixon and Reagan expanded upon what Goldwater had started out of the west to win landslide reelections. And these Republican candidates were winning higher-educated, higher-income, suburban voters in high-growth western states. But with the loss of the populated Pacific Coast states after Reagan, and now Nevada and Colorado in 2008, higher-educated voters in sprawling metropolitan and suburban areas are a key component of Democratic success for the presidency and Congress. Moreover, despite the question of race in this historic election, Obama performed better with white voters than any Democrat since 1976 winning a majority of young white voters for the first time in over three decades.

Clearly, the unpopularity of the Bush administration, the war in Iraq, and the financial collapse helped Obama and the Democrats with voters in 2008, just as the war on terrorism and cultural issues helped Bush and fellow Republicans in 2004. But population growth, demographic changes, and diversity in the west and elsewhere currently favor Democrats. Just as the New Deal coalition gave way to the Reagan coalition, we may one day speak of the long-term impact of an Obama coalition, coalescing in the critical election of 2008. Of course, the decisions that the Obama administration makes in light of the crises before us will affect any future interpretation.

Winning the White House reflects our changing electorate, societal, and cultural transformation. On his way to Washington, DC, and an historic inauguration, Barack Obama's personal journey took him from the farthest western reaches across the Pacific to the Northeast shores before heading for the Midwest urban center of Chicago. It is a uniquely American pathway through an Electoral College regional map as much about the changes across our nation as the candidate elected to represent them.

Notes

1. Chuck Plunkett, "Obama Speech Puts West in Front Row," *The Denver Post*, August 7, 2008, p. A1.
2. Larry Rohter and Jeff Zeleny, "Candidates Look to West for Undecided Voters," *New York Times*, October 26, 2008, p. A31.
3. Dan Balz, "With Pick, McCain Reclaims His Maverick Image," *Washington Post*, August 30, 2008, p. A10.
4. V. O. Key, Jr., "A Theory of Critical Elections," in Jerome Chubb and Howard Allen, eds., *Electoral Change and Stability in American Political History* (New York: Free Press, 1971), p. 43.
5. See Walter Dean Burnham, *Critical Elections and the Mainsprings of American Politics* (New York: Norton, 1970).
6. Kristi Anderson, *The Creation of a Democratic Majority, 1928–1936* (Chicago, IL: University of Chicago Press, 1979).
7. Rick Perlstein, *Before the Storm: Barry Goldwater and the Unmaking of the American Consensus* (New York: Hill and Wang, 2001).
8. Kevin Phillips, *The Emerging Republican Majority* (Garden City, NY: Anchor Books, 1970).
9. Everett Carll Ladd, Jr. with Charles D. Hadley, *Transformations of the American Party System: Party Coalitions from the New Deal to the 1970s* (New York: Norton, 1975).
10. Ruy Teixeira and Joel Rogers, *America's Forgotten Majority: Why the White Working Class Matters* (New York: Basic Books, 2000).
11. John Petrocik, *Party Coalitions: Realignment and the Decline of the New Deal Party System* (Chicago, IL: University of Chicago Press, 1981).
12. Paul Light and Celinda Lake, "The Election: Candidates, Strategies, and Decisions," in Michael Nelson, ed., *The Elections of 1984* (Washington, DC: CQ Press, 1985), pp. 83–110.
13. See Robert Dallek, *Ronald Reagan: The Politics of Symbolism* (Cambridge, MA: Harvard University Press, 1999).
14. Stanley Greenberg, *Middle Class Dreams: The Politics and Power of the New American Majority* (New Haven: Yale University Press, 1995).
15. See Mark Rozell and Clyde Wilcox, *God at the Grass Roots* (Lanham, MD: Rowman & Littlefield, 1995).
16. Francis E. Rourke and John T. Tierney, "The Setting: Changing Patterns of Presidential Politics, 1960 and 1988," in Michael Nelson, ed., *Elections of 1988* (Washington, DC: CQ Press, 1989), pp. 1–24.
17. See Gerald Pomper, ed., *The Election of 1992* (New York: Chatham House, 1993).
18. See Gerald Pomper, "The Presidential Election," in Gerald Pomper, ed., *The Election of 1996* (New York: Chatham House, 1997), pp. 173–204.

19. Brett Scruton, "Spotlight on Alaska: Youths Are Excited about a New Age of Politics," *Anchorage Daily News*, October 24, 2008, p. D4.

20. Mary Barabak, "Women May Call Election: The Gender Gap May Be Reemerging," *Los Angeles Times*, October 23, 2004, p. A20.

21. Cathleen Decker, "California Gives GOP the Blues," *Los Angeles Times*, November 6, 2008, p. A1.

22. Stanley Greenberg, *The Two Americas: Our Current Political Deadlock and How to Break It* (New York: St. Martin's Press, 2004), p. 127.

23. Ibid., p. 110.

24. Karl A. Lamb and Paul A. Smith, *Campaign Decision-Making: The Presidential Election of 1964* (Belmont, CA: Wadsworth, 1968), p. 59.

25. Greenberg, *The Two Americas*, pp. 154–159.

26. John B. Judis and Ruy Texeira, *The Emerging Democratic Majority* (New York: Scribner, 2002), p. 85.

27. Paul R. Abramson, John H. Aldrich, and David W. Rohde, *Change and Continuity in the 2000 and 2002 Elections* (Washington, DC: CQ Press, 2003), p. 104.

28. Ronald Brownstein and Kathleen Hennessey, "Latino Vote Still Lags Its Potential," *Los Angeles Times*, September 25, 2004, p. A1.

29. Rudolfo de la Garza and Louis DeSipio, eds., *Awash in the Mainstream: Latino Politics in the 1996 Election* (Boulder, CO: Westview Press, 1999).

30. Kirk Johnson, "Hispanic Voters Declared Their Independence," *New York Times*, November 8, 2004, p. A1.

31. Richard Alonso-Zaldivar, "Bush Snags Much More of the Latino Vote," *Los Angeles Times*, November 4, 2004, p. A30.

32. Quoted in ibid., p. A30.

33. Alicia Caldwell, "Defining the Latino Voter," *The Denver Post*, August 24, 2008, p. D1.

34. Marjorie Miller, "Obama Banks on Latinos," *Los Angeles Times*, October 26, 2008, p. A1.

35. John C. Green, Mark J. Rozell, and Clyde Wilcox, eds., *Prayers in the Precincts: The Christian Right in the 1998 Elections* (Washington, DC: Georgetown University Press, 2000).

36. See also, Jim Wallis, *The Great Awakening: Reviving Faith and Politics in a Post-Religious Right America* (New York: Harper One, 2008); E. J. Dionne, Jr., *Souled Out: Reclaiming Faith and Politics after the Religious Right* (Princeton, NJ: Princeton University Press, 2008).

37. Laurie Goodstein, "Obama Made Gains among Younger Evangelical Voters," *New York Times*, November 7, 2008, p. A24.

38. John Wildermuth and Demian Bulwa, "Prop. 8 Backlash Grows; Pride and Protest," *San Francisco Chronicle*, November 10, 2008, p. A1.

39. Cara DiMassa and Jessica Garrison, "Why Gays, Blacks Are Divided on Prop. 8," *Los Angeles Times*, November 8, 2008, p. A1.

40. Dana Milbank, "Bush, Cheney Tout Job Growth in Ohio, Nevada," *Washington Post*, June 21, 2004, p. A5.

41. Molly Ball, "Economy, Jobs Top List of Nevadans' Concerns," *Las Vegas Review-Journal*, August 24, 2008, p. 3A.

42. Kate Linthicum, "Out to Boost Obama's Nevada Odds," *Los Angeles Times*, October 14, 2008, p. A8.

43. David Sarahson, "A Wide Open West That's Still Wide but Not So Open," *The Oregonian*, August 26, 2008, p. C4.

44. For a geographical analysis of such differences, see Richard Morrill, Larry Knopp, and Michael Brown, "Anomalies in Red and Blue: Exceptionalism in American Electoral Geography," *Political Geography* 26 (2007): 525–533.

45. John Kenneth White, *The Values Divide: American Politics and Culture in Transition* (New York: Chatham House Publishers, 2003), p. 167.

46. David Brooks, *Bobos in Paradise: The New Upper Class and How They Got There* (New York: Simon and Schuster, 2000), p. 43.

47. Alec MacGillis, "Candidates Running Closest in the West; Demographics Shifting in Mountain States," *Washington Post*, August 25, 2008, p. A26.

48. Molly Ball, "Obama Swept Away Nevada," *Las Vegas Review-Journal*, November 6, 2008, p. 1A.

49. Nicholas Riccardi, "Party Seeks a Mountain West Ascent," *Los Angeles Times*, August 24, 2008, p. A22.

50. See Judis and Teixeira, *The Emerging Democratic Majority*, p. 81.

51. John Ingold, "Newcomers Help Color the State Blue," *The Denver Post*, November 10, 2008, p. A19.

52. Karen Crummy, "Battle for the West Rocky Footing for Candidates without the Independents," *The Denver Post*, June 29, 2008, p. A1.

53. Amanda Paulson, "Obama Strong in Long-Red Colorado," *Christian Science Monitor*, October 27, 2008, p. 25.

54. Timothy Egan, "An Evolving Identity Helps to Leave Five States in Search of a President," *New York Times*, October 30, 2004, p. A15.

55. Morris Fiorina, *Culture War? The Myth of a Polarized America* (New York: Pearson, 2005), p. 106.

56. Stephen Ohlemacher, "Obama's Victory May Show the Way to Win in the Future," *Associated Press*, November 8, 2008.

Index

Note: Page numbers in *italics* indicate tables.